A MILLION ACRES

MONTANA WRITERS REFLECT ON LAND AND OPEN SPACE

Edited by

Keir Graff

With contributions from

Rick Bass, Alexis Bonogofsky, Christine Carbo, Janet Skeslien Charles, Gwen Florio, James Grady, Keir Graff, LeDoux Hansen, Jamie Harrison, Eric Heidle, Sterling HolyWhiteMountain, Allen Morris Jones, Carrie La Seur, Maxim Loskutoff, Antonia Malchik, Maile Meloy, Caroline Patterson, Jim Robbins, Russell Rowland, and Joe Wilkins

Photography by

Alexis Bonogofsky

The Lost Get-Back Boogie by James Lee Burke was first published in 1986 by Louisiana University Press. Excerpt reprinted by kind permission of the author.

"Eleven Kinds of Sky" by Joe Wilkins was originally published in the January/February 2012 issue of *Orion*. Reprinted by permission of the author.

The Home Place by Carrie La Seur was first published in 2014 by William Morrow and Company, an imprint of HarperCollins Publishers. Reprinted by permission of the publisher.

"The Last Drowning" is an excerpt from an untitled novel by Jamie Harrison that will be published in spring 2020 by Counterpoint Press. Reprinted by permission of the author.

An earlier version of "Nothing More Than Everything" by Antonia Malchik was published as "Bitterroot" in the Summer 2015 issue of *1966: A Journal of Creative Nonfiction*. Reprinted by permission of the author.

"What You Do for Fun" by Maile Meloy was first published in *Montana State Parks: Complete Guide and Travel Companion*, by Erin Madison and Kristen Inbody (Great Falls Tribune/Riverbend Publishing, 2014). Reprinted by permission of the author.

"A Fine Spring Day" by Allen Morris Jones was originally published as "A Fine Spring Day, with Regrets" in the Spring 1998 issue of *Big Sky Journal* and anthologized in *The New Montana Story*, edited by Rick Newby (Riverbend Publishing, 2003). Reprinted by permission of the author.

"The Beast in Me" by Maxim Loskutoff was first published on August 18, 2018, in the *New York Times Sunday Review*. Reprinted by permission of the author.

An earlier version of "Fourteen Ways of Looking at the Clark Fork" by Caroline Patterson was published as "Thirteen Ways of Looking at the Clark Fork" in the Winter 1997 issue of *Big Sky Journal*. Reprinted by permission of the author.

ISBN 978-1-60639-121-1

Designed by Bruce Capdeville,
Real World Design, Helena, MT

Printed in South Korea

2 3 4 5 6 7 8 9 10 C&E 25 24 23 22 21 20

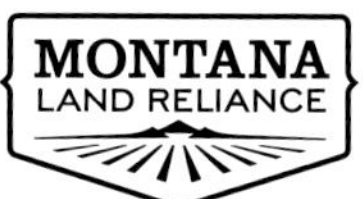

PO Box 355, Helena, MT 59624
406-443-7027 • mtlandreliance.org

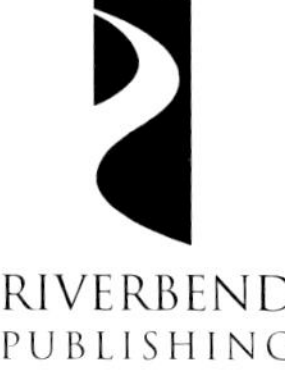

RIVERBEND
PUBLISHING

PO Box 5833, Helena, MT 59604
866-787-2363 • riverbendpublishing.com

The wind was blowing up the Bitterroot Valley, and the leaves of the cottonwoods trembled with silver in the bright air. I watched the fields of hay and cattle move by, and the log ranch houses chinked with mortar, and the drift of smoke from a small forest fire high on a blue mountain. The creek beds that crossed under the road were alive with hatching insects, and the pebbles along the sandy banks glistened wet and brown in the sun. Damn, Montana was a beautiful part of the country, I thought. It reached out with its enormous sky and mountains and blue-green land and hit you like a fist in the heart. You simply became lost in looking at it.

–James Lee Burke, *The Lost Get-Back Boogie*

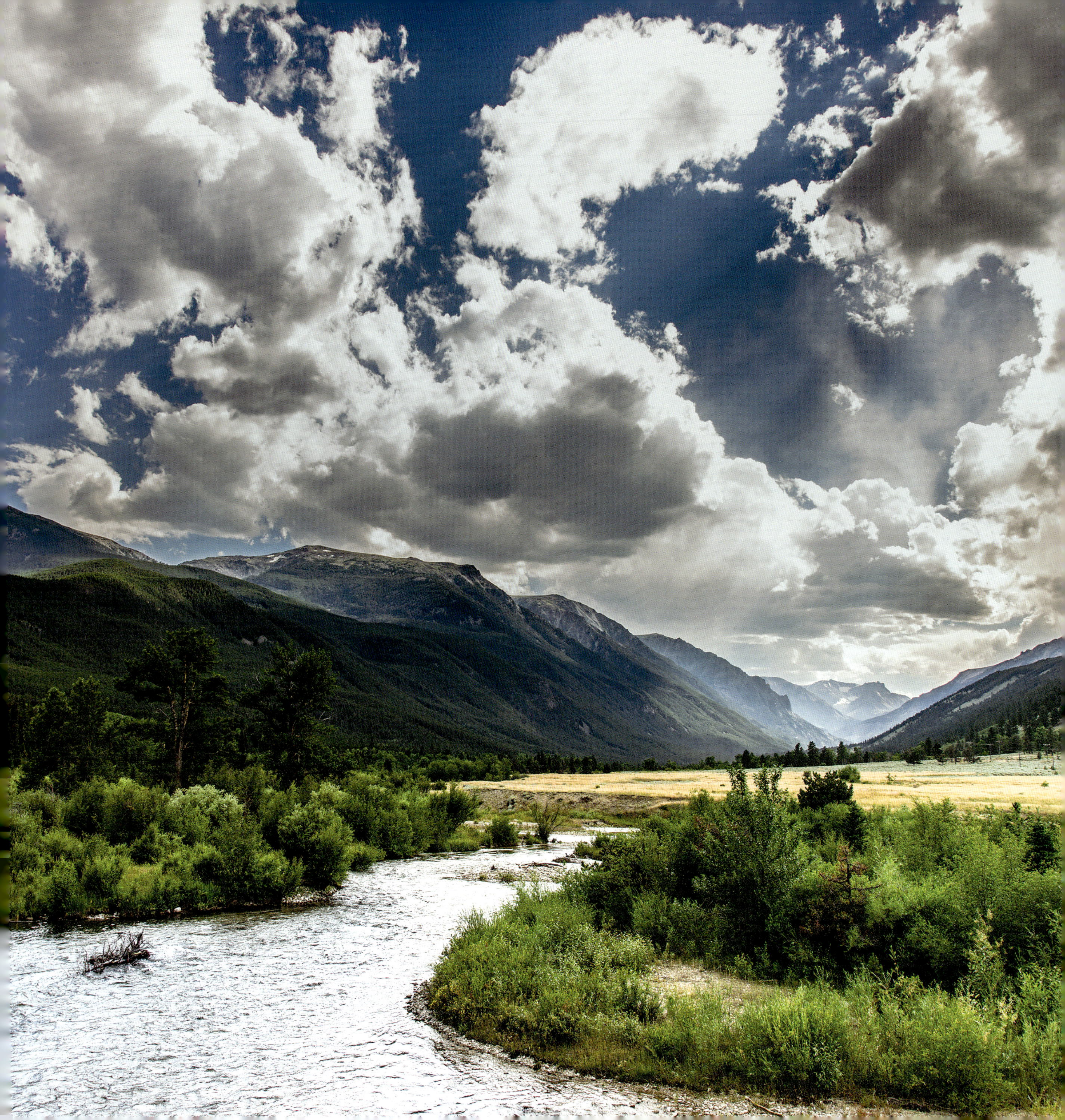

CONTENTS

INTRODUCTION

Keir Graff

For many people, the value of land has long been easy to define. Parceled, claimed, and fenced, a plot derives its worth from what can be erected on it, grown in it, or extracted from it. Ownership, under the capitalist system—and if you ignore, as we too often do, more complicated questions of use and occupancy—is as straightforward as determining whose name is on the deed and who owns the mineral rights.

Land has value, land is currency. Wars have been fought over it and will always be fought over it. Our thinking about land is often acquisitional, avaricious. As Mark Twain reputedly said, "Buy land, they're not making it anymore"—a joke taken seriously by everyone from pioneers to real-estate developers.

But the Montana Land Reliance mission is about something more than ownership. It is about partnership and the uneasy concept—at least in our culture—of sharing. Their mission statement: "The Montana Land Reliance (MLR) partners with private landowners to permanently protect agricultural lands, fish and wildlife habitat, and open space." Protecting farmland protects our food sources and a rural way of life. Preserving fish and wildlife habitat supports animal populations for both their own good and for the recreational activities of fishing and hunting. And all of these protect the vistas that define the Montana experience for residents and visitors alike. It is these last two words—*open space*—to which my mind returns again and again. How do we calculate the value of open space? It's only slightly less difficult than determining who owns the wind.

Born and raised in Montana, I have lived the last two decades in Chicago, a teeming metropolis that in days of rail and steam was once a major point of departure for settlers headed west. There is a significant Montana expat community here and, both before and after Norman Maclean, a fair amount of two-way traffic. (Read Caroline Patterson's essay, "Fourteen Ways of Looking at the Clark Fork," for a primary-source account.) I take my sons home to Montana every year for vacation, determined that they will absorb at least some of it through osmosis, and that the smell of summer-hot sap and pine needles will be familiar to them (if not, perhaps, as familiar as the scent of ozone on an urban heat island). That the sudden chill of a summer evening at altitude is something they know to expect. That brown hills backgrounded by blue mountains frame their understanding of beauty.

It's worked to some extent. On a long hike in Glacier several years ago, my older son exclaimed, "This is the most beautiful place I have ever been," and those words thrilled me like few others he has spoken. Both sons may live their lives far from Montana but will always carry a little bit of the state along with them, like burrs on their socks.

As for myself, riding public transit in the nation's third-largest city, working long hours in front of a screen at the magazine that has been my vocation and on the books that are my avocation, each return to Montana is a soul-cleansing sigh. Last summer I felt an unalloyed delight at watching the bars disappear from my cell phone as we dropped down into the Grasshopper Valley. It takes a while for the stress and cares of the city to be cleansed from my body but always, on every visit, there comes a time when I feel I have remembered who I was, who I truly am.

Without diminishing the people who raised me, this is largely down to land and space. I grew up in town but played on a mountain and swam in a river. Family trips allowed the peculiar Montana luxury of annoyance at occasionally having to share a trail or a shoreline with several other people. (Lake Michigan beaches are as crowded as Coney Island in comparison.) As an adult, whether I'm letting the wind whip through the car on a lazy drive across Camas Prairie, hiking in a sun shower along the soggy Bowman Lake trail, or simply beholding the majestic Rocky Mountain Front—my soul is nourished by the views, yes, but also the room. Space means absence. The fourth-largest state is forty-eighth in population density. One of the things that makes it special is simply that, outside of a few tourist hot spots, you're not being elbowed aside by all the other people who think it's special.

And that is where my conundrum comes in. It's one thing to protect specific habitat for an animal or plant. It's another to set aside land for hiking, boating, fishing, and hunting. But when it comes down to protecting space, we face what feels almost like a logical fallacy: for the benefit of the most people, we need to carefully limit the way most people, their worst instincts unchecked, would use it. It can feel greedy, or even elitist, to suggest how people ought to use their land. Sometimes the last to arrive are the first to suggest closing the door. And isn't there still plenty of land left?

In a crowded world, Montana still has lots of room. Chicago, which due to its size is not even a particularly densely populated city, has nearly twelve thousand people per square mile. Montana has seven. But Montana cannot become Chicago. If you litter the valleys with one-point-five-acre ranchettes, with everyone chasing their own slice of Montana, you don't have Montana anymore. If everyone carves a sliver off a towering ponderosa, everyone gets a toothpick and nobody gets shade.

Still, what right do we lucky Montanans, we fortunate few, have to stop and say *that's enough?* What right does someone like me—I'm no outdoorsman, my knowledge of flora and fauna distressingly average—what right do I have to lay claim to any of this, even to say that my enjoyment of broad twilit valleys and lonely two-lane roads must be preserved?

Land management does require making choices with foresight for the future. Given the state of the world's environment and of Montana's—from Colstrip to the Berkeley Pit to the attics and groundwater of Libby—it's clear we should have started making those hard choices long ago. And this is where another key word, *partnership*, recurs. There are many avenues to protecting the outdoors we all love, most of them worthwhile, but MLR's approach is a powerful addition because it's opt-in. Not all will make the choice to preserve and share the unique qualities of the land they steward, but many will. And the million acres protected by MLR conservation easements since its founding in 1978 are a testament to that progress.

Imagine that: a million acres. That's the size of the entire Yaak Valley Rick Bass writes about with such urgency in "The Ark of the Yaak."

There are very real things at stake here. Climate scientists will attest to the value of carbon sinks and reforestation. And there is some kind of equation by which megalopolises must be offset by forests and plains and lightly used swaths of land for the occupants of this planet to survive. But there is also an emotional or spiritual component. I believe nature is a healing force for the human psyche, both for those who live in it or adjacent to it and those of us who live trapped in urban sprawl. We need access to it. We need to allow children and elders alike to know the awe and humility that comes from standing alone in a place indifferent to our human wants and needs. Those Montana Office of Tourism ads that periodically blanket Chicago and make me wince when I think how many people will descend upon the place I still think of, selfishly and wrongly, as *my* state—we need those, too. We need everyone to visit Montana, at least once, to see the beauty of it.

To know what is worth saving.

What we are protecting is in many ways absence, but it is only our absence. It is also everything: earth, water, sky.

When I was asked to edit an anthology celebrating The Montana Land Reliance's millionth protected acre, to say I jumped at the chance would not do justice to how hard I bumped my head on the ceiling. As with the previous anthology I was involved with, *Montana Noir*, I knew this would be a chance to spend more time in the best place on earth. Some of that time would be physical, but most of it would be mental, as I filled hours, days, weeks, and months with the project—and if I can't be in Montana in person, being there in my mind is the next best thing. Knowing well Montana's abundance of talented writers (I've long maintained it's difficult to throw a rock without hitting a good writer there, though out of respect for the writers, I keep the rocks in my pocket), I knew I would have difficult decisions to make along with the excitement of discovery.

Think of the book you hold in your hands as a gorgeous, hardcover, coffee-table-sized literary journal. Most of the pieces are essays, works of nonfiction, but I've included a handful of short stories as well, one song you can read as a poem, and of course you will gaze upon the stunning photographs of the remarkable Alexis Bonogofsky.

My instructions to the contributors were purposely somewhat vague: I told them I wanted to read about "the great outdoors." I wanted to know what the land meant to them and how they related to the land in their writing. What I received—and what you are about to read—reflects a wonderfully diverse range of thoughts, feelings, experiences, and perspectives. They wrote of natural beauty and their joy at beholding it, they expressed their love for Montana and their happiness at making it a home. There is humor here, too, but also heartbreak. There is darkness in these woods and plains because to love something intensely means to fear for its survival and to mourn its loss. As Sterling HolyWhiteMountain writes in his eloquent essay, "one of land's meanings to Indian people is loss."

You'll find voices familiar and new here. Most of them are Montana natives, but several are not, and their perspectives are equally valuable because they help us see with fresh eyes. Reading Gwen Florio's essay about finding her way to Montana from the East Coast reminds us how many people become citizens of a place not by birthright but through love. I read her first draft on a Chicago Transit Authority bus and felt a powerful ache, because I was now the one on the outside looking in.

Jim Robbins, like Gwen a veteran journalist and an Easterner by birth, has traveled the world but settled in Montana by choice. Most at home in the mountainous western part of the state, in his contribution he takes a deep dive on a long drive into the prairie, exploring an ecosystem to its very roots and wondering if he can learn to love that landscape, too. And Janet Skeslien Charles, who grew up on her parents' farm near Shelby, now reflects on what it's like to return home from the bright lights of Paris.

Some writers here use classic outdoors activities as their starting points. In a short story paying tribute to the legendary Edward Abbey, Eric Heidle's protagonist carries her father to his final resting place on cross-country skis, encountering snowmobilers and a wounded elk. Jamie Harrison shares an excerpt from her untitled forthcoming novel in which a happy rafting excursion on the Yellowstone quickly turns deadly, reminding us of the beauty and danger of rivers. Maile Meloy's account of her family's annual Smith River float speaks with wry humor to the way Montanans use the outdoors to evaluate friends and partners. Christine Carbo gives us a fictional account of the very real threats and fears women can face when hiking and camping alone. Allen Morris Jones gives us a haunting fishing story in which a young boy asks an essential question about the ownership of natural things. And Maxim Loskutoff recalls a close encounter with a grizzly while hiking in Glacier Park, reminding us of an oft-forgotten truth: we're animals, too.

Running throughout all these essays and stories is an exploration of the way we are shaped by land and open space. These themes are more explicit in some than others. Joe Wilkins masterfully captures a childhood in the Big Dry, a "summer country because if there was hope for us it was in a summer's work." Photographer Alexis Bonogofsky trades her camera for a keyboard, offering poetic vignettes illustrating lifelong lessons learned from the land. An excerpt from Carrie La Seur's debut novel *The Home Place* is set in a Billings trailer park but is steeped in a sense of the land and focuses on a wrenching possibility: selling the home place. Russell Rowland looks back to a summer spent working on his uncle's ranch to explore the way the quietness of eastern Montana contributes to a stoic stereotype that carries its own dangers.

Bridging past and present, Caroline Patterson's family history reflects on a remarkable range of subjects, centering on the river that connects and divides Missoula. And in his inimitable style, James Grady gives us a whirlwind tour of the whole state, dotting it with literary and historical turnouts, before ending with an indelible portrait of his hometown Shelby.

And, yes, some writers focus on threats to the land they love and the pain of losing it. Antonia Malchik writes lyrically of land, grief, loss, and fear for the future, getting at an essential truth: for many, land is everything. Her mother LeDoux Hansen gives us the cowboy song whose refrain is heard in Antonia's essay. Sterling HolyWhiteMountain shares a resonant Indian perspective on land, loss, and conservation that is necessary reading for all of us.

Finally, Rick Bass tackles what's next, writing about environmental challenges in the Yaak Valley, climate change, and the climate refugees—swans—who are already arriving. For my own contribution, I've written a new story exploring the mental cost of life on an endangered planet, and nature's capacity to heal both us and itself.

This book has been both a challenge and a delight, and to play a role has been my privilege. These wonderful writers have all generously given their time and their words to support the preservation of open space in Montana—and by purchasing a copy, you've done something, too.

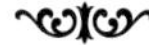

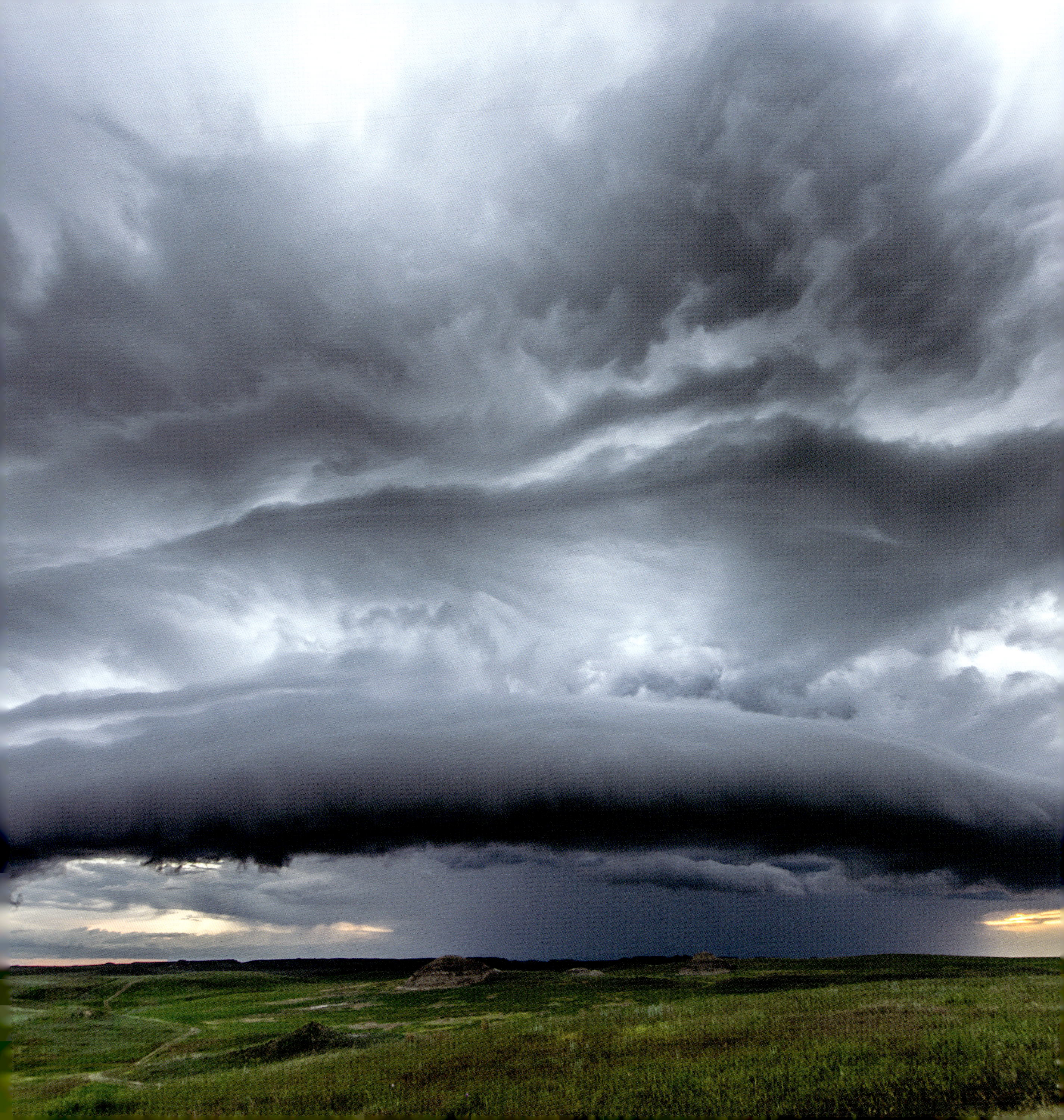

ELEVEN KINDS OF SKY

Joe Wilkins

SLATE

Sometimes it is okay, in the half-dark of an early midsummer morning, to climb out of bed, to leave your little brother slack-jawed and small and tangled in wool blankets, to pad quietly in white-footed pajamas down the hallway, through the bathroom's all-night odors of hard water and drying towels, and on into your parents' room.

They leave the window open at night, to breathe the good prairie air, so it is breezy and cold, and you slow and shiver. The floor is plain wood, and the floral print wallpaper peels where the seams come together. On your mother's dresser there are a few framed snapshots and a crucifix, some bright necklaces and rings, a blouse or two. On your father's chest of drawers there is nothing save his silver watch and jackknife, his cracked snakeskin wallet. Yesterday's work jeans are draped across the foot of the bed, his old brown belt still strung through the loops. And the two of them: they are mountains of cream sheets, of musky warmth, of slow breath, slow breath, slow breath.

You crawl—quietly, so very quietly—up onto the bed between them. Without a word, they make room for you, and you slide yourself between their scratchy sheets and pull the blankets up tight to your chin. You try to be as still as can be, as quiet as the sky. You wait and wait, nearly holding your breath with stillness—until slowly their bodies ease and their breaths slip and deepen—and then you can relax, for they are asleep once more. They need their sleep. They work hard. You understand that to be a boy in this bent-back, make-do world is to be a shadow, off to the side of things and out of the way. Though here, for a sunrise span of minutes, you are the center of the unfolding universe.

Your father faces the wall, his back a sheer, rising ridge, his white T-shirt stretched thinly from shoulder to shoulder. With the tips of your fingers you feel now the tight, black curls of his head, so unlike the dishwater mess you brush from your own eyes. Oh, it is something to be this close to him, to touch him, to breathe with your big-shouldered father. You breathe with him.

But you are more like your mother, you think, turning to look at her soft, sleeping face. Not just your lank hair, but the way she is facing you and is not ridges but hills and sweeping fields. That's how you feel on the inside. You feel like plain old hills, a dry swath of buffalo grass, like you can turn your back to nothing and must face everything.

You aren't worried about this. Not yet, at least. Your father's hair didn't go dark and curl until he was in the

Army. You've heard the story many times, how he blames a shampoo his sister sent him. It'll be that way for you, too. It will happen, this alchemic transition to manhood. You must be patient. Until then, you'll watch him. That's what you do: watch things, think about things. That's how you'll make your way through.

On the ceiling—it catches your eye, always—there is a twisting pattern of cracks and water damage. It looks like some shovel-headed, bent-nosed man. You don't like it, are even scared of it, but the accident of that grim face holds you. You can't look away. You stare and stare, and the man stares back. You are about to squirm—to make a noise and wake your parents—when the first morning meadowlark calls, and you can suddenly, thankfully look away.

You crane your neck to see out the window, to follow the bird's clear song. The gauzy curtains lift and fill, the green-silver leaves of the plains cottonwood in the front yard ripple like water. And beyond, the very sky comes alive—all blue and slate and brightening smolder.

SHEETING

It was a summer country. Not because we didn't have a winter, for we had a long stretch of near-arctic time, from mid-October through mid-April, when the sun stayed low in the sky and set in the late afternoon and the temperature dropped in mere minutes to negative twenty-three with the wind coming cold and hard from the north and west. Everything under that wind weathered. Storms piled snow as high as our sheep shed, some twenty feet, though in the days to come the wind would scour the drifts down again to hard, dirty patches. The freeze then worked deep into the body of the land itself. There was no use trying to dig a posthole or even work a good throwing stone from the gravel. If a blizzard was on the way, you cut your fences so your stock could keep moving and maybe stay alive. If it was just bone cold, you stacked a load of square bales on the back of a pickup and drove out to winter range and called the sheep from the fields.

It was a summer country because when the wind finally twisted and eddied and came warm down the hills and across the plains, there were only a few days of mud—and then there was the season of sun and work and dust. Under the wide, sheeting sky the real work was done: fields plowed and planted, sheep sheared, cattle branded, alfalfa irrigated, hay put up, a steer butchered, a garden harvested, tomatoes and beef tongue canned, the long winter readied for.

It was a summer country because if there was hope for us it was in a summer's work. With enough rain we might make the bank payments, might lease another section of land, might buy a new tractor or a hundred head of yearling ewes, might even get ahead of things for once. It was a summer country because it was then we might curve the cycling seasons of our lives ever so slightly up and corkscrew toward some further hope, whatever that might be.

After a long winter of bone cancer, my father finally died on February 17, 1988. The following summer was hell's own season: the height of the drought and the worst of the grasshoppers. It was a time when the flat turning of the seasons would otherwise have been a blessing.

STORMY

First thing in the morning Donnie Laird turns his welding rig onto our road and comes raising a rooster tail of dust fast down the gravel and bangs on the screen door with his ham of a fist and announces to my mother that he'll go ahead and fix the boys' basketball hoop.

The other Saturday I'd wanted to lower it so my brother and I could dunk. My mother was at work, and I took the pickup keys without permission and with the tailgate down backed over the cement pad and up to the pole. I planned to stand in the pickup bed and loosen the high screws and slip the hoop down the pole. In the rearview mirror I aimed the truck and carefully tapped the gas, but the truck fairly bucked beneath me and the wedge of the tailgate slammed into the pole, which meant the new basketball hoop and level cement pad we'd begged and begged our mother for was just-like-that useless.

But Donnie couldn't have known this. No, he came by because that's what my father's old friends are always doing: stopping by sad-eyed and grim-mouthed, their feedstore ball caps twisted up in their hands, staring at their boots and asking if there's anything, anything at all, they can do. Most of the time my mother thanks them and sends them away. Though they are strong, they cannot haul my father up and out of this dry ground. Though they are fine farmers and ranchers, a day on the tractor or a night in the lambing shed won't mean much in the long run. Though they, too, loved my father, they are like us bewildered and brokenhearted. They ask not for us but for themselves—they ask out of the selfishness of grief.

Which is fine and probably as it should be. Donnie most likely stepped out of his rig that morning and saw the bent hoop and knew right then and there what he could do. He might have even thought for a moment, before he put his fist to the screen door, about the boy who did it and what it would mean to have such a mistake erased. For I imagine shame and expiation are on his mind, what with his stink of liquor and tobacco spit and day-old clothes. When my brother and I pull on our tennis shoes and go out to help, I see the pillow of greasy coats in the cab and the pile of beer cans in the back and think that Donnie has probably not been home for days, has not seen his wife and daughters—who go to our church and live up the road from us in a double-wide trailer near the river—in a long, long time.

Donnie tells my brother and me to work on the scarred metal around the bend with wire brushes while he readies the welder. Other than my grandfather, I don't often see grown men up close anymore, so while I scrape I sneak looks over at Donnie. He must be over six feet tall, and though his face is round and wide, his eyes and nose and mouth are pinched close together. His skin is umber from the sun, but when he takes off his cap, there is a stark white line across his forehead. My grandfather is always telling me, stepping back and putting up his fists, that he's right at fighting weight: one hundred and eighty pounds. But Donnie looks twice as big as my grandfather; he must be close to three hundred pounds. He is thick across the chest, and his arms and legs are muscled and enormous. And he wears a cotton shirt, dark blue, almost as black as a stormy sky, the very kind my father wears in the picture on the piano in the front room, which makes me wonder if this is just what you do when you are a man: get big and thick and wear a blue shirt to work.

Once Donnie has the welder in order, we put our shoulders to the pole and bend it straight again. Donnie gets out his level just to make sure. He breathes heavily and his untucked shirt waves over the full, hairy sack of his stomach. We put on welding masks and flip the visors down and the day goes dark until Donnie sparks the torch. He lays, like I thought he would, a thick bead directly on the metal scar, but then, opposite that, where the pole looks more or less straight and fine, he welds a long rectangle of tempered steel perpendicular to the pole, the width of it sticking six inches straight back. I think a fin, a wing, maybe Donnie's signature or bit of artifice, but I am so happy to have the evidence of my wrongdoing made right that I don't ask any questions and so don't discover that this steel wing is a kind of truss that carries the whole weight of the hoop, that will basket after basket keep it from slowly folding over on itself.

I don't understand all the forces at work here, the principles of tension, moment, and node. How twice the strength is needed to come straight at something. How at times what is still is charged and what is hastened is dead. How bread becomes flesh, how flesh becomes dust, how the heart is bread and flesh and dust—the way Donnie cools the weld with a five-gallon bucket of water and picks up his clanking tools, and we thank him and shake his heavy, trembling hand, and though he will in a few years abandon his wife and daughters and dedicate himself to liquor and other oblivions, we think of him kindly and often.

CEDAR-CLEAN

For three days it has rained.

The little creek we're camped on rushes straight down the valley, ditch-fast and muddy. The limbs we drag back to camp are so green with sap or rotten with rainwater they will not burn. We cannot light a fire. We have caught no trout. We huddle at the table with musty blankets draped over our shoulders.

We are here, a hundred miles from home and holed up in our tiny camper, because my father is dead. Or, rather, we are here because when my father was alive he took us every summer to the Beartooth Mountains. Some scorched July week, my father would park his tractor and pack the old forest-green Coleman cooler and drive us all up to Mystic Lake, where we'd fish for cutthroat and hike switchback trails and look down over thousand-foot-high vistas of sheer rock and cedar-clean sky. On those good days, the mountains were like the many stone hands of God, the sun always bright, and the air crisp and cool. Come evening, we sat on stumps and hunks of granite and stuck marshmallows on long willow sticks. My sister toasted them lightly over the coals, and I blackened them in the flames, and my brother sat far back from the fire and ate them raw, one after the other, and my mother and father too sat back from the flames and sipped their beer and laughed and told stories—the wavery dome of firelight illuminating all that mattered in the world.

We are here because my mother grieves hard as iron for my father and his fatherless children, and so she has by herself hitched the secondhand camper trailer to the pickup and packed the tackle box and the cooler and hauled us west across Montana to the smaller but closer Castle Mountains—where each day since, the rain has come at us hard and slantways, where each day we fish the creek and fail, try a fire and fail, where we huddle now in the camper, play another hand of cards, which my sister wins like always, where dinner is again cold canned chili topped with cheese and onions.

Yet what a time it was. Like a slanting rain, I want to whisper across the years: it was enough. There was a mountain. Fir and cedar leaned in around us. Even for the rain I had a can of strawberry soda cooling in the creek. Astonishing, that we made it there at all, that in the years to come we would make it back most every summer. Mother, I don't know how you did what you did. It would have been easy to say, Enough. To say, I'm tired. To say, I tried. Most everyone expected it, expected you to let whatever rain came soak us and whatever wind blow us like dry weeds across creation.

But here you are, with a fire in your hands. You'd gone down the road, in the rain, and found someone who'd been camped there for weeks and had a load of good kindling. You must have begged an armful—what force and fury, I think now, to knock on their camper door and beg an armful of good, dry wood—for when we peek out, we see you kneeling in the rain, kneeling before the ring of black stones, a fire leaping up before you, rising from your outstretched hands.

That fire burns hot and high all night. And the creek in the next valley, we discover, runs deeper and colder. In the morning we go out with jigs and hoppers and corn kernels and catch a mess of brookies. Back at camp, you gut them and dust them with flour and fry them with their heads still on in a slick of bacon grease. The pink flesh falls hotly off the bones. We eat it and are filled.

WASHED

My grandfather leans out the pickup window and says he'll be having coffee at the Lazy JC. "And Ed," he adds. "Try not to scare the boy."

Ed sucks his teeth, eyes me up and down. "Shit, Jim, it ain't up to me if the boy gets scared or not."

As my grandfather grins and drives away, Ed waves me around the corner of the house. We weave through a sloping dirt yard spotted with tough bunchgrass and piles of bolts and rebar and blown tires and engine parts and make our way up to a windowless, tin-roofed shed slumped near the back fence. Ed yanks on the strap of hide stapled to the door—the gray boards biting into the dust as the clanking knock of steel chains and wood comes from somewhere inside—and despite his age and bulk slips gracefully into the dark yawn of shadow. After a moment, I follow.

What light there is falls thinly from cracks and knots. Motes of dust hover and spin in each wedge and shaft. The air tastes of rot and spice. The floor, like the yard, is hardpan dirt, a few pale weeds twisting for the light. The ceiling is just high enough for a man to straighten himself, and the clanking comes from the rows and rows of steel traps hung along the walls: the slender curves of number ones like the wings of sparrows; solid number threes; the massive, menacing jaws of number sixes, like the jaws of the bears they snare.

Ed is big as a bear, but slumped and pudgy and bald. He studies the rows of shelves along the far wall. I stare at the stubbly back of Ed's neck. His shoulders rise and fall with each breath. He must be searching his memory, I think, for the shelves are not labeled, and neither are the glass bottles that crowd them: some green, some brown, some purple, some a washed sky-blue, some with droppers for lids, some with burnt driftwood corks. He is taking a long time, looking back and forth, and I imagine he enjoys remembering, that there is a story that explains each one: which ridge and what kind of sky, how the coyote snapped and snarled. These are Ed's blue-glass stories, these bottles and vials he considers—first this one and then that one, clinking like bells as he thumbs through them.

For Christmas my grandfather gave me three good steel traps and half a dozen snares. Two of the traps are number ones, and I have caught quite a few prairie dogs with them—but prairie dogs are easy, will practically fall into a trap or sniff out and tangle themselves in a snare. My other trap is bigger, a number three, and I have set it where my grandfather told me to, along a dry wash up north. I have not yet caught a coyote, but I am hoping, which is why I'm here. Though my grandfather has trapped a fair number in his time, he is no maker of potions. He, too, came to Ed Dempsey, or before him Buster Knapp, for the promise of a tincture squeezed from the pea-sized glands of a coyote and mixed with rabbit piss and cow's blood and left to ferment for a good thirty years.

Ed takes up a small brown bottle and holds it to the light, then twists off the cap and gives it a sniff. He holds it out to me. I sniff, too. It smells of wet fur and oranges and what I think is sex. I would like to keep smelling it, but Ed pulls it back and caps it and wraps it in burlap and hands it to me, saying, "What you do is you break yourself open a bone, any bone, and dribble some of this in the hollow—just a drop or two now—and then set that bone right at the edge of a cutbank. You've got your trap set on a cutbank, right? Or a dry wash? Right, okay then, set it right at the edge, just past your trap—maybe in a sagebrush or something where it's hard to see or get to—and you by golly ought to have yourself a coyote come morning."

I nod and thank him and step out into the white light. Ed follows, pushing the wooden door shut and wrapping the length of hide tight around a nail. We make our way back up to the house, a two-story that like most in town has seen better days. Ed is old, too, and past his body's best work. He is now the mayor of Melstone. Though in his dark shed he still milks the bladders of skunks and muskrats, he spends his days dealing with school levies and zoning laws. I don't ask him how he reconciles these two lives, don't tell him how I hope for nothing so much as to trap a coyote, to steady the rifle at my shoulder, and as the coyote snaps and gnashes at its own bone-raw and bloody leg, shoot it cleanly in the head. Or why, after finishing Steinbeck's *Tortilla Flat* days before, I felt somehow bigger than myself and kindly toward all the world, even this one I feel most times I don't belong in.

I don't say any of these things. I shake his hand, say, "Thanks," and make my way down the gravel road to the general store, little scuffs of dust rising with my every step. And no one but Ed Dempsey knows I'm carrying in my pocket a glass bottle of magic.

FISHBELLY

In my Aunt Edith's studio I am quiet.

I have not been told to be quiet, I just am, for her studio—with its intricate tools and brushes and long-necked lamps on benches, its smells of paint and standing water and shaved pine—seems a place to be watchful and reverent.

I shut the door slowly and stand off to the side. I lean up against the wall with my hands behind me. I feel with my palms and fingertips the whorled, rough-cut boards, and I watch my Aunt Edith. Her back is to me and one lock of silvery hair hangs off the side of her head, obscuring her profile. With her calloused hands, nearly as big as a man's, she pulls the wet print from the face of the wood—all orange and fishbelly and pale blue, maybe the scab hills south of Billings at daybreak—and studies the colors and densities and textures, and finally hangs the print up with the others to dry. She is slow and deliberate, and maybe this is why I am quiet: her attention demands my attention; her care says there is something happening here beyond work or play. And the prints themselves, which seem like the best of stories, fairly pull the breath from my lips. I look at them. And look again.

"Oh," Aunt Edith says, turning, her wrinkled face sliding into a wide smile. "I didn't hear you come in. Goodness, how quiet you were! Shall we get some ice cream? Hmm? I think maybe I would like a bowl of ice cream. What about you, Joe?"

I am too old to be fussed over, but Aunt Edith, who is really my great aunt, my grandfather's older sister, has no children of her own and doesn't know, so I don't mind. Also, I very much want a bowl of vanilla ice cream dotted with raspberries fresh from her garden.

"Yes," I say. "I think I would like a bowl of ice cream, too."

Later, we go to dinner. I get ready in the third-floor bathroom. Aunt Edith's house is grand and yellow and sits on the rimrocks above the Yellowstone River and the city of Billings. You can see forever out this window, clear to the Bighorn and Beartooth mountains. You can see as well downtown—the thin streets and tall hotels and shiny bank buildings—which is where we're going for dinner. I scrub my face with soap, comb my hair, tuck my shirt into my jeans, and lace up my best sneakers. I rush down the first flight of stairs, which curves around the cone-topped turret of the house, and step more carefully down the next flight, in case Aunt Edith is ready and waiting for me.

She isn't. I stand around and study the framed photo of Aunt Edith's dead husband with his long, bearded face. He looks kind enough, I guess. Maybe a little disappointed. He failed, I have heard, at farming, and Aunt Edith supported them by teaching school. After he died, Aunt Edith started painting and making prints instead. Her work hangs in all those bank buildings downtown now, up at the Yellowstone Art Museum, too, and is all over the color inset pages of the journals she has stacked on the far end of the kitchen table. My Aunt Edith is an artist. It's thrilling and obscene to say it. *Artist.* It is a word that sounds like the look of red wine in stemmed glasses or pictures of Spain. Aunt Edith is as well an atheist. I know an artist makes things, but I don't quite understand what being an atheist entails, though I think it means her dead husband will not be waiting for her in heaven, like my mother says my father will be waiting for me.

"I've been waiting for you," I tell Aunt Edith, as she steps from her room wearing dark slacks and a long-sleeved, silky blouse, her silver hair pulled back in a tight bun. "Thank you. That was very kind." She smiles and looks in her finery both like my Aunt Edith and not like my Aunt Edith. "Shall we have some dinner?"

Dinner is at a Chinese restaurant downtown. It is the first time I have ever eaten at a Chinese restaurant. It is the first time I have ever eaten anywhere there are reservations and menus without prices and waitresses who don't write anything down. Aunt Edith orders for both of us, and while we wait for our food we talk about which things I like to study in school, about her artwork, about the news, about books. The waitress comes with steaming tea and some kind of sour soup, plates of rice and orange-colored chicken, thinly sliced beef with red strips of pepper. It's all new and strange and beautiful. Before we eat, I say, "Wait!" I look up at my Aunt Edith. "What are the names? I want to know the names of everything."

DARKENING

What you do is open slowly the thick furnace door, for just as soon as it is cracked the coal fire roars and oily smoke and sparks rush out. You take a long metal tool—which has a looped handle on one end and another handhold in the middle that you twist to open and close the claw on the far end—and reach into the fire and lift the clinkers, the tortuous looking byproducts of burnt coal, and drop them one by one into the ash can, a rusty black metal bucket in front of the furnace. Then, your face and hands and neck bathed with dry heat, you hang the claw back up and take a thin, long-handled shovel and scoop up the cinders and loose ash, though much of it lifts, rolls, and eddies in the fire's twisting wind, and shovel it too into the can. You latch the furnace door and breathe a moment. In the crook of your arm, you wipe your ashy, blasted face.

You are not done. You pick up the ash can by its handle and climb the basement stairs—careful not to let the hot metal bottom bump against your legs—and shoulder your way out the front door. The cold October wind fills your lungs as you haul the bucket out to the gravel road, where you dump the still-burning clinkers and ash in a rut, cinders leaping and wheeling and settling.

The sky is darkening, for it is usually right before dinner when you clean the furnace, and you look back at the house, with its lit windows and coal smoke slipping out the chimney, and you know it is warm in there and good. You understand then something of necessity: that a coal furnace gives an even heat, that one day the ruts of the road will fill with ash. That the world works like this: you shovel a pickup load of coal, you clean the furnace, you empty the ash cans, and you and yours stay warm. Though this is absolutely what you want, you stare at the dying glow of the clinkers, wind licking at your ears and wrists, and the stark fact of it shivers and braces you.

GONE

We rode into the world in the backs of pickups.

Say sitting atop what's left of a load of Bull Mountain furnace coal, my jeans blackening and greasy as my grandfather turns his Ford down the gravel road to our house, splitting this load of coal like the last between his stone cellar and our earthen one.

Maybe coming back from the ranch, my grandparents up front so my brother and me in the bed with our backs up against the cab, some old wooden posts and a thick-linked chain beneath us, the highway wind wheeling dust and straw.

Or letting the GMC idle where it will through the snow-swept north pasture, clambering into the back and cutting the twine and tossing a good ton or two of alfalfa hay flake by flake to the sheep.

Or the backs of our thighs burning against the tailgate as my mother drives us all down to the river for an afternoon swim.

Or a bunch of boys piling into the bed of my old GMC after school and riding down Main Street to the Lacy JC for Gatorades and beef jerky before basketball practice.

Or that boy, the one who seemed so certain the world would not ruin him, climbing out the back window of the cab and into the pickup bed at seventy-five miles an hour, tossing can after can of Mountain Dew behind us like bombs onto the highway.

Or the night my friend drank too much up at that summer basketball tournament in Reed Point. We were in the junior varsity division, on a team with some boys we'd played against during the previous season, and after we lost out, one of their older brothers told us to jump into the back of his sleek little Toyota pickup, and we did, and he drove us up into the Absaroka Mountains, where there was a fire of pine and cedar spitting hot sap and sparks, a radio turned up loud, cans of Bud Light and a bottle of vodka going around and around. We couldn't have been more than fourteen. We had been best friends since third grade—though in a few months my friend's mother, scared for her life, would leave for Kentucky in the middle of the night with him and his sisters, and we would lose touch.

That night, shoulder to shoulder in the pickup bed, where I'd made him lie down after he'd pulled on that bottle one too many times, my friend told me he wished his father would just die, that God was asleep at the wheel up there letting a son of a bitch like his father live, that it would be a whole lot easier if someone would just murder the bastard.

For the mountains and tall pines and ragged firelight, I couldn't even see the sky.

INKED

The dry heat of the day has finally risen. Grasshoppers scratch in the cheatgrass. A streetlight snaps on. Someone smacks a basketball against the blacktop.

There are probably thirty or so of us up at the outdoor court in Lodge Grass, on the Crow reservation, some hundred miles across the mountains from where I live. We are lounging on car hoods and listening to rap music, waiting for someone to get a game started. The court, with its new rims and clean square of cement, belies the rest of town: all the streets here fade into dust and ruts, razor wire rings the school building, and there's scarcely a business open. The basketball court, though, is beautiful. And so are Bruce and Randy, these two older boys I start shooting around with at a side basket.

Bruce's family used to live on a small hay farm down the river from us, but they moved a few years ago and run a large ranch along the Little Bighorn now, the river the Crow call the Greasy Grass. Bruce used to be my best friend, or at least I called him my best friend. Bruce had lots of friends. He was a grade above me and seemed to know everything: he taught me how to box in his basement, let me borrow his Metallica CDs, made sure I'd seen all the R-rated movies a boy should see. He went out with the prettiest girls and when he broke up with them told them they should go out with me. Some of them even did. But Bruce is different now. He speaks softly and looks not in your eyes but down and away. He's quieter, reined in, not at all the boy who once chugged fourteen cartons of chocolate milk in forty-seven seconds. And Randy is without a doubt Bruce's best friend now. I haven't seen them apart the whole time I've been here. Bruce has even become part of Randy's clan in a ceremony, which makes them—though one is white as me and the other the burnt-copper color of the sandstone cliffs in the distance—brothers.

Once the games begin, they go on for hours, everyone yelling and cheering, people smoking and drinking, players fighting, the rhythmic thump of hip-hop knocking through the dark prairie night. The winners stay on the court, so we wait a long time to get a game, and once we're on, the play is fierce—but we stay on. Bruce is thick in the chest and strong. Though a few inches shorter than me, he can take two dribbles and hammer the ball through the iron. Randy is tall and quick. He looks all elbows and knees but spins like the wind. His long hair flying, he slips through swaths of streetlight and rolls the ball off the backboard and in. It doesn't take long before whoever's playing defense on me starts sagging back to help out on Randy, who usually scores anyway. Near the end of our fourth or fifth game, Randy slices into the key and leaps and, for some reason, kicks the ball back out to me. I bobble it but am so wide open it doesn't matter: I have all the time in the world. I dribble, aim, and shoot. It's a three-pointer. I hit it. My first bucket of the night. Randy brushes back his long black hair, points at me and lifts his chin, says I shoot like an Indian.

I leave the Little Bighorn the next day and drive home. Bruce and I write a few more letters, but we lose touch.

I don't really mind. I've seen now how things can change, how distance and difference remake us. I study as hard as I always have, and in my senior year I apply for every scholarship I can find and even get quite a few of them. I lie in the tall grass in back of the house, the susurrus of cottonwood leaves above me, the pages of a novel my sky.

And I think of that single shot. I almost held onto it, almost waited until Randy was open again so I could pass the ball back to him. If it had been Bruce who passed it to me, I might have done just that. But it wasn't. And I didn't. I shot it. I see the ball arcing above us, turning and turning, at its zenith disappearing for a moment in the high prairie dark before dropping again into the light.

BRUISE-BLUE

If there had been a flood, a true flood, the dark and frothing waters slewing across the plain, our house would certainly have sheared from its moorings, drifted like a drunk, and sunk.

The foundation was bad. There was a great long crack in the stone and cement of the basement's south wall. When a summer storm thundered through, or when a chinook wind came whistling up from the south and the snow melted in a matter of hours, water sieved from that crack. The plaster fell away in chunks and the water came even quicker, muddier. My brother and I swept the water to the sump pump in the corner and shoveled out the mud. More than once, the pump burned out trying to keep pace with the rain. Then, until we could get to town to buy the right part, the whole basement would fill and mosquitoes would breed. Beyond the sodden books and ruined rug and shorted-out freezer—those hundreds of pounds of bloody, stinking, worm-rank meat—we knew the house itself might not hold. The south foundation wall might buckle, causing the house above to lean so far as to fall.

One summer I dug a trench around the perimeter, some three feet down, and dumped in bag after bag of powdered bentonite, which hardens when water hits it, and then packed dirt over the top. I didn't know what I was doing. I was hoping the bentonite would waterproof the foundation, though with every afternoon storm, thick clouds shouldering across the suddenly bruise-blue sky, the rain coming hard and fast, a gully washer, muddy water still ran and pooled in the basement.

My mother had a contractor pour a wide sidewalk around the foundation, but that didn't help, either. The contractor told us the only thing left to do was lift the house up into the air, tear out the foundation, and redo the whole thing. We didn't have the money for that. We shut the basement door. Let it flood, hoped the walls would hold.

And the foundation was just one thing among many. We had mice in all the closets, ants in the sugar drawer, mealworms wriggling in the flour, millers and other moths hatching eggs in the ceiling. In the summer, our little air conditioner cooled maybe a room and half. In the winter, we rubbed our stinging eyes and coughed as coal smoke rose from the vents. The kitchen counters were knife-scarred and stained with coffee and blood and burnt sugar, the wallpaper in the bathroom peeled off in sheets. Yet through it all, our old house weathered and stood. The waters never rose high enough, I guess, and the stone below, even broken, was stronger than it looked.

CLOUD-SHOT

I find the notes folded and shaped to the curve of my back. They must have slipped some time ago through this tear I have just discovered in the left pocket of my old red-checked jacket. The first note is from a small pad, folded once right down the center and faded now to a rinsed sky-blue; the other has been folded many times and is nearly worn to nothing along the creases.

Deep in the day's cares and worries, finishing up graduate school in a few weeks and on yet another plane to yet another job interview—Baltimore, this time—I can't make any sense of the first. *Masking tape and overshoes*, it says. *Stock salt. Steel posts. Handsaw. Claw hammer. 10-inch frying pan.* The script is my own, I think, but the list is utterly unfamiliar. I don't own a handsaw. What's this about stock salt? The second is just three names: *Donnie Laird. Clyde Brewer. Wade Kincheloe.* I read it again. And once more. These men were my father's friends. They were, like my father, hay farmers and sheep ranchers who drew their irrigation water from the Musselshell River. Like my father, all are dead. Yet my father died years before Wade or Donnie or Clyde, which made him a kind of sad legend. And legends—due to the teller's good-hearted dishonesty, the tale's anecdotal lack of detail—are something less than real. Though I fished this jacket years ago from the back of my father's closet, though my shoulders now fill the spaces his once filled—to me he has never been more than some sad-eyed farmer's beer-sour breath, the dusty photograph atop the front-room piano no one ever plays, my mother's Sunday morning tears.

Yet here, now, in my own two hands are these lists: the very things of a day, a season, a life. Was he on his way to Tractor Supply up in Billings? Or maybe the stockyards across the river? Did my mother, still in her nightgown and patching once again his old pair of overshoes with the last of the masking tape, remind him all morning not to forget? Did he owe Clyde money? Or did Donnie owe him? Were they all thinking of going in on some rangy Wyoming sheep? Maybe signing up for a truckload of good alfalfa hay? Was he just waiting for the irrigation water to roll to the back fence, sitting at the kitchen table and sorting things out with pen and paper and a cup of black coffee while light rimmed over the far hills and trees?

I stare at the lists through takeoff. Rub my thumb along the many creases, over the few still-sharp corners. The plane begins to level. Bright, upswept clouds slide beneath us, alternately obscuring and revealing the roads and rivers below. I trace carefully the slanted letters, so strangely like my own. Then, just to feel the syllables further, I say, out loud, "Clyde. Wade. Stock salt."

The woman sitting next to me frowns. I say again, louder this time, "Stock salt."

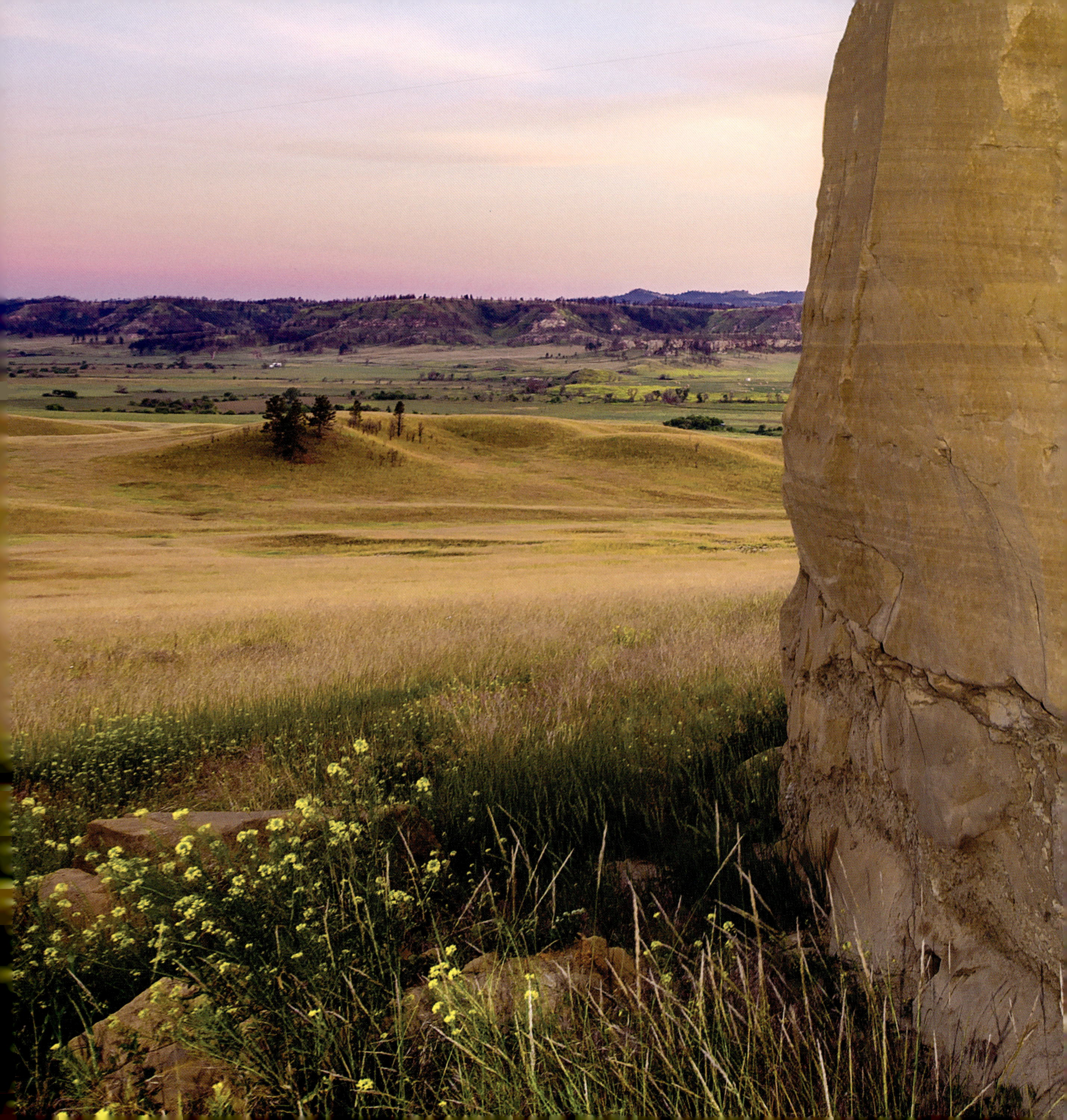

IN THIS PLACE

Alexis Bonogofsky

45°35'42.5"N 108°31'11.3"W

We are driving down a gravel road in Old Blue, my dad's Ford pickup, south of town on our way to a dryland wheat farm so he can fix a tractor tire. He is wearing his uniform, a light blue long-sleeved shirt and dark blue work pants. His name is written in cursive on a small patch over the front pocket.

I am eight, nine, maybe ten, and it is hot. Today the heat tastes like the fine eastern Montana dust that is coating my tongue and billowing up behind the truck. It will linger in the air; our path can be seen for miles around. I watch the road through a hole beneath my feet where the floor of the truck has rusted away.

The windows are down. My dad calls this "North Dakota air-conditioning." It feels like a giant blow-dryer is pointed straight at my face.

He has a bag of salted sunflower seeds between his legs. He puts a big handful in his mouth and then spits the shells out the window, one by one. He gives me a handful and it takes me a lot longer to get through them; my teeth and tongue are not as adept at removing the seeds. I try to spit my shells out the window like he does but most of them end up on the floor or the side of the door. I use my shoe to scrape them out the hole in the floor.

Shakespeare is lying between us but his head rests on my lap, panting, his eyes closed. His drool soaks my jean shorts.

The tractor is alone in a field when we get there.

"Why isn't he here?" I ask.

"Who? Steve? 'Cause he's smart."

I don't understand what my dad means by this, but I don't ask for an explanation.

He gets to work. I sit cross-legged in the middle of the dirt road and throw rocks. Time passes. I'm not sure how much. In this heat, seconds feel like hours.

"Dad. Dad!" He can't hear me over the air gun and compressor as he takes the lug nuts off the wheel. I get up and walk over. I'm hesitant to tap him on the shoulder but I do it anyway.

"What?" His face is red and his shirt is already soaked through with sweat.

"What can I do? I'm bored."

"Look around, kid. You can do whatever you want."

I look around. I see hot. I see dry. I call Shakespeare. Maybe he wants to play fetch. Then I remember: dogs named Shakespeare don't play fetch. He looks at me, his tongue lolling out of his mouth farther than you can imagine, and then turns and crawls under the pickup for shade. I consider joining him, but I notice a corral off in the distance and start walking toward it.

With every step I take through the sagebrush, some of it reaching my chest, dozens of grasshoppers leap onto me and bounce in front of me. I try to shoo them away but it's futile. I walk more slowly to see if they will calm down, but they continue to dance around me, flying up in long, graceful arcs into the never-ending blue sky. I pretend they are escorting me, announcing my arrival to the grasshoppers ahead.

A thunderhead builds on the horizon. I want to feel the raindrops on my face and tongue. I want to eat the clouds. The thunderhead is bright white on top, with shades of gray closer to the ground, almost black on the bottom. I feel a slight change in the air, maybe only a half-degree drop in temperature, but it feels as though the world has changed underneath my feet. A slight breeze brings the clean smell of sage. I hear distant thunder.

The cloud climbs itself, growing taller and taller as I watch—a wild invitation.

Grasshoppers begin to land on my shoulders and arms and legs. I don't brush them off. They are invited, too.

The thunderhead expands up and out, coming toward me. We will meet somewhere in the middle.

I walk faster and the grasshoppers leap higher in ever-widening circles reaching out across the world.

In this place I learn to see beauty where it lives.

45°43'26.8"N 106°41'02.0"W

In the early morning and evening, light travels quickly through sandstone formations that emerge from the prairie like sentinels, illuminating the ancient geology of the land. Here, you can see the entire sky. I like to walk in this country. I like to chase the light.

Right now, I am walking with a young mule deer buck. He is moving westward in the open prairie toward the Little Wolf Mountains. Nick, the rancher who is letting me hunt on his place, calls it the "Big Open."

We walk together for almost an hour, hundreds of yards apart. Occasionally, the buck glances over at me while he grazes. I watch him watch me. I am not hidden at all. Even if there were cover, I'm not sure I'd take it. Right now, I'm more interested in walking with him than hunting.

Eventually, we pass on either side of a small hill. I arrive at the other side first and sit behind a large sagebrush. My heart starts to beat faster. There is a decision I have to make.

A few moments later, I see him emerge from a draw. He sees me lift my rifle to my shoulder and stops seventy-five yards away from me, broadside.

I take the safety off and put my finger on the trigger.

I think.

Run.

I think.

Run.

I think.

Run.

I think.

I won't shoot if you run.

He watches me.

My heart is thumping in my chest. It is all I can hear.

I aim just behind his shoulder.

I watch him watch me. I inhale. Exhale. When my breath is almost gone, there is stillness in my ears, my heart, my lungs.

I think.

Run.

I squeeze the trigger.

Anyone who knows, knows what it looks like when your aim is true.

He drops to his knees and then gently set his back end down. His head slowly lowers and rests on the ground. I watch him through the scope. His body rises and falls with breath that slows until there is no movement.

I cry.

In this place I learn that sadness and gratitude sometimes feel the same.

48°24'06.9"N 105°00'19.5"W

Standing in a blizzard in the middle of the prairie is a remarkable thing.

It is cold. It hurts to breathe. The wind is brutal; I turn my back to it. I can barely feel my hands and feet. My quilted Carhartts are not enough to keep me warm. My teeth are chattering. The only light comes from truck headlights illuminating a large corral. A couple dozen people huddle together in groups around the other vehicles.

It is almost midnight when we get word that the semis hauling the Yellowstone bison have just crossed the Missouri River and are on tribal lands. They will be here soon. The drums and the singing begin to welcome the bison home.

In this place I learn about restoration.

→ 45°43'41.6"N 108°32'22.5"W →

I walk out my back door, through the yard, into the north pasture all the way to the first slough, and keep going until I end up in our dog graveyard. I never call it that, but that's what it is. When someone asks, I say it's the place we bury our dogs. That sounds less morbid.

When I go there I remember two moments.

I see my dad dressed in an old Big Sky State Games T-shirt, Wrangler jeans, tennis shoes, a ball cap, and his aviator sunglasses. He is digging a deep hole in the ground under a small hill.

Next to him, wrapped in a blanket, is Max, his German Wirehaired Pointer. Max the Great. Max, there has never been another dog like him. Max, the dog who would retrieve any bird no matter what. Max, who went to work at the tire store with my dad every day and had his own doggy door so he could move freely in and out of the shop. That Max.

He is black-and-white and has a beautiful beard and he is dead.

I am standing next to the skid steer that holds a bucket of rocks from the Yellowstone River that I brought up to cover his grave. I watch as my father picks Max up and gently lays him in the ground. I stay quiet as he grabs the shovel to fill in the hole.

Everyone who knows, knows the first shovel of dirt is the hardest.

You are wondering what the second moment is.

It is a Saturday morning in late September. I sit on my four-wheeler in the clearing. On the back of the four-wheeler is my cat Dustin. He is in a box. He will be the first cat to be buried in the place where we bury our dogs, a worthy honor for a cat who most likely thought he was a dog.

My dad calls my cell phone. We start talking about smoking meat. He had a custom smoker built out of a stainless-steel cooler he bought at an auction when a restaurant closed in Billings. I am using it today to smoke beef brisket for a friend's wedding. I ask him to come down to the farm and help me.

"You don't need me, honey. You can do it yourself," he says.

I bury Dustin next to Max.

The next day my dad dies.

You don't need me, honey. You can do it yourself. I leave those words in that clearing on my farm. They stay there. If I want to remember them, I take a short walk.

In this place I learn that the land holds memories for us when they are too hard to carry by ourselves.

→ 45°36'21.1"N 106°16'52.3"W →

It is a cool, early June evening and we are all standing in a parking lot waiting to eat. Burgers sizzle on a grill. People mill about, chatting in groups.

We were all there to speak at a public hearing on the proposed Tongue River Railroad, which, if built, would haul coal from the Otter Creek Valley to coal ports on the West Coast. I think about the three hours we all just spent in the school auditorium: the Northern Cheyenne, the ranchers, the Amish.

Their words echo in my head.

“My name is Otto Braided Hair. Very emotional. We have spiritual ties to this land. One of the things that I was told is that every creek, every drainage, has some of our blood in it. If they weren’t buried there, they were killed there. In this whole area, this whole region. That’s why it means so much to us.”

“My name is Clint McRae, my family and I ranch on Rosebud Creek and the ranch borders on the Tongue River . . . . You claim that one residence will be displaced. I’m assuming it will be one of the Amish houses that the railroad is supposed to go through. Has anyone actually gone and talked to the Amish and visited with them? The answer is no.”

“My name is Brad Sauer. I ranch down the creek here. I want to say to my neighbors the Northern Cheyennes, thank you for showing me what free speech looks like and sounds like . . . .”

I sit down on the curb. I watch people laugh. I watch them eat and drink together. I watch them pat each other on the back and I know at that moment we have won. The Tongue River Railroad and Otter Creek coal mine will not be built under their watch.

In this place I learn about community.

45°43'26.8"N 106°41'02.0"W

Find a place to sit down.

Sit down.

Be quiet.

The sandstone rock I choose looks like an ocean wave. I take off my hunting pack and lay my rifle down in the grass. There is no way that I’m the only person who has ever slept on this rock. It is too perfect.

The air is cold but the sun is warm and I climb up onto the rock and find a spot where it gently wraps around my body. I close my eyes. There is a heavy feeling to the sun’s light in November. It presses into you like a wool blanket.

Anyone who knows, knows that the naps you take while hunting are the best naps.

The only sounds are a light breeze moving through the grass and my heart beating.

I drift off.

I dream that I place my hand on the sandstone and feel it expand, like lungs filling up with this sacred air, and then slowly release.

I wake with the words of a W. S. Merwin poem in my head:

> *If there is a place where this is the language may*
> *It be my country*

In this place I learn that the earth breathes.

⟶ 44°58'52.7"N 109°26'29.6"W ⟶

So far I have spoken only of prairies. But now I will speak of a mountain.

I was once a child struggling to keep up with the long strides of my parents as we hiked down to this mountain lake and now here I am, holding my niece Lila's hand while she bounces from one rock to another as we cross a wide swath of snowmelt in our path.

My sister is in front of me, holding my nephew Liam's hand, and my mother is up ahead taking photos of wildflowers on her phone. My border collie Lena is at my heel.

My dad is in my backpack. Part of him, anyway.

We make it down to the lake. It feels like it is our lake.

Four-year-old Lila takes off her shoes, then her socks, and finally her pants. She steps into the icy water. I hold her hand as she takes a couple of steps, seizes up from the cold, and then bounds out, knowing I'll catch her.

"I told you it was cold," I say as I use my shirt to dry her legs.

She asks me if I think mermaids live in the lake.

"Definitely," I answer.

She nods her head seriously, then looks up along the snow embankment.

"Why is the snow red?" she asks.

"It's algae."

"How did allergies get on the snow?"

I love her so much. We fish. Seven-year-old Liam catches brown trout with a fishing pole with Elsa from the Disney movie *Frozen* on the reel.

We have a picnic.

We have one more thing to do.

"OK guys, we have to talk," I say as they both nod. "When people die, some people, instead of being buried, get what we call 'cremated.' They are burned in a fire and turn into ash. Grandpa Tom loved this place, so we are going to leave some of his ashes here."

I don't think they understand but they nod again.

I take out the thick plastic bag that holds a small portion of my father's ashes. It is rolled tight and has lots of tape on it. I finally get the tape off and unroll it. The ash is finer and whiter than I imagined it would be. It looks like powder.

I'm not sure what to do next. I look at my sister and my mom. We never talked about how this would work.

I ask the kids if they want to put the ashes into the lake. They say yes and start to argue about who gets to do it first.

Liam takes the bag first and walks to the little creek that flows from the snowbank. He slowly tips it upside down. He is gentle with it. Not much comes out. My sister helps him. Fine white ash floats down the stream and into the lake. He does half and then it's Lila's turn.

She grabs the bag and dumps the rest directly and unceremoniously into the lake.

"He looks like a ghost in the water," Liam says, looking up at me. "Is he a ghost in the water now?"

"Is he?" Lila asks.

They look at me and then my sister and then my mom.

"He looks like smoke spreading out in the water," Liam says.

"He'll be up here with the mermaids," Lila says.

There is joy to be found where you would never think to look for it.

In this place I learn that grief and love are the same feeling.

45°46'12.6"N 106°28'26.6"W

I cannot end this story on a mountain because my heart lies in the east, "where the sky comes down the same distance all around."

I am hiking up a hill. Lena is right behind me. It is almost dawn in the early fall and there is a blanket of fog covering the land. Where I'm headed is high enough that I think I'll break through the mist and be able to look out over the country when the sun rises over the horizon.

Elk are bugling in the pine trees below me where the land gets rough. The prairie is broken by scores of coulees, startlingly beautiful sandstone formations, and layered buttes.

Countless times I have seen the sun come up over the prairie and I am amazed that I have been allowed to witness such moments. I have seen all the prairie sunrises I need to be happy and yet I have not seen enough of them. The land begins to lighten. The sun will be here soon.

Lena and I get to the top.

I think.

Find a place to sit down.

Sit down.

Be quiet.

There is no time to waste.

In this place I learn what hope is.

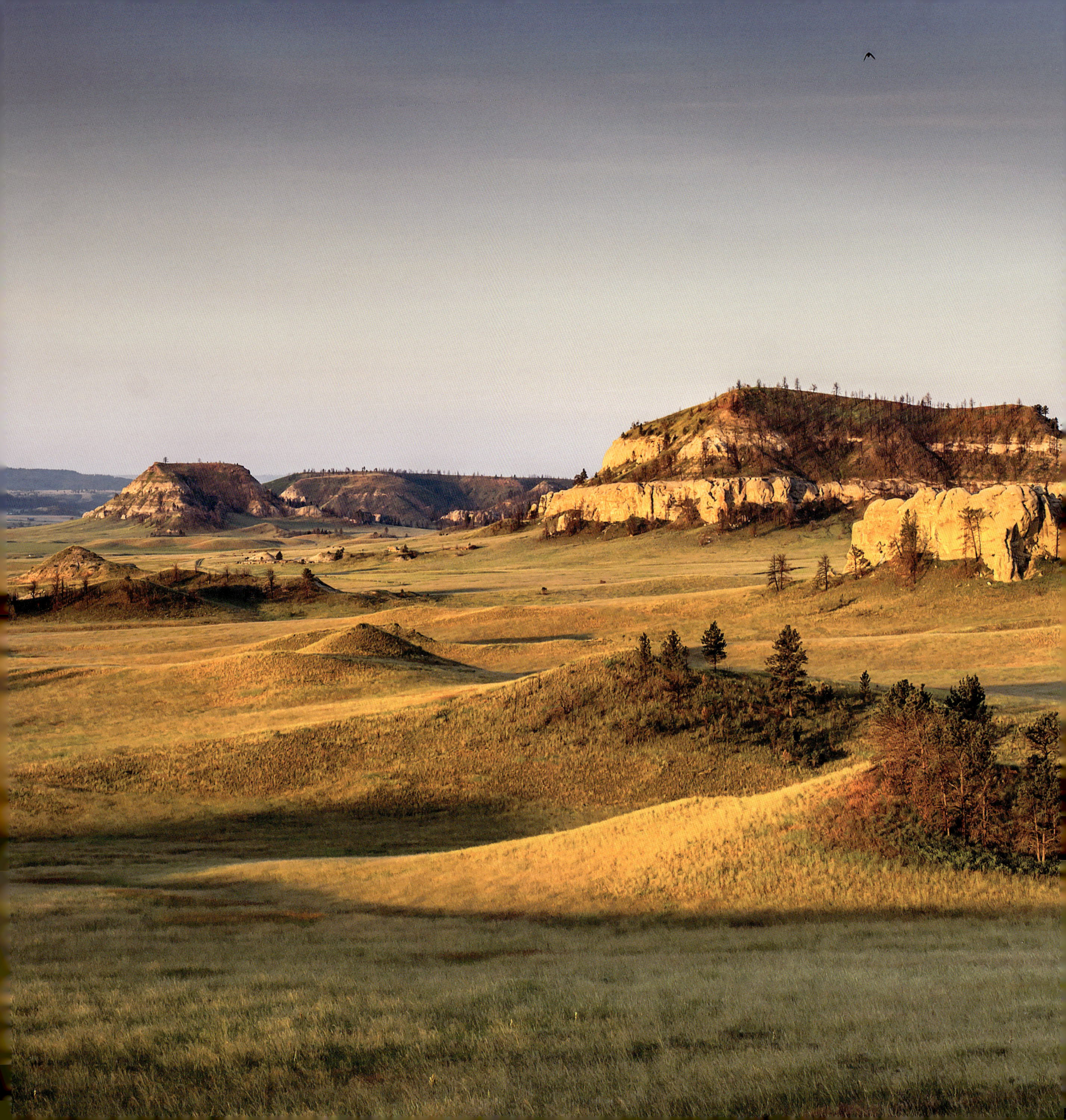

BREAKING THROUGH THE FENCE

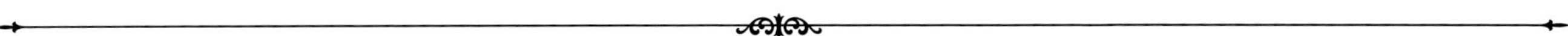

Russell Rowland

Stiff and tired, I climbed down from the mail truck, pulled my bag out of the back, and waved goodbye to the driver, who had not stopped talking since she picked me up in Ekalaka two hours earlier. This was 1974, a time when you could still catch a ride with the mail, and I had been traveling all night from Billings to my grandparents' ranch in southeastern Montana. For the first leg of the journey, about two hundred miles, I had been wedged between the driver and another passenger, and at sixteen years old was horrified by the thought of falling asleep on a stranger's shoulder. So when the second driver wouldn't stop talking, all hopes of a nap went out the window with her first mail sack. Dawn was just breaking as I approached my grandparents' house on the Arbuckle Ranch.

I hadn't slept a wink and all I could think about was crawling into bed. But my Uncle Lee rushed out of the house, clearly alarmed. "Take your bag inside," he told me. "There's a fire at the Thomas place."

I swallowed my complaints as we drove to the Finger Buttes, a few miles from the ranch. With an ad hoc fire crew consisting solely of neighbors, we spent the next several hours dunking burlap sacks into barrels of water and beating that fire until our hands were chapped. We prevented the fire from spreading to the dry grass below the butte, where there was no telling how quickly it would have spread. I was exhausted by the time we finished. But I also felt an incredible sense of pride and accomplishment, feelings that would become very familiar over the next six weeks. After we had contained the fire, people joked with one other and teased the landowner about pulling them away from their work. Relief brought out the humor in everyone—this would also become a familiar dynamic.

For the next month and a half, I spent ninety percent of the daylight hours working: stacking hay, driving heavy machinery, riding, and branding. It was my first job and it remains the hardest one I've ever had. And in many ways, it was the best experience of my life. As a sixteen-year-old kid, I had very little sense of what it meant to earn my way. This was also the first time I had been away from home for an extended period, and I grew up fast.

I lived with my Uncle Lee and Aunt Maggie, and they proved to be marvelous guides as I made this transition. Lee was demanding, but never cruel, and Maggie made me feel like part of their family. There was a great deal of laughter and discussion at the dinner table. Lee had attended an Ivy League college and served two stints in the Peace Corps, first in Colombia and then Bolivia, where he met Maggie, who was Bolivian and had attended schools in America. They were people of the world, anomalies in this isolated ranch country.

So along with the manual labor, I was challenged intellectually, too.

Lee was the first adult in my life who talked to me as though I were also an adult. One day when we were riding horses out into the vast emptiness that is eastern Montana, he turned to me and asked, "So what is it that keeps you going, Russell? What prevents you from putting that proverbial gun to your head?"

The question shocked me. No one in my family ever brought up such touchy, emotional subjects. But he followed it with an infectious laugh, and I could only laugh along with him as I pondered the question.

As you would imagine from a boy of sixteen, my answer wasn't profound, but it stays with me: I told him I liked my future. I can't remember why I said that, but it has sometimes been a comfort to me that I once felt that way. It took a while for me to find my way after that summer. After a bout with alcohol and a few detours around the country, I eventually made my way back to Montana, first through the written word, and then by settling down there again.

One day, Lee announced that two of his bulls had broken through the fence and made their way onto a neighboring ranch. He told me to ride out and fix the fence, then retrieve the bulls and move them back to their pasture.

My grandparents' ranch was huge, roughly twenty-five thousand acres, and the corner in which these bulls were pastured was about as far from the house as you could go. It was a job that would take a good part of the day, but I loved riding, so I took my time getting there. When I got to the broken fence, I set to work mending it. In the distance, the bulls watched as if they knew what to expect and weren't the least bit interested. After I finished, I ate the lunch Maggie had packed for me, then found the gate about fifty yards down the fence line. I went through and left it open so I could guide the bulls back where they belonged.

Then came the hard part. I had moved plenty of cattle in the previous weeks, and it was a job I enjoyed, but I had never dealt with bulls before. That day, I found out how stubborn they can be. Each time I got them moving toward the gate, one or the other—or both—would suddenly trot off in a different direction. It took a good hour to finally coax them along the fence to the gate. And when we got there, they wouldn't go through without lumbering around me a few more times.

Fed up, I threw out a few swear words as I closed the gate and climbed back into the saddle. The sun was dropping, but I figured I could make it back to the house by suppertime.

I started back but, halfway across the pasture, turned to take one last look at the bulls. They had broken through the fence again, in the same damn place as before.

My first thought, I'm embarrassed to admit, was to ride back to the house and feign ignorance when the call inevitably came. It would have been perfectly plausible that the bulls busted through after I left. But I had the foresight to realize that, when it came time to fix the fence and retrieve the bulls again the next day, the job would fall on one person and one person only.

I turned around.

Lee died of lung cancer, although he had never smoked in his life. He contracted multiple sclerosis the year after I worked for him, and although he lived another forty years with that disease, it became impossible to run the ranch as he would have preferred to do. Instead, he worked for the US Agency for International Development, living in several different Latin American countries to help develop co-ops and credit unions in agricultural communities.

He and Maggie moved back to Montana after he retired, and he continued to be a guiding force in my life. During his final year, I helped him write his memoirs, an experience that brought us closer together and gave me more insight into the way he saw the world. But there was always a slight distance between him and other people that I never quite understood. We were nearing the end of the project when I finally heard something that helped explain it.

When Lee was ten, he was riding around the ranch with George, one of his Arbuckle cousins, when they decided to go for a swim in a reservoir one of his uncles had built to provide more water for the livestock. My grandfather had warned Lee never to swim in this particular reservoir, but the boys were hot and feeling adventuresome, so they stripped down and dove in.

George was not a strong swimmer, and once he got in over his head, he began first to struggle and then to panic. Lee swam to him and offered a leg to hold on to, thinking he would tow George to safety. But after grabbing Lee, George thrashed around so much that he started to take Lee under with him. Lee had to break free in order to save himself. As he told me what happened, some sixty years later, I could hear the deeply felt, unresolved pain in his voice.

After they fished George's body from the reservoir, family and friends gathered at the house. Lee was inconsolable; not only had he been unable to save George, he had created the danger in the first place by defying his father's rules. He was sitting on the stairway sobbing when George's older sister, Rieta, sat down next to him.

"Lee, you're not helping anyone by carrying on like this," she told him. "You're making things worse. For my mother, especially. You need to stop."

I had always known about the drowning, but when Lee told me this part of the story, it hit me like a stone. His guilt and grief explained so much about who he was. And the way he shared this advice from Rieta—as if it was the best advice he ever got—told me how he'd become a man who spent a lifetime warding off his emotions.

Lee took her words to heart and never allowed himself to fully feel the sadness of what happened that day. Driven to succeed, be became an all-state football player and valedictorian in high school before earning two masters' degrees from Dartmouth. His mind was always working: when telling a story, he would veer off into tangents that could last half an hour, about the economic instability of Colombia in the 1940s or the contempt he held for Che Guevara. He had an encyclopedic mind, and in some ways used it as a shield. It was as if he spent his whole life running to stay one step ahead of the feelings evoked by that day.

One day just before he died, while we were still working on his manuscript, Lee turned to me and said, “I’m glad we’re related.” It was the closest he ever came to telling me he loved me.

Because he was the patriarch of that generation, we often followed his lead. Most of my family is bullheaded and struggles to tap into the emotional well that all of us have whether we like it or not.

But Lee set a positive example, too: he was curious about the world. He was my godfather and took the role seriously, counseling me on my choices more than my own father did. I left Montana in my late twenties and lived in twelve different states over the next twenty-five years. Part of my motivation was the need to avoid facing myself, but most of it was a sincere desire for adventure. I went to graduate school in Boston and served my country in the Navy.

During my travels, I always had a strong feeling that Montana would call me back someday. It started in my work: all my books are set in Montana, and I never really considered writing about anywhere else. What I found myself exploring in my writing was how such a brutal and unforgiving place shapes the people who live in it.

There is a quietness in Montana, especially in the eastern half of the state, that surrounds you and fills you up, eventually becoming part of who you are. The act of talking becomes an effort that is too much for some. Especially talking about difficult things. And so much of life here is difficult.

What we learn here is that everything is unpredictable. A sudden hailstorm can wipe out a years’ worth of work in a few minutes. A lightning strike in the buttes can threaten your entire ranch. A summer dip can change your life forever. Not having control over the unknown is a constant source of stress, but it also makes people here adaptable. The fear of being a nuisance by talking about our feelings can motivate us to get out and do something to change our lives. It’s when that fear becomes too much that it becomes a danger. I know this was true for me for a long time. It was a big part of why I drank.

We learn that we can’t let fear of the unknown keep us from doing our jobs. Or from simply living. Because along with the unpredictability, this wide-open land also promises that anything is possible. And sometimes we have to break through the fences around us to find those possibilities.

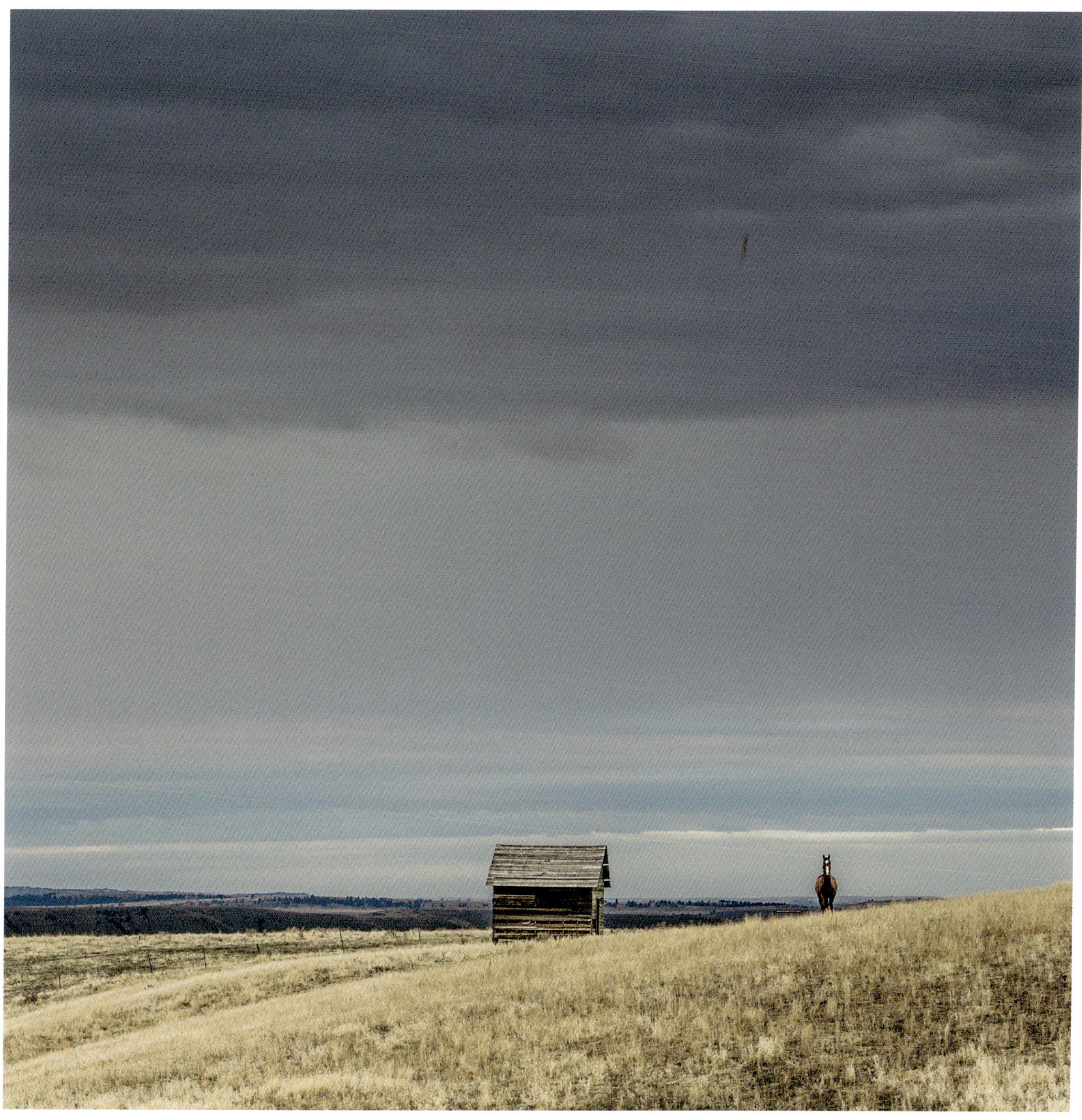

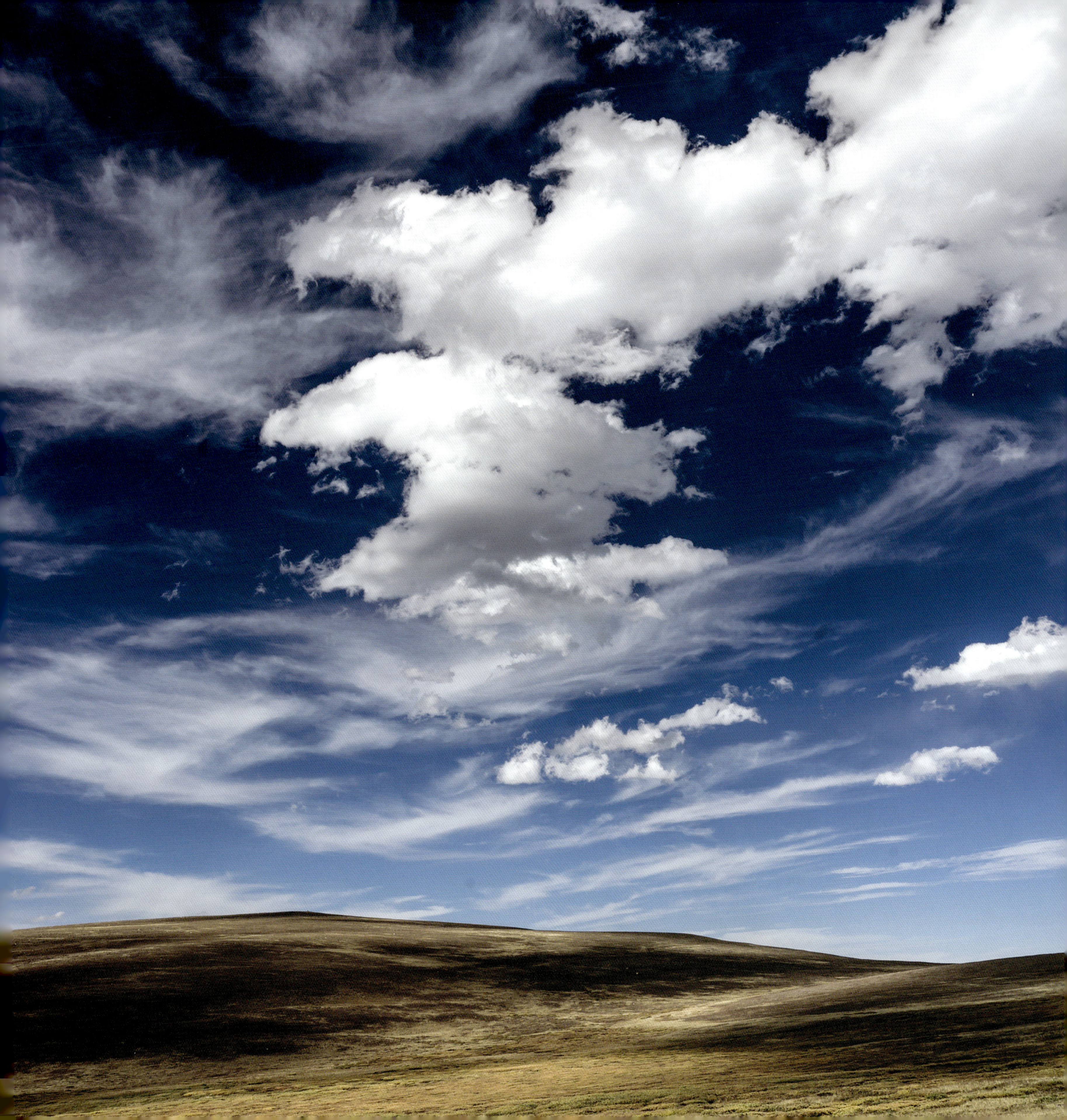

THE SOUL OF THE PRAIRIE

Jim Robbins

On a warm, sun-washed summer afternoon too many years ago to count, I topped a ridge in Glacier National Park's backcountry and peered for the first time into another world. In the brilliant, high-altitude sun, ribbons of water poured over ledges and splashed onto rocks below, spraying in the air before tumbling down to an improbably turquoise lake in the valley bottom. The air was delightfully moist and cool as I hiked down to the lake, nearly ten degrees less than the temperature in the front country where I'd started. Mountain goats peered down from above, unalarmed, cocking their heads with wide-eyed curiosity. Grizzly bears were out there somewhere and the possibility of an encounter added an element of uncertainty, an edge of fear that stoked alertness. I peered up at a nickel gray, snow-draped peak towering above and felt a rush of insignificance. A kid from the urban East, it was my first foray deep into Glacier and I was overwhelmed. More than forty years later, I still backpack almost every summer into its wild mountain lakes and I am still in awe.

To get to western Montana from the East Coast, I had driven across eastern Montana, a landscape that registered only as long hours of windshield time and treeless hills before I got to Missoula, a place where mountains formed the kind of sculptures I wanted to live among.

I didn't give the prairie much thought. It wasn't until decades later that I traveled back to the grasslands, on assignment for a national magazine, to take a deep dive into what was going on there. "Anyone can love the mountains, but it takes a soul to love the prairie," wrote Willa Cather, the nineteenth-century prairie prophet. I guess I am one of the anyones she refers to. My assignment, then, wasn't just to write an article, but to search for my soul.

It's not far from where I live to the beginning of the prairie. One fine spring day, I drove east from Helena, away from the mountains. I planned to explore the prairie, to dig—literally and metaphorically—beneath its surface. It's a harsh, extreme world, this broad sweep of American outback, with "the nation's hottest summers and coldest winters, greatest temperature swings, worst hail and locusts and range fires, fiercest droughts and blizzards, and therefore its shortest growing season," according to Frank and Deborah Popper, married scholars from Rutgers. Their 1987 paper, "The Great Plains: From Dust to Dust," was the first argument for turning the plains away from farming and back into its natural state as a kind of giant wildlife preserve.

One of the arguments they made was that farming on the prairie has largely failed; where it does exist, it is propped up by generous federal subsidies. Even with them, many towns have shrunk or been abandoned.

Martinsdale seems to fit that bill. It's a town on the wind-scoured plains between the snow-frosted Castle and Crazy mountain ranges, going but not yet gone. As I got out of the car to walk along the main street, the wind nearly tore the door off its hinges. It was once a stop on the transcontinental railroad and its residents clearly believed prosperity was right around the corner, as evidenced by the stout, red-brick Stockman's Bank. When I visited, it had been boarded up so long, the paint was peeling off the boards. The wind howled through the smashed-out windows of a crumbling train station long since abandoned, its rails torn up and carted away. The Martinsdale hotel and the grocery store were over, though the green neon sign above the Mint bar was glowing and someone was washing the windows at the closed café. Winds howled through the broken windows of an abandoned school, cars rusted in front yards, old signs creaked in the wind, empty stores were boarded up, and to complete the scene, a tumbleweed cartwheeled across a field. In a story repeated across the plains, as farms and ranches got bigger, the people who once lived on them migrated out.

As I continued east and then angled north toward the Hi-Line, the plains were in many places flat and featureless with nothing to break the monotony, so empty they conjured a faint longing. This is the kind of country where you could, as they say, watch your dog run away for three days. A tree was a cause for celebration. "Trees were so rare in that country, and they had to make such a hard fight to grow, that we used to feel anxious about them, and visit them as if they were persons," Cather wrote in *My Ántonia*. The unrelenting space that rolled away in every direction, the isolation and remoteness and relentlessly howling wind caused a malady among some early pioneers called "prairie madness." People wept and raved, sometimes walking off into howling blizzards never to be seen again.

That I couldn't muster much enthusiasm for the prairie at first, I came to realize, was largely because of what our species and our great machines have done to it: much of it is now overgrazed pasture or featureless farm fields devoid of most native life forms.

In the past, though, it was very different. Lewis and Clark wrote eloquently about an incredibly bountiful land. I headed northeast, along the Missouri River east of Great Falls where they had explored. "This senery already rich pleasing and beatiful was still farther hightened by immence herds of Buffaloe, deer Elk and Antelopes which we saw in every direction feeding on the hills and plains," Meriwether Lewis wrote in his journal.

There are three kinds of native American prairie. Short- and mixed-grass prairies run from central Texas to southern Saskatchewan, including Montana, and parts of Alberta and Manitoba. Some seventy percent of the native grassland in the northern Great Plains is gone, though only a third has disappeared in Montana. Tallgrass prairie was once found in eastern Texas, eastern Oklahoma, eastern Nebraska, and on up to the Dakotas. Tallgrass refers to the five species that make up the mix and they are indeed the tallest species, though they don't always reach great heights. Intact mixed-grass prairie without invasive species is rare.

Conservationists have taken a worldwide inventory of imperiled ecosystems and concluded that of the world's biomes, native grasslands are the least protected. For example, just one and a half percent of the northern

Great Plains has been set aside, while anywhere from eight to ten percent of tropical grasslands and tropical forests is protected. There is an ongoing campaign to set aside grass preserves across the plains and Montana has several.

It's not just about grass. The protein-rich plants are at the bottom of the Great Plains food pyramid and sustain a variety of wildlife. Prairie dogs are an essential element of the ecosystem and were once scattered by the millions across the West, living in socially complex communities. On a previous trip, near Greycliff, I had watched a town of prairie dogs go about their daily lives, running around like the cartoon chipmunks Chip and Dale, nervously chattering and scurrying about.

In many places war has been made against prairie dogs because they can seriously damage grazing land or farm fields, and vast numbers have been done in by poison, hunting, and the flooding of their burrows. One man invented something called "Dog-B-Gone," a truck with a vacuum hose that sucks the little guys out of their hole, the idea for which he said came to him in a dream. Varmint-hunting outfitters that go by names such as "Seekers of the Red Mist" and "Headhunters" offer trips where people can dress up in camouflage and shoot unsuspecting rodents as they stick their heads up out of their holes.

Conservationists, on the other hand, are trying in many places to protect this much-despised animal because prairie-dog towns are the grocery store for myriad species, from swift foxes to coyotes, wolves, ferruginous hawks, and the unusual-looking weasel with the face coloring that makes it look like a burglar, the endangered black-footed ferret.

Ferrets are predators of the plains, living in the same burrows as their only prey, the prairie dogs, which they kill and devour when the prairie dogs are asleep. One ferret eats about one hundred forty prairie dogs each year, or one every three days. When the prairie dog was nearly wiped out in the 1970s, the ferret was thought to have gone the way of the dodo.

In 1981, however, a dog named Shep on a ranch near Meeteetse, Wyoming, brought home a dead ferret. Ranchers John and Lucille Hogg, puzzled by the strange creature, took it to a taxidermist who recognized it and called federal officials. Eighteen ferrets were found living on the Hoggs' ranch, the last of their kind. The ferrets were carefully trapped and bred in captivity. There are now around 500 extant, including some in north central Montana.

As the grasslands have declined, so have the songbirds that voice the famed prairie symphony, from Baird's sparrow to McCown's longspur to Sprague's pipit. The numbers of these and other grassland-dependent birds has plummeted and there is concern for their future.

At the romantic heart of the Great Plains restoration movement, though, is the largest land mammal in North America: the bison. Tens of millions of the brown, shaggy-headed beasts roamed the plains from northern Mexico almost to Alaska. The herds were so large that many early explorers questioned their sanity upon seeing them. The bison were hunted until they were on the edge of extinction—but just before they blinked out, they were bred back into viability.

While there is disagreement about whether bison are better for the land than cattle because they graze differently, the real difference appears to be how the animals are managed. Grazing, ecologists say, is a necessary part of the Great Plains ecosystem. Bison that roam freely graze different areas with different intensity, creating a mosaic of varied habitat for multiple species.

Bison create wallows, for example, that become small prairie potholes with a diversity of species in and around them. When bison die in the wild, their carcasses rot in place, becoming a nitrogen-rich pile of bones. The places they graze heavily appeal to the mountain plover, and the places they don't graze at all appeal to Baird's sparrow.

We tend to focus on the charismatic species, but at the bottom of this mind-bogglingly productive system, of course, was the prairie itself, a natural perpetual-motion machine that renewed itself again and again to produce a vast crop of protein-rich wild grasses each year. The little bluestem, needle and thread, and other grasses evolved in reaction to fire, drought, and cold, growing stronger and more resilient as the years passed. Where there was tallgrass prairie, the stands were so dense and so tall that newly arrived settlers sometimes thought people riding through fields on horseback were walking.

Farming and ranching have crowded out most of the ancient native prairie grasses. So much water has been pumped out of some aquifers that rivers and streams have been diminished or even gone dry and wind has carried away much of the soil. "We were given a gift from the last ice age," a scientist told me, "but in some places thirty to fifty inches of topsoil has disappeared since."

In their paper, the Poppers proposed deprivatizing the plains and replacing a fading agricultural economy on taxpayer-provided life support by playing to the prairie's strengths—using native grasses that are already adapted to the harsh climate and need no federal subsidies, fossil fuels, herbicides, pesticides, or pumped water to grow.

They envisioned bison and other disappearing species, from ferrets to prairie chickens, roaming freely on a vast landscape: an American Serengeti called the Buffalo Commons. People living in and around the Commons, they suggested, could subsist on tourism and hunting. As they conducted a series of meetings on the Great Plains, their proposal sparked enormous controversy. They were vilified, shouted at, and in some places almost run out of town. It seemed like an intriguing, if somewhat radical, idea but nothing more.

But the prairie winds have shifted. The seed the Poppers planted has grown as biologists, NGOs, Indian tribes, the federal government, and even Ted Turner have in the last thirty years reassembled pieces of the prairie, especially here in Montana. They are just pieces so far, and how far the re-wilding goes remains to be seen, but from Canada and Montana to Kansas and Texas, herds of wild bison have been, or will soon be, brought back to roam vast acreage. Frank Popper is tickled. "What was such a fantasy in 1987," he told me, "has steadily materialized ever since. No one is more surprised than I am."

One of the places where the Buffalo Commons has come into being is the American Prairie Reserve in north-central Montana with large parcels on either side of the Upper Missouri River Breaks National Monument. As I drove from Lewistown toward it, the sky darkened to the ominous color of a deep bruise, and the radio station interrupted the country and western music I was listening to with a tornado warning. Though more common further south, these dark dervishes are fairly rare in Montana. Without the protection of a storm cellar—or a "fraidy hole" as a friend calls them—the best strategy, I had heard, was to lie in a ditch, though giving up the protection of the car seemed worrisome. Fortunately, a tornado never appeared.

By the time I reached Malta, the sun had come out and its effect on the land was electric, illuminating the green spring grass until it seemed to glow. I drove to the ranch on a muddy road and watched as a truck full of bison was unloaded, the animals kicking and snorting as they were set free on the landscape. The preserve has now raised more than seventy-five million dollars to buy private land adjacent to federal holdings and create a new bison home on the range with ten thousand head roaming three and a half million acres. They have built yurts for overnight visitors and they allow some hunting. It is the Buffalo Commons realized.

It has not gone over well with some. Many cattle ranchers in the region see a threat to their way of life if federal land is turned over to bison. They have launched a campaign to "Save the Cowboy—Stop the American Prairie Reserve."

If the population of Phillips County continues to dwindle—according to each census since 1920, it has lost ten percent of its population, declining from 9,600 to around 4,300—a vast wildlife refuge could be an economic engine.

The American Prairie Reserve's mission isn't just to bring back the bison, but a restored prairie ecosystem home to everything from prairie dogs to foxes. Perhaps even grizzly bears, someday. Once a prairie animal, they are growing in number and making their way back out to the grasslands as far east as Two Dot and Shelby, though they haven't reached Malta—yet.

The undulating blankets of grasses, I would learn later, are not at the very bottom of the prairie ecosystem. The soul of the prairie, the engine that powers the grasses, the buffalo and prairie dogs that eat the grasses, the eagles and coyotes that eat the prairie dogs—indeed every living thing—has largely been overlooked.

A few years ago, I interviewed Janet Jansson, director of the federal Microbiomes in Transition research initiative (MinT), based at the Pacific Northwest National Laboratory in Richland, Washington. MinT is a collaboration of scientists around the world charged with looking at how "perturbations"—disruptions such as climate change and pollution—are affecting the planet's microbiomes, not only in the soil, but in the oceans, on land, and even in humans. It's no small task. In the Earth's crust and water there are an estimated quadrillion quadrillion microorganisms. One of the most vital biomes is in the soil.

Jansson says there are about two billion microbes in a teaspoon of soil, divided into five thousand different types, thousands of species of fungi, viruses and protozoa, nematodes, mites, and a couple of termite species. How these myriad pieces all fit together is still largely a mystery (it's often called a "black box"), but experts know there's a giant, bustling factory belowground with a vast array of workers. Each little critter has a highly evolved role to sustain the soil ecosystem and the plants aboveground.

There is a crash effort to figure some of this out. Microbes are key players that perpetuate not only the prairie, but all life on the planet, providing numerous ecosystem services and serving as a major bulwark against environmental changes. The soil microbiome is critical because it is the foundation on which the house of terrestrial biodiversity is built. Without healthy soil ecosystems, the world's food web, including those things humans eat, could have serious problems. The problem is that it's one of those things we know very little about.

Another researcher, Dr. Elaine Ingham, is a soil scientist who has, over more than 30 years with the US Department of Agriculture, painstakingly picked apart the tiniest dynamics of the food web, examining the complex ecosystem in Jansson's teaspoon of dirt. She has shed new light on how the world beneath us keeps all of creation alive.

Just as there are ecosystems aboveground, there is one below. Say a tufted hairgrass plant realizes it needs iron. It is, like all plants, stationary, and so has evolved a system to have what it needs make the journey to it. The grass calls on an intermediary. One of the key ways a plant signals the myriad organisms around its roots is by emitting highly desirable sugars, known as exudates. The grass emits a sugar targeted to attract and grow bacteria and fungi that solubilize, or extract, iron from rocks, silt, and sand. Then predators in the next trophic level up, things like protozoa, nematodes, and microarthropods, gobble up the bacteria the plant has husbanded and excrete the iron the tiniest creatures have extracted. Plants do this for forty-two essential nutrients, from cobalt to sulfur to copper.

Soil microbes developed their relationships, Ingham says, over three billion years. Then, somewhere in the neighborhood of a billion years ago, plants showed up and began partnering with the soil. "This is evolution," she says, "the plants and critters have worked this out."

In the nineteenth century came the steel plow, "that slices, dices, crushes, and destroys the complexity. It's Hurricane Katrina hitting New Orleans," Ingham says. Following that, pesticides and herbicides killed off many members of these sustaining systems.

That's why some people want to see a farming economy based on the native plants that are already adapted to live on the prairie. Wes Jackson is a much-lauded scientist, a winner of the MacArthur "Genius Grant" who runs an experimental farm called the Land Institute near Salina, Kansas. He saw potential in the prairie grasses, naturally resistant to frost, weeds, insects, and disease—though shy on nutrition for humans—and set out to breed an edible, nutritional prairie, a project still undergoing its own evolution. Decades in the making, it has produced its first commercial grain, a perennial strain of wheatgrass called Kernza.

On my drive back to Helena, I stopped to climb to the top of a buffalo jump that overlooked a vast swath of prairie. I imagined a herd of huge bison clawing the air frantically as the ground disappeared beneath their hooves and they tumbled toward the earth below. I noticed wobbly-legged antelope fawns ducking their heads down to hide in tall grass, prairie dogs scurrying and chattering, shrikes swooping, and a coiled rattlesnake warming itself in the sun, not too far off the trail.

The prairie, I realized, is something like an ocean. From a distance it looks like it's just a sea of grass, but that's only the surface: if you take the time for a deeper dive, worlds upon worlds of life are revealed.

Even after working hard on the relationship, I can't say I love the prairie the way I do the mountains—though I did come away with a new appreciation for its beauty. And did I find my soul? Nope. That still lives in the mountains. But I caught a glimpse of the soul of the prairie.

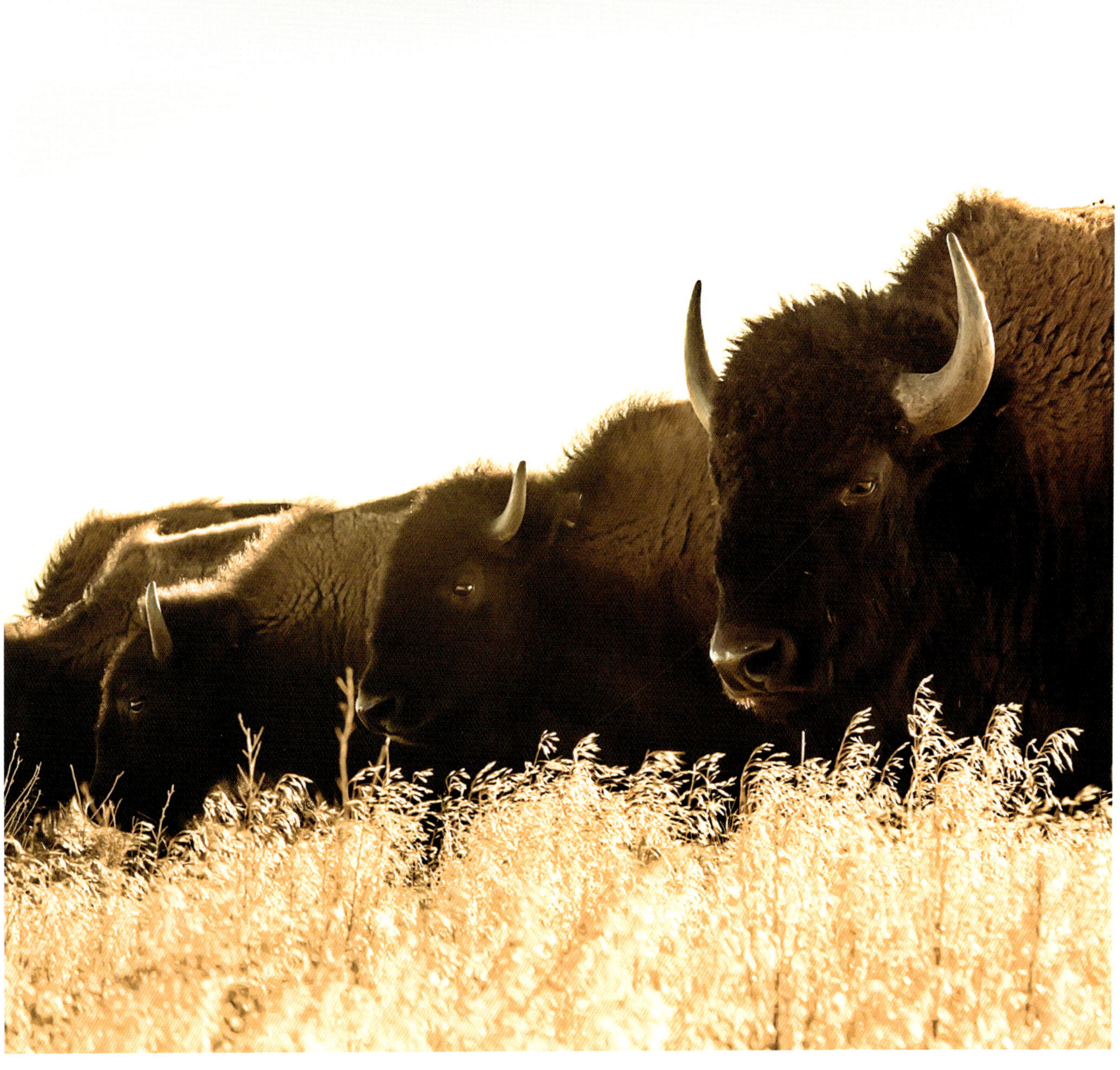

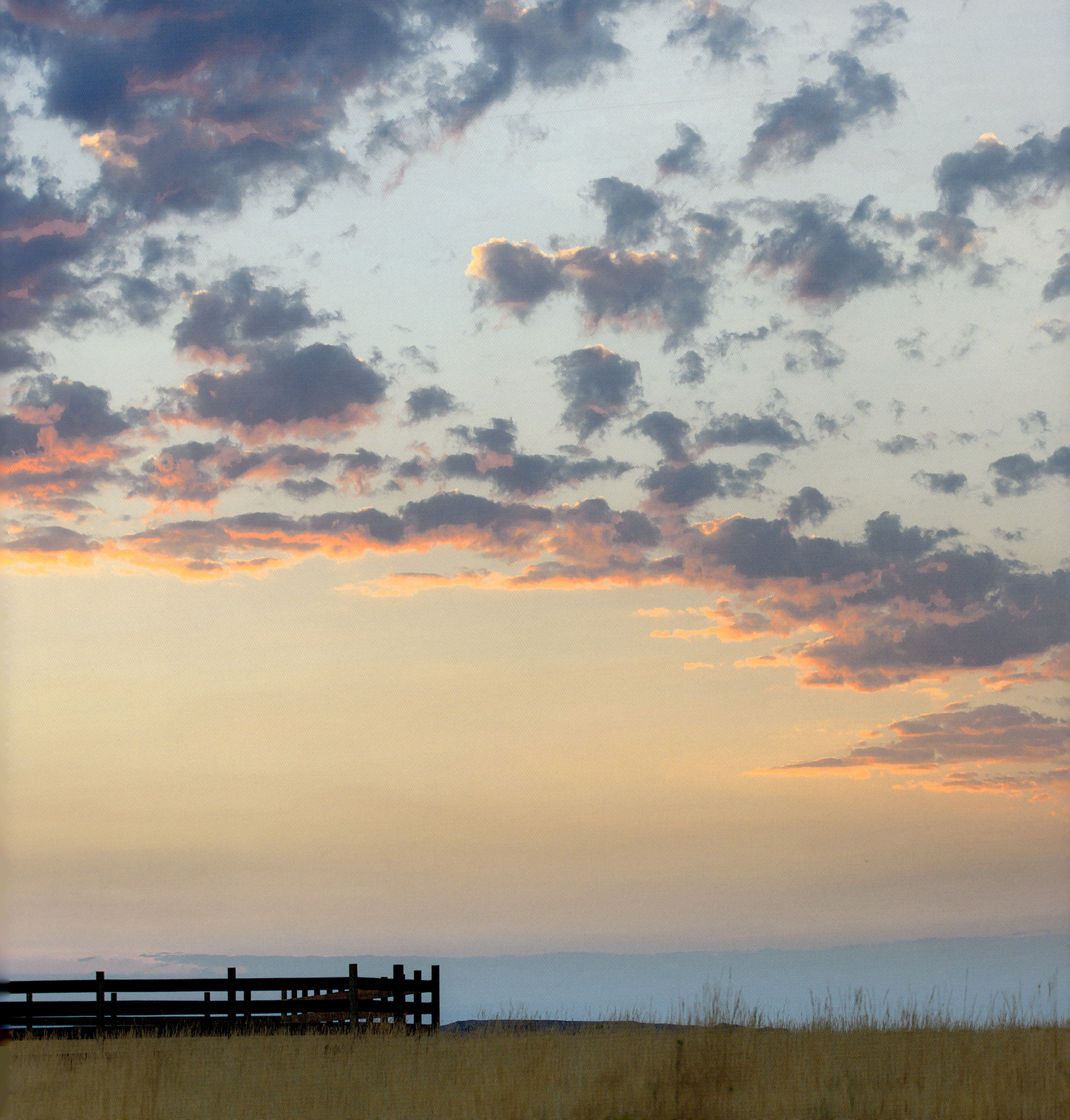

EXCERPT FROM
THE HOME PLACE

Carrie La Seur

After leftovers are put away and Brittany is bowed over the second Harry Potter book, dug out of her ridiculously small bag of belongings, comes the last trip of the day, to Maddie's. Brittany is quiet on the long drive to the other side of town. They speed along the rims with the dim, snow-laced city below, the refineries beyond twinkling like Christmas trees. Alma can just make out the dark line of the Yellowstone, where her parents let all three of them get as filthy and muddy as they wanted, even as other parents pulled their children back from the river's edge to warn about ruining their shoes. In her childhood, there was never much worry about staining a shirt or breaking a plate. Those things had no real value. The family was what counted. And then there was no family.

Alma looks up just in time to steer back across the center line. She shakes off the memory and starts to contemplate what she knows about people who could have been near Vicky the night before, if this horror turns out to be murder instead of the perpetually cruel hand of God reaching out to take her sister. Vicky hardly needed help to do herself in. The thought of murder—someone putting hands on Vicky to end her life—feels like a vulgar joke. Too much, from a universe that has already asked too much of this family.

Brittany has fallen asleep in the passenger seat as Alma drives, taking Alma back to winter nights when her little sister crept into her bed in their shared room to cuddle close for warmth and ask for tales out of the well-stocked family larder of wildlife stories. "The one about the bear in the car," she'd say, or "The one about the camp coyote," or "The one about the bighorn sheep in the fog." Alma almost smiles at the warmth the memory still holds. Vicky would fall asleep on Alma's pillow every time. That image—not the cold, bruised body on the gurney—is what she will hold close.

Maddie's place is a double-wide trailer in a nicer trailer park on the west end, bought after her stroke but before Al died. She and Al moved into Billings off the ranch to be near family and medical care. She gets around with a cane, her left side weak but not useless, and from her flowered recliner watches her shows. Alma glances through the front windows into the living room and sees the television tuned to a new game show she doesn't recognize. To her left, almost obscured by the darkness, are the raised garden beds Walt built after his father died. Maddie had called Alma just to tell her. Now that death had ended Walt's long feud with Al, Maddie could make coffee for her only surviving son in her own kitchen, pat his shoulder, send him home with bread or pie. He didn't come around all that often—he was still Walt, after all—but he did little things for her, and Maddie was exultant.

Alma opens the storm door and raps on one of the three small rectangular windows in the door. Maddie startles and looks up fearfully, then smiles and reaches for the cane. "I'm comin,' honey!" she shouts. "Just give your old grandma a minute."

Alma tries the door, but it's locked. This is new. Maddie and Al never used to lock their door. In fact, they had trouble finding the house keys to lock up when they went to Arizona to overwinter in the Airstream.

After a slow progress from her chair, Maddie unfastens a chain and turns a deadbolt. "Well look at you! Skinny as ever, I guess. Still workin' too hard out there in the big city. And ain't you pretty. You look just like me when I was your age!" As Maddie reaches up to hug Alma, who's at least six inches taller, she gets a good grip on her ribs to measure the extent of the skinniness. "Good lord, don't you eat? Come on in—you too, Brittany, get out of the cold, girls—and have some brownies. I made a pan when you said you was comin'. You can tell me about your trip." Alma exhales in relief. She should have known that there would be no emotional scene with Maddie, especially with Brittany present. At some point, they will talk about Vicky, but first there will be welcoming food and the calm of her grandmother's house. They will reveal as little pain as possible, and in that way overcome it.

Maddie is already moving at her deliberate pace to turn off the TV. The house smells of dust in unreachable places; meat and potatoes cooking; a little white cockapoo that has left behind its hyperactive days and now wanders in a senile daze, peeing occasionally on a potted fern in the front window; and the homemade lilac potpourri that Maddie has always used in overabundance, like incense. There's something else that Alma doesn't remember and takes a moment to place: not the decay she smelled on Helen, just age, perhaps, settling over her grandmother like a shroud.

"There's not much to tell, Grandma. It was an easy flight. Much better now that they've stopped crossing the mountains in turbo props. Listen, you don't need to bother, I ate at Helen's."

Maddie snorts. "Sprouts and organic carrots, that's all you'll get over there. Supposed to be purifying her system and all it does is make her crabby. You need something that'll stick to your ribs. I'll fry up a few pork chops." Maddie ignores Alma's protests and takes out plates and cups. "I sure am glad you came out right away. And Brittany, I'm so happy you're here, hon. I would've brought you right over here if I still had my license. I don't know that Helen's in any better shape than I am, but the state of Montana thinks so and that's what counts."

Maddie's words flow together in the patterns Alma learned as a child—little grammatical glitches, dropped or added consonants, a twang and a drawl. The slow, John Wayne cadence affects her like the sweep of sky visible from the airport. Hearing it, Alma knows she's home. Maddie's voice speaks of place almost as much as the place itself, not the word but the land made flesh. Maddie is a child of Big Horn County herself, who grew up in town as the sheriff's daughter, just a generation removed from ranch life. She dropped out of high school to get married, as you did back then when a landholding man like Al Terrebonne proposed. The transition to the Terrebonne home place held few surprises for her. It was a stretching out of what had been contracted in Hardin, relearning the deep textures of place, the intimacies of soul-mapped land, every rock named, every season a new geologic layer of meaning. Brittany cuts herself a large brownie and disappears into the guest room down the hall. Her watchful, withdrawn silence is starting to feel like a ghostly presence, almost—Alma rejects the thought as soon as it crosses her mind—like Vicky is with them, waiting to see what Alma will do.

At the table with her hands on the worn vinyl tablecloth, Alma pushes her hair back and turns her face toward Maddie. If only it were as easy as dropping a decade of training to speak to her grandmother in the same dialect, the song of that soft western voice. She made such an effort to lose it in college out East, where they made fun of the way she talked and dressed, and laughed at her for being so proud of being from Montana. She wonders what kind of woman she would be if she still talked like that. Not the same person at all. Would it be someone she'd want to know? Someone she'd like better?

Alma tries to think of something positive to say about Helen's condition and fails. "Helen doesn't look good to me. I mean, I'm sure she's reeling from the news, but physically she's deteriorated a lot since I last saw her. Do you see her much?"

Maddie pauses in slicing the rest of the brownies. "Well, I—you know I try to see her, but we've been distant so many years now, and Walt, my poor sweet boy—he was like a stranger since he and Al fought after the war, until he started to come around a little these last few years. They bought that house up in the Heights, you know. None of our family has ever lived out there. It's so far." With her infallible country girl's sense of direction, Maddie stares at the northeast corner of the living room, facing the Heights, as her face slips momentarily into sadder lines than the ones imprinted on her face. Her resemblance to Walt is suddenly very strong. Her voice grows soft, barely a whisper. "Al was so harsh with them, you know. It's the way he was raised. It just rolled off Mikey, but Walt—he always took everything to heart."

To Alma, this is a new window into Walt's dark, surly character. Her dad never spoke much of his childhood, but his bond to the home place and his father was unquestioned. Alma remembers Grandpa Al as a benevolent patriarch, ever ready to pull a quarter out of her ear.

"Did Vicky and Brittany spend much time with them?" she asks. "Walt and Helen, I mean." This is history Alma doesn't know well, beyond the time when Vicky cut her off. Their mother's dislike for Walt was catechism, but to listen to Maddie is to hear another story altogether. Alma realizes with a sudden, disorienting shift in perspective that Maddie remembers only the gentle giant she raised, the sensitive boy who never came home from the war. She recalls for the first time in years how Maddie used to have a special place next to her good china for Walt's Silver Star and Purple Heart, dug out of the burn barrel at the home place where Walt threw them years ago. Glancing over at the cabinet, Alma spots the boxes behind the glass.

"Walt had a soft spot for Vicky, and now Brittany. He tried to look after them, I'm sure he did, but Helen took a dislike to Vicky early on, thought she was wild, didn't want her around. I wanted to bring her out to live with us, but you know how things were between Al and Walt. They couldn't even discuss it. I remember Helen talking about how Vicky lied before anybody else noticed it. Sometimes I think Vicky just fulfilled Helen's prophecies about her. I never trusted Helen. I know she's failing, but I think she milks it a little, trying to keep Walt close this way when nothing else ever worked." She gestures with the knife, seeming unaware of its threatening flight as she talks about Helen, then slides a brownie onto a paper napkin decorated with red and green bells and hands it to Alma. She glances down the hall, where Brittany has shut herself in the guest room. "That poor, poor child. I—I just don't know what to say about Vicky, honey." Her tears come down quickly and copiously as they always have. "It sure ain't the world I grew up in. As much as I worry about you out in Seattle and it's right here in Billings that . . ."

The whistling teakettle saves Maddie from further words. She gets out the jar of Taster's Choice and makes them each a weak cup, then remembers and opens the jar to add another heaping scoop of brown powder to Alma's. "I wish I could have done more," she says as they sit. "It never seemed like that girl got a fair shake."

Alma folds her hand around the thin porcelain in a vain attempt to take the chill from her hands. "Everyone was always trying to help Vicky. It never did any good. She was so angry all the time." She wonders briefly where her own anger is hiding, in what tense body part it has taken up residence.

Maddie lets her coffee sit, cooling, while she examines Alma, pausing on the diamond earrings, the bare ring finger, before going back to the subject of Vicky. "She was trying to get things together this last year or so, you know. She's been helping me out, coming by to fix meals. She took me to the doctor a few times for checkups too, and she'd go out Sarpy once in a while to check on the house. Of course, Pete's always helped out a lot, but Vicky was trying, she really was." *Which means,* Alma says to herself, *that Vicky's been doing her grocery shopping in your kitchen and helping herself to your prescriptions.* God knows what's going on out at the ranch. The house. The home place. The land. Even the Circle E—the brand Charles bought for Eliza as a wedding present, still owned by the family. Like the Inuit and their dozen words for snow, the Terrebonnes name and rename the most important thing.

"I'm sure she was, Grandma," she affirms as she sifts through the Sunday *Gazette*. If the paper is still as doggedly reliable on local crime as it used to be, the story on Vicky will show up tomorrow. Alma hopes they won't say much. They'll repeat the ugly verities the police have given out: unattended death, autopsy, automatic homicide investigation. It might not hurt to call the paper and ask for a little discretion, for the family.

"These last few months, though, there was something going on," says Maddie, interrupting the reflection. "She was upset, didn't want to talk about it. She used to talk to me when she was little, but lately she'd just get all cutesy and say, 'Don't you worry, Granny, I'm a big girl!' Huh. She never was a big girl. You knew that. Never could take care of herself like you were born doing. It all would've been different if the kids hadn't died like that. Terrible thing." For a second, Alma is confused: *The kids?* But Grandma means Mom and Dad, of course, her lost son and daughter-in-law. Maddie grips her cup and stares into the dark liquid, looking for something that isn't there but should be. With a grunt, she presses both hands on the table to force herself upright. She picks up her cane from the back of her chair and moves to the refrigerator. "And she'd talk about the home place. She had this idea maybe we ought to sell out, after all this time."

"Sell the home place?" Alma gasps. "How could she . . . Grandma, are you sure? Could you have misunderstood her?"

Maddie doesn't open the fridge, but puts a hand on it for support. "She didn't make no sense sometimes. She'd say one thing, then another. There's this fellow who wants our mineral rights, so they could mine right up near the place. I told him no way no how, but then Vicky, she thought since nobody's out there now, maybe we oughta go ahead. She says they put it all back the way it was after."

"*Grandma . . .*" Alma's voice is low, scandalized. Such a thing is beyond imagining. She's terrified that next Maddie will say that she's already signed.

"But I just don't see how that could be so," Maddie continues, straightening up with the support of the fridge and the cane. "We lived out there so long. All you kids know every ridge and coulee. I just don't see how they could come through and put things back like they was. And where do all the animals go while they're at it? We've got winter range for elk out there, sage grouse leks, even those black-footed ferrets, they say. They can't graze and nest and mate in a big hole full of dump trucks. So I told her that."

"What did she say?"

"Well, she come back a few times with different ideas, how they could mine different parts of the place to move across to Crow land. That's what they want, I guess. But then she started to talk about the other families out there, how she didn't think it was right the way the land agent was pushing them around. She had all these notes of stories they told her, people I've known all my life getting threatened. She started saying she just wanted to get the company to leave us alone."

"Really?" A chill hangs on to Alma in spite of the hot cup in her hands. "So she changed her mind about signing?"

"She was a good girl, Alma." Maddie smiles, opening the fridge at last, as if the subject is settled. "I don't want you to think bad of her. I just wanted to tell you about that business with the coal company in case—in case it turns out to matter somehow. I think she might've hatched some plan of getting them to pay her off to keep quiet about their methods of getting folks to sign. She always had some kind of fool notion about getting rich, always playing at something. I'm afraid of what might've happened if she crossed the wrong person. I tried to look after her, Alma. I sure wish I knew what I should've done different." Maddie's eyes are very like Alma's, clear and bright and green. Looking at her is like staring into the funhouse mirrors that show your eyes in a different face, Alma thinks. But when she speaks of Mike, or Walt, or Vicky, the undertow of sadness in those eyes is nearly too much to resist. Alma averts her gaze to take in the rest of her petite grandmother. Maddie's carefully styled and colored hair is a late-blooming, endearing vanity in a woman who spent years many miles from the nearest salon, but her neat, matched outfit is vintage Maddie. At the home place she was always at breakfast in a tidy housedress, hair combed, even if she'd been up half the night pulling calves in Al's bibs. The hand she stretches out toward Alma across the counter is knotted and spotted, but when Alma goes to her and takes it, the grip is powerful.

"I don't think there's anything any of us could have done," Alma says. "As hard as anybody ever tried to help Vicky, she just pushed us away harder. I don't know how many times I've called her since Grandpa's funeral. If she even picks up, everything is always fine fine fine. She'll tell me about a concert she went to or some joke she heard but not that they're about to cut off her phone, so I have to find out by getting the disconnect message."

"Oh, that was Vicky all over," Maddie says with the beginning of a laugh that dies. "Never admitted anything was wrong, and always thought everyone was out to get her. She used to drive me plum 'round the bend sometimes." Maddie is pawing through the freezer now, tossing Tupperware and aluminum-foil packets on the counter.

"What are you doing, Grandma? Do you need help?" Alma asks, fielding frozen items that threaten to sled onto the floor.

"I'm making you pork chops. They thaw out quick in the microwave and I can fry 'em right up. You haven't had a decent meal all day. Got some string beans in here too somewhere, that I froze last summer. Here we go." Maddie shuts the freezer, tosses the bag of garden beans onto the stove, and moves to the microwave with the chops.

"Really, Grandma, I'm fine." It's not the time to tell Maddie that Alma is a vegetarian now. Besides, the girl who learned how to field-dress a moose isn't squeamish about the origins of meat, just scrupulous about what she puts in her body. Maddie's meat has always come from some friend's hunting trip or farmyard. "I was just going to do a little work before I go to bed. There's a lot to keep up with."

"Mm-hm," Maddie mutters. "I think I'll make up some mashed potatoes, too. You always like that pork gravy I make."

Alma smiles and shakes her head as Maddie pushes the canister of flour along the counter toward the stove. The word *no* won't do any good now. Alma bends to get out pans and utensils, saving Maddie the effort.

"I'm sorry about the instant potatoes," Maddie says. "It's easier for me with the bad hand, but I know it don't taste the same."

"It'll taste better than takeout, I guarantee."

Alma takes over the mashed potatoes, and together they soon fill a plate with the classic Terrebonne homecoming meal. Alma sits down over the food and breathes in its moist warmth, the erotic smell of her grandmother's thick pork gravy. God, it's good.

"Listen, Grandma, I'll go out Sarpy tomorrow and make sure everything's snug around the home place, okay?" Alma breaks the silence as she finishes off the second chop. She hasn't eaten like this in months, and she hadn't realized she was hungry.

Maddie nods. "That'd be nice. I always liked it out there this time of year. Real peaceful."

"You ought to come with me then, along with Brittany. It'll be good for her to spend time with you, too. We can have lunch in Hardin like we used to. If we have time we can stop and see some of your friends."

Maddie reaches out and pats Alma's wiry hand with her scarred, wrinkled, soft one. Her agate rings glitter even in the low-wattage glow of the dusty overhead fixture. Grandpa Al's hand-polished stones still speak to Alma of days on the river with him and his bamboo fly rod, standing thigh deep in rushing water, casting into dark, glowing pools. They all slept in the camper on the back of his old blue Chevy, or in an army-surplus pup tent if he wasn't too worried about bears. Grandpa knew how to keep the rain out of the tent in a spring storm, clean fish without attracting bears, start a fire in any conditions, and, if necessary, kill a charging moose with a low-caliber bullet through the head at close range, which Alma saw up close once.

Pete and Vicky were farther downstream, but she'd wandered past Grandpa, almost around the upstream bend. The moose came charging past a shelter of thick pine, suddenly upon her at full speed, and Grandpa, flying faster than the moose, grabbed his old Winchester from shore and downed the massive beast with a single shot. The crack of the rifle ricocheted over the water like thunder after a close strike of lightning. The moose dropped to its front knees in shallow water ten feet from her, let out a long, echoing groan, and died. Blood ran out of its head with the water and she felt the sticky warmth engulf her bare calves.

Grandpa walked out in his waders and stood over the animal. It was a full-grown bull with a rack on each side wider than Alma's arm span. It would have killed her. She wanted to go to Grandpa and feel his protective arm around her, but she couldn't move.

"It's a damn shame," Grandpa said. He levered another bullet into the chamber and walked up around the bend, just to be sure, then came back to pick up Alma and carry her to the pickup. "What did you do to make that moose so mad?" he asked.

"I don't know, Grandpa. I'm sorry." Alma didn't entirely understand what had happened, but she felt Grandpa's sadness. "I'm sorry you had to kill him."

"I didn't have to kill him. I chose you."

Grandpa fished avidly, but he didn't hunt for sport. He'd hunted as a child, for food, out of genuine hunger. For him, that was the only ethical justification for killing, aside from self-defense. He'd grown up a rejected, beaten-up white boy on the Crow reservation. For a white man he had an exceptional sense of the sacred, along with a vicious uppercut.

As Alma and Pete helped Grandpa cantilever the carcass out of the river with ropes and the winch on the pickup's front bumper, she felt unworthy. Something was born in her that day, a small knot of determination that would one day change the course of her life. They ate moose steaks, sausage, jerky, and stew all through the coming winter, and Alma had to choke down every bite.

After clearing up, Alma helps Maddie to bed. The bedroom is decorated the same way as in the old ranch house, right down to the faded prairie-rose sheets that match the china pattern. Maddie gets into her button-down polyester nightgown and sits down on the bed for Alma to unbuckle her leg brace. Alma picks up the hairnet and thick foam headband from the bedside table and settles them around Maddie's salon-golden hairdo. "Grandma," she says as they struggle, laughing together, to do up the Velcro closure, "what in the world do you do when I'm not around?"

"Brad Pitt comes by most nights to help me," Maddie deadpans. "He's such a nice boy."

"Brad Pitt, you don't say?"

"Oh my, yes. Your old grandma's still got it."

After leaving Maddie, Alma tiptoes to the door of the tiny back bedroom. The door is shut but not latched. It opens on well-greased hinges to reveal Brittany asleep in the bright light of a waxing gibbous moon. Even in her great-grandmother's warm house, Brittany has gone to bed in her stained army-navy surplus coat. Alma kneels to help her out of it. Brittany is limp as a baby, allowing Alma to move her limbs without the slightest protest.

"Poor thing," Alma murmurs, "no wonder you're worn out." As Alma settles Brittany's arms under the blankets, she notices that even in deepest sleep, Brittany clutches something under the dirty fingernails of her right hand. Alma peels the fingers back enough to see a faded photograph, torn in half but reattached with tape that has begun to dry and yellow, clutched against her own dog-eared business card. She recognizes the photo. It's Brittany as a toddler, in a Sears portrait paid for by Alma as a Christmas present, posing with Vicky and Dennis, like the cozy nuclear family they never were. They're all in Christmas sweaters knit by Maddie, scrubbed and combed, a smiling catalog family. Alma claps one hand over her mouth to muffle her sigh. With the other hand, she closes Brittany's fingers back over the precious photo.

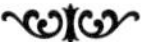

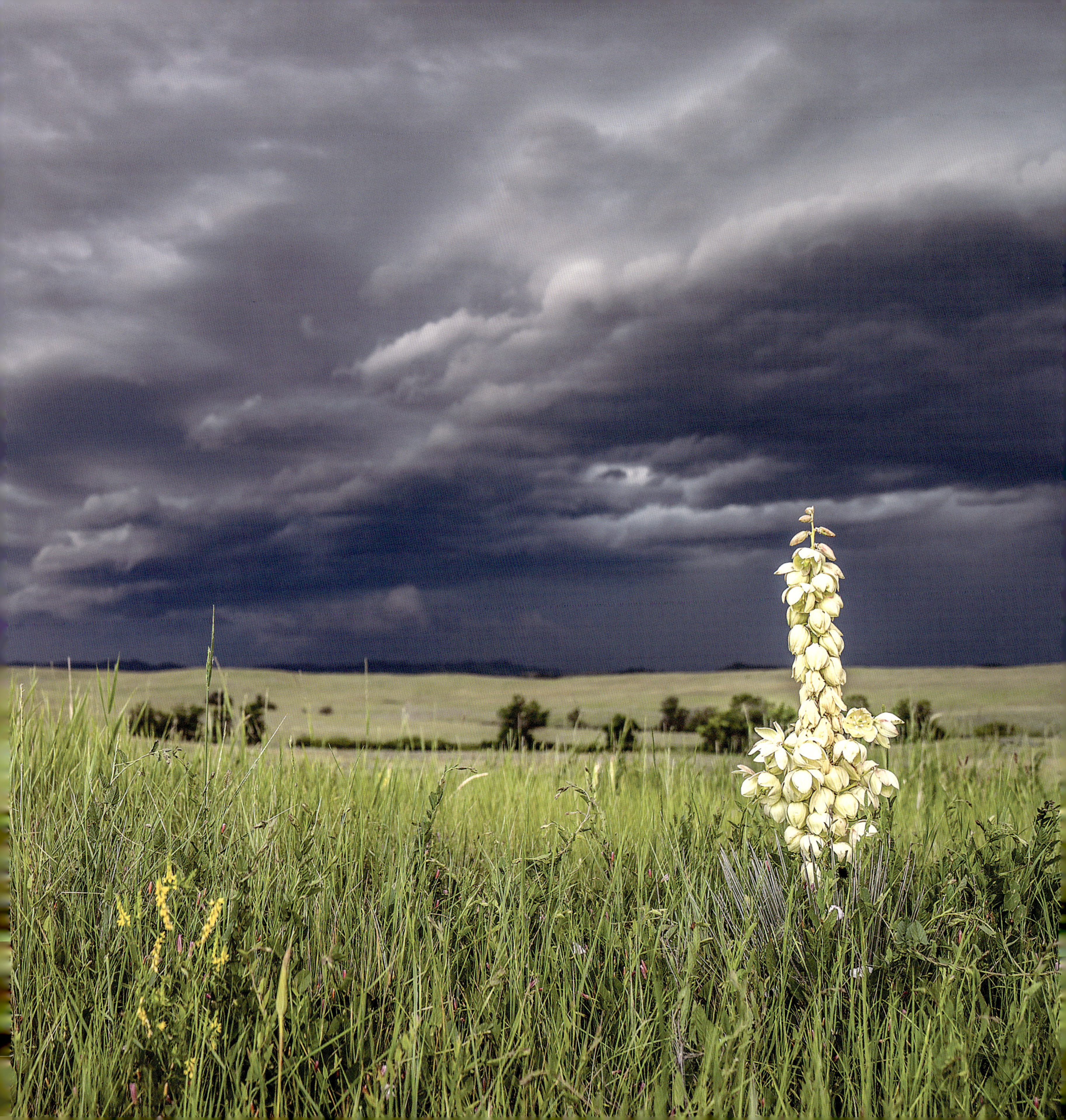

NOTHING MORE THAN EVERYTHING

Antonia Malchik

She hasn't lived there in over forty years, but every now and then my mother still brings up "the ranch." Each scant member of my family knows what "the ranch" refers to: that spread in the wrinkled draws of eastern Montana where my mother was raised, where she learned to drive an eighteen-wheeler and ride a horse, and to love, under the tutelage of her father, every particle of the block of virgin prairie resting in the middle of several thousand acres devoted to wheat and cattle. Made of sharp rises and hills, curious with old teepee rings and buffalo wallows, that pastureland stayed virgin because her own grandfather wanted it that way. When my mother was fourteen, her father bought a Cessna and taught her to fly; when I read the memories she's written down, they often feel sketched from this vantage in the forever sky, with descriptions of the prairie's buttercups and yellow bells specked among the cattle ranging over the pasture.

It's that bit of prairie my mother yearns to protect these days, even more than she longs for a lost life of wind over the fields. "Who owns the mineral rights on that prairie block?" she asks, the words burdened with longing to hold this one little bit of earth, to know it will be safe to love, if not ours to own. My grandfather worked the land as long as he could, but finally sold up in the early 1990s. You can only do so much when you've got one nonfarming child and three granddaughters immersed in books instead of soil.

"I don't know," I tell her truthfully. After my great-aunt and then my grandfather passed away, that piece got snarled in a legal muddle, and in any case plenty of people in the American West don't own the mineral rights to their land. It could be the family who currently farms it, it could be a third cousin we've never spoken to, it could be some faceless resource-extraction company. The last thought is terrifying: someday my mother will wake up in her house over the mountains, listening to the coal trains pass by, and know in a place more vital than heart or gut that a drill—for oil, for natural gas, for fracking fluids, for coal-bed methane extraction—has pierced the soil she is made of.

She asks me because, in a fit of alcoholic mistrust almost a decade before he died, my grandfather rewrote his will to leave his money to my sisters and me, cutting our mother out. The ranch was sold before I knew Grandpa as anything but a tall, blue-eyed alcoholic—with a passion for Montaigne and a hacking cough from a lifetime breathing wheat chaff—who made a packet investing in risky wheat futures and used to startle the house awake with tequila-fueled, midnight renditions of "Git Along, Little Dogies." The legal documents offer little clarity; blindly, we hope the prairie block's true state of being will someday seep through.

We're used to thinking of sustainability in a short-term way, centered around the virtues of a farmer's market or the comforting prospect of renewable energy. But take this one spot of land, the one my mother treasures almost as much as she does her grandchildren. Sustainability means it can provide for human life: food, water, shelter, and warmth for as long as geologically possible. Once we've stripped it for resource extraction or exhausted its agricultural potential with herbicides and pesticides, that possibility is gone. Within a few short years, even in human terms, so are the jobs that made the sacrifice attractive.

We all know these arguments. If not, we should. What we are not allowed to talk about is the loss of a human's love for her landscape, for the dirt under her feet, for the contours of the land that have shaped her breath, her worldview, her heart. When this is lost, we have sacrificed her ability to connect with something that is—for lack of a better word—holy. Land that sustains not just the body, but the soul.

I was born in Bozeman, at that time a humdrum cow town whose highlight was the soggy Sweet Pea festival in midsummer. Montana still felt isolated then. When we visited my grandparents in their little house near "the ranch," the four-hour drive rolled across highways that were almost always empty. There were so many lacks in my childhood—transportation, jobs, culture—that I grew up believing the home I loved could never change in any material way, and the qualities that made it whole and beautiful would prompt in all people a desire to treat it gently. I grew up believing in my bones that the land under my feet would always be there.

Now, as a friend put it, Bozeman's crapped itself out all over the Gallatin Valley. Like most things, it's not all bad. The wealth that's poured into the area's scenic beauty made possible a shocked residents' 2002 stand against the opening of a new coal-bed methane mine. Still, there are only so many obscenely large housing developments you can build before those clear mountain streams are drained dry and nobody's got a view of the ranges anymore. To those of us who grew up with the tiniest aftertaste of the pioneers' hardships in our mouths, it seemed like the sheer weight of money crushed whatever freedom was left.

Back in my teenage years, it used to frustrate me when my mother talked about these things, especially the way she compared herself and the ranchers she'd grown up with to Native Americans—more victims of a culture that recognizes ownership in terms she doesn't believe in. I got annoyed at the way she went on about what land means to those who have grown up enmeshed in it, and I met mentions of "the ranch" with a reflexive eye-roll. I could not share in feeling bereft or stunned at the ease with which those who cared so little for it could seize the soil that formed her home to rip out fuel and leave only waste, while over the mountains those with wealth earned elsewhere built manicured suburbs of Houston and Hoboken. The loss of the prairie is one I have only recently understood. Now I, like my mother, have watched my Rocky Mountain home eaten by heretics, watched hills I once walked freely closed to me by the fences of people who will never know or love them as I do, people moved by the thrill of possession, not the humility of awe. I know now how my mother felt when the land she thought was safe was handed over to others who would be able to "make something of it."

"Montana, like all frontiers, is about seeing ourselves in the midst of possibility," my mother once wrote in an essay on conservation easements for a now-defunct local magazine. "We will transform the land, use it, but never use it up; our steers will fatten, and the grain will grow; we can dam the rivers, and they will still hold fish; forests will give timber and never be eroded or scarred.

Now that same landscape we looked to for eternal youth seems to be telling us our choices are running out."

She wrote those lines in the early 1990s, at a time when gated communities of million-dollar homes seemed the greatest threat to what was left of our wilderness and waterways. That was before the explosion in oil production fracked its way around towns near the North Dakota border and started moving west. By 2012, the extraction companies were test-drilling for oil and gas among the tiny, rare purple bitterroot flowers hiding along the Rocky Mountain Front, a landscape so beautifully fragile I can almost feel my heart tear with a desire to protect it. The housing developments that ate up my hometown only scar the surface; the drilling would bore the heart out of yet another piece of Montana landscape that makes me believe in something never-ending.

⟡

I will say something sacrilegious here. When the planes flew into New York City's twin towers on September 11, 2001, I mourned deeply for the lives lost and families broken. But I did not think that I—or my country, my way of life—had been attacked. This was the refrain heard all over the news: "they" had attacked our values, our lifestyle, and what makes our society cohesive.

I could not accede to that claim. My life, as I was only beginning to understand then, was tied to the vitality of the dirt I'd been raised on, not the urban landscapes under assault. I was living in Boston at the time and watched colleagues and friends hold one another and cry. Heretically, I wondered: *Will this one day help them see how my mother feels? How I feel?*

Every time a new hydraulic fracturing operation is opened, every time I see land broken and raw for the sake of the coal or copper beneath, every time a development of multimillion-dollar homes plops onto one of the mountains I love, a vital part of me is attacked. The communities I feel the most solidarity with are those like the Shuar people, whose land will be sacrificed to enormous open-pit gold and copper mines swallowing their ancient homes in the Ecuadoran Amazon; hardworking farmers in North Dakota and Pennsylvania whose free-range cattle are being made sick by the natural-gas fracking fluids seeping into their soil and water supplies; and the Blackfeet tribe whose teepee rings still mark the prairie land my mother loves so much. Those with no respect for older, deeper values have always believed they can put the land to better use than those who live in symbiosis with it. They can use it, and use it up, destroying its ability to sustain life for generations. They drive machines into that which I hold sacred, caring only for short-term economic gain, feeling nothing for what is lost and irreplaceable. And every one of us is complicit in the act.

⟡

In 2012, Montana Fish, Wildlife, and Parks lauded the success of a stream remediation project over twenty years in the making. For the first time in decades, there are enough westslope cutthroat trout in Silver Bow Creek near Butte that FWP was able to allow catch-and-release fishing in a waterway previously so toxic with heavy metals that fish trying to swim into it just up and died. Smelters, concentrators, and precipitation plants operating from the late 1800s to the early 1900s dumped enough mine tailings and sewage into the creek to contaminate the water at least twenty miles downstream, earning the area a Superfund designation in 1983. Montana's governor noted on the announcement of the westslope cutthroat's comeback that nobody had been able to fish in Silver Bow "since our great-great-grandparents."

You can bet that anyone trying to stop toxic dumping at the time would have been accused of being anti-jobs and labeled a kook, if not run out of town. The same response is heard these days in places like Appalachia. In Erik Reece's book *Lost Mountain*, which chronicles the environmental devastation wreaked by mountaintop-removal mining, one coal miner's wife asks, "What use are the mountains to us, other than coal?"

What use was Silver Bow Creek, after it had become so polluted you wouldn't dare eat a trout from it, even if one swam its waters? If only our great-great-grandparents last fished there, how many generations of families lost out on catching their own dinner or drawing the water running by their front doors? How many children couldn't cool their ankles under the cottonwoods on hot summer days?

"We need to find a new way to see ourselves and our possibilities in this landscape," my mother wrote in that essay on conservation easements, in a more hopeful time before man's appetite for energy consumption gained new life through cheaper technologies and—let's face it—a backlash of resentment against the environmental movement. "Not just for the people who are still fortunate enough to live on the land or the professionals whose vocation is in the natural world but for the rest of us: the nurses, prep cooks, attorneys, real estate agents, and mill workers—all of us who once held a piece of forever and are beginning to feel ourselves displaced. Because if this isn't home, we ask, what is?"

My mother's writing has a tang that can only come from a childhood spent on the land, whether a farm, a homestead, or a backcountry cabin. When you grow up watching bugs with your feet in the dirt, spend dark winter mornings tending to the animals and afternoons squinting over the wheat fields, your words can smell of April's wet-snow Chinook winds or taste like dust on a hot August afternoon when the earth is gasping from drought. This intimate relationship with nature, not always a pretty one, is something we are on the verge of losing even in our literature. Raised in a town, with memories of sidewalks and day hikes and fights with my sisters—and later a sense of some connection missing, something my mother had that I could only ever crave—I cannot write like that. And I can't make up for it as an adult. The land doesn't talk to me in the same way it talks to her. Once a little girl with unruly blond curls, squinting at a camera with the prairie spread out behind her, now she is a senior citizen setting up in the local farmer's market to sing about land and loss, ownership and virtue, about the coal mining and hydrofracking among the unkempt foothills of her youth. Her songs are heavy with the twisting, bitter pain of knowing the world is run by people who see the land she loves as nothing more than a product to be assigned a market value.

Our society's writers occasionally produce books that force us to see the dying birds, the lungs damaged by power-plant particulates, the burst in cancer rates downstream from chemical factories; these seem to be the only tools that awaken the national consciousness to our dependence on a damaged ecosystem and remind us that a "growing economy" cannot sustain us forever. This knowledge has an urgency for me, yet the writing I do—so unlike my mother's—feels short of the mark. *My father and I stood once / on a piece of bluestem prairie / under a cold sky* begins one of my mother's poems. "Shouldn't this beauty belong to everyone?" ends an essay I once wrote about the wreck of my hometown. I know which of these speaks to the heart. The way I write about the land and all the self-sustaining, energy-conserving skills I shore up for survival in an uncertain future will never have my mother's spirit. But it's all I've got to offer.

When the last person is gone who grew up crunching across frozen mud with the slap of winter in her face, and who knew from girlhood the scent of a thunderstorm about to break, how the ground creaked when it was thirsty, the fear of a lost cow on the far pasture—when there are no more childhoods like this, humanity will have been struck a blow that will change it forever.

The land that can shape this kind of life is shrinking daily. Some of the very swathes of wide-open prairie and grassland moved into conservation at the time my mother was writing about the popularity of easements were the same ones test-drilled by hydraulic fracturing operations for oil in early 2012. The land trusts that sought to preserve that space had no rights to the energy resources resting underneath the wildlife and wildflower habitat; more crucially, they have no right to keep the mineral owners from drilling.

What does it mean to live on this earth, in Big Sky Country or anywhere else, and to plan futures for our children, if none of our activities can provide livelihoods for more than a generation or two, and if our choices preclude sustaining life for our grandchildren?

Five generations of my family have lived in what's called the Last Best Place—*Montana*, the word itself making me feel like a lovesick teenager, all weak-kneed and fainthearted. My young son and daughter have become the sixth, and I feel wary about giving them a life that opens them to the magnitude of this loss. Of teaching them to treasure what can't be saved.

My mother wrote a folk song a few years ago about an old cowboy dying in his trailer and refusing to leave his land to the oil company. The refrain, *I'd rather give up heaven than Montana*, speaks to me of heartache and loss, offering a bare speck of hope that we might yet salvage what is vital. For those of us who want nothing more than land to sustain our love, and a simple life for us and our children ("Nothing more?" my mother noted upon reading this essay; "Isn't that *everything*?"), this is a war we are always on the verge of losing, if we haven't already lost. It is a war in which women like my mother have given battle cries again and again, only to be muted by the voluntary deafness of a society that finds their truth uncomfortable. But no amount of locally grown heirloom tomatoes or organic wheat, no number of wind turbines or carbon offsets, will in the end make any difference to this landscape's ability to sustain us if we do not learn to value even more our relationship with the land, our love of home.

Whenever I send my mother money—repayment of what should have been her share of my grandfather's leavings—I write *spirit of the prairie fund* on the check's memo line. It started as a briskly scrawled joke, but over time it has grown in unspoken importance for both of us, as if between us we were keeping the prairie-rapers at bay. Keeping the prairie alive, and through it, ourselves. My pioneer ancestors' bloodline that homesteaded "the ranch" with care and caution has petered thin, but the love of the land runs through my mother and me like a vein of some mythical unadulterated and unchangeable metal, never corroding, never degrading, never fading. Beyond love, beyond passion, it is a connection so deep that losing it feels like facing my own death.

Once I was old enough to understand what I had when it was taken from me, then I knew what it was, and the creed my mother tried to teach me. I know that wildness, too, can be a religion, and its sacred places can be stolen from those of us who, in our hearts, truly own it. Our gods can die.

I'D RATHER GIVE UP HEAVEN THAN MONTANA

LeDoux Hansen

An old cowboy lay dyin' in his trailer
The one he bought in 1942
That last damn cigarette's still burnin' in his hat
The bottle's empty, but his eyes are blue

The lady from the Charitable Sisters
Has come to save his soul from fires of hell
She says, "Brother, if you can,
just leave your soul in Jesus's hands
And your land here, to the Oil Man when you sell."

The cowboy raised him up on his good elbow
And brushed aside that helping hand of bone
He said, "Ma'am, if you don't mind,
before we leave this world behind
I've got a little place here, of my own." He said,

"I'd rather give up heaven, than Montana
When it comes the time to cross that great divide
I'll stick with what I know: the shaggy buffalo
The prairie wind, whose arms are open wide.

"There ancient warriors guard the sacred mountains
And spirit holds a story man can ride
I'd rather give up heaven, than Montana
I'll see you, darlin' on the other side.

"When God made all creation, and the prairie
He saved the last place for the best of all
I'd rather give up heaven, than Montana
I'll see you at the roundup in the fall."

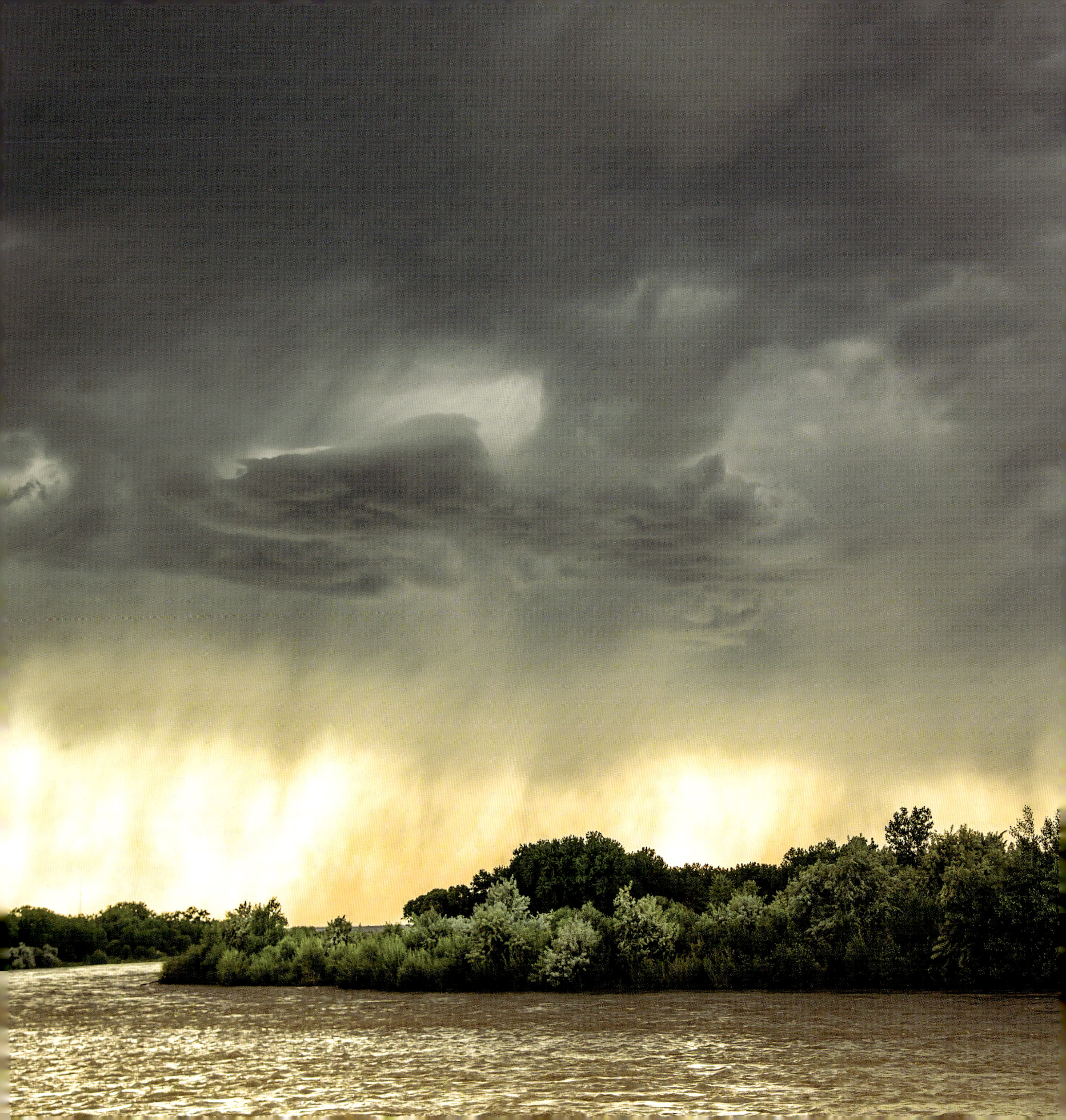

THE LAST DROWNING
EXCERPT FROM AN UNTITLED NOVEL

Jamie Harrison

On June 28, eleven people had headed out to the Yellowstone River, putting in at about three in the afternoon just south of Livingston for their first float of the year. The river was still a little high, but the group was trying to stay just ahead of the summer onslaught of tourists. One drift boat held two people who were delusional and naïve enough to think they could fish in the cloudy, turbid water, a large raft carried seven others who only wanted to have fun, and a couple chose a double kayak.

An older crew had talked about going but bowed out—Vinnie Susak, who owned the raft, was dealing with a client's suicide attempt in jail; Polly and her husband Ned had a doctor's appointment in Bozeman; Josie Murray and Polly's cousin Harry Swanberg had decided to enjoy their affair on dry land. There would be nothing relaxing about a float when the river was flowing this fast. But many of this younger group had gone down the Colorado and the Salmon, and all of them were athletic, the wedge of the new West. They'd floated the Yellowstone a dozen times the summer before and now they would see which channels had deepened or filled during high water, where pools or beaches had formed or banks had collapsed. They packed beer, cheap champagne, fried chicken and coleslaw. They brought coats, though when they shuttled cars to their take-out, on the east end of town, it was ninety degrees. When they put in, ten miles down the valley south of town, it was only slightly cooler, with a puff of clouds to the west.

They passed many downed trees, some blocking their way, some hard to see in the milky water. The people in the raft and drift boat—bartenders, teachers, carpenters—watched the kayak, worried, but the youngest of the group, Ariel Delgado, was experienced and careful, and Clark Mackleby, a Seattle kid who'd been in town since January, said he'd spent his childhood on Puget Sound and the Columbia River.

They saw two bald eagles, one golden eagle, many ducks, cliff swallows, a fox, dozens of whitetails, hundreds of cows. Someone's goat ran along the riverbank, watching the flotilla. Clark said he saw a bear, but no one believed him. The river was too violent to hear much; they shouted conversations. Hail loomed when they were an hour in, nearly to the canyon. They could feel a sudden sharp edge to the air even before an extreme darkness appeared to the northwest. The threat passed quickly, with just a little wind, and though the people in the raft and the drift boat decided to get home, Ariel and Clark pulled over on a pretty island.

And just like that, Ariel disappeared from the world.

Something awful happened every year on the river. How could it not? Even during a spring when the flow wasn't record-breaking, whole trees shot down like Pooh sticks. A stiff, dead baby bison had floated through town a few years earlier with its own golden eagle riding on top, the bird watching the world between nibbles.

People loved the Yellowstone for coolness, prettiness, peace, food, wildness, a dare, but touching it meant buying a lottery ticket. Using it was like driving on ice, flying a small plane, walking out of a bar with a stranger. It was easier if the unlucky person was someone from out of town, someone middle-aged or otherwise mundane, but usually it was someone local, because people who lived here loved their river. This year it was Ariel, who'd been born here, gone to school here, played soccer and trombone, tested high, generally been beloved. She was a lovely girl, funny and smart and ready to give the world wonder for decades. Or not: Who knew what she would have been? Dead was all the things that wouldn't happen. It had been her twenty-second birthday, and the rumor was she'd wanted Clark Mackleby to take her out to dinner.

When he said he couldn't afford it, someone had stepped in with the idea of floating.

When Clark was able to talk, he told Cy Merwin, the county sheriff, that they'd almost made it though a bumpy, braided section of the river when a branch from a submerged tree hit the kayak just right, just at a dip, sweeping both of them from the kayak. Clark said he'd seen Ariel's face underwater, but given the opacity of the river, this was delusion. He'd crawled up a bank with water in his lungs, bleeding from cuts on his head and limbs, and a raft of stoned college students had found him there an hour later.

He said they'd let their friends go on ahead so they could make love.

By then it was six o'clock. The others had shuttled home, assuming that Ariel and Clark had lingered on a sandy bank. After a deputy finally managed to translate what Clark—who was crying, though he would not cry again—was saying, Search and Rescue was ready to go within a half hour. Polly's cousin Harry, who had dated Ariel's mother before she found God or had Ariel, was already in a boat with Ned before they understood they'd be looking for someone they knew. On the solstice, at this latitude and longitude, it was light enough to try to see blue shorts and white limbs until 10:30, but there'd still been no time to mount a true search before dark. Flashlights glittered on the riverbank all night.

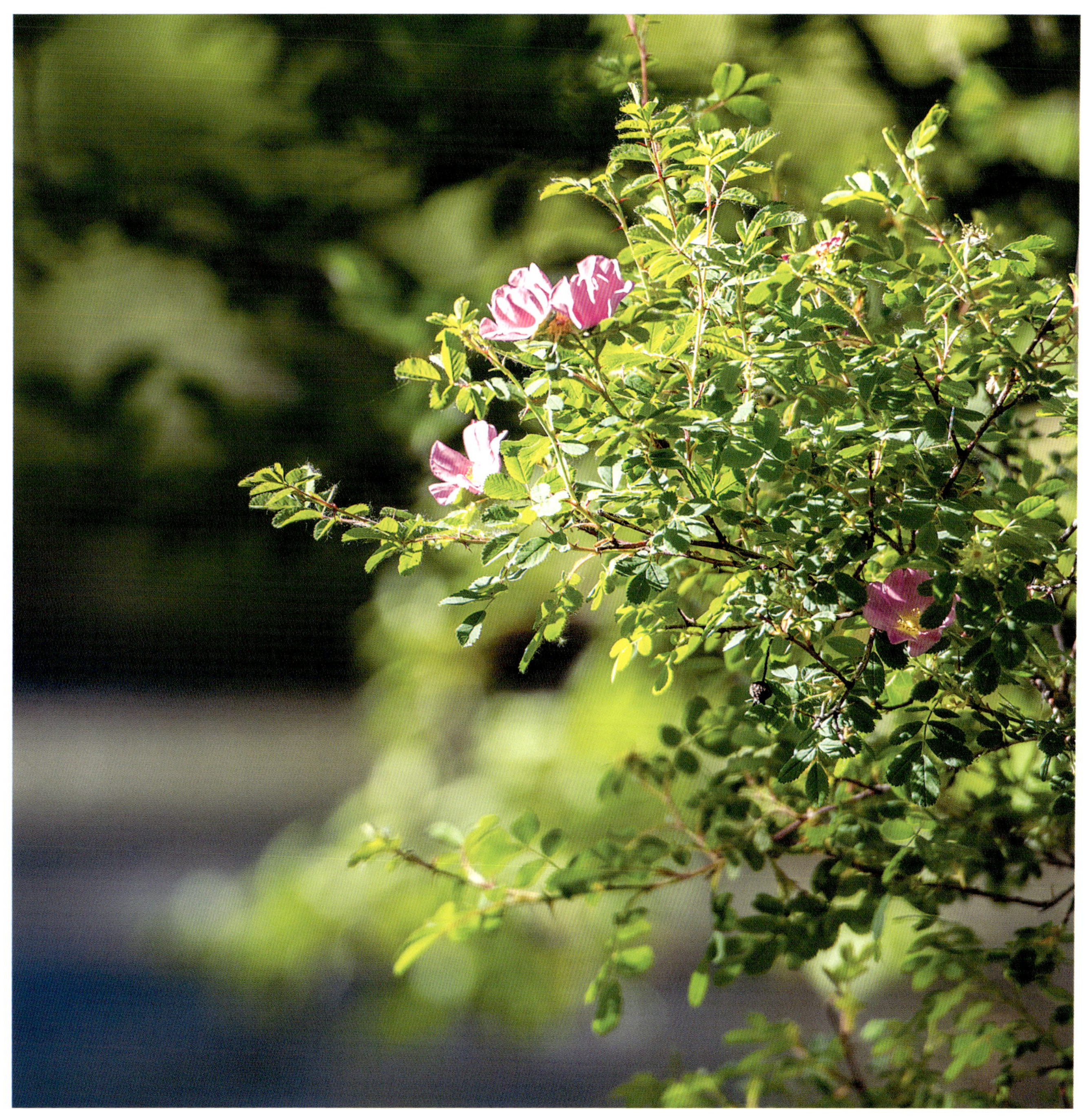

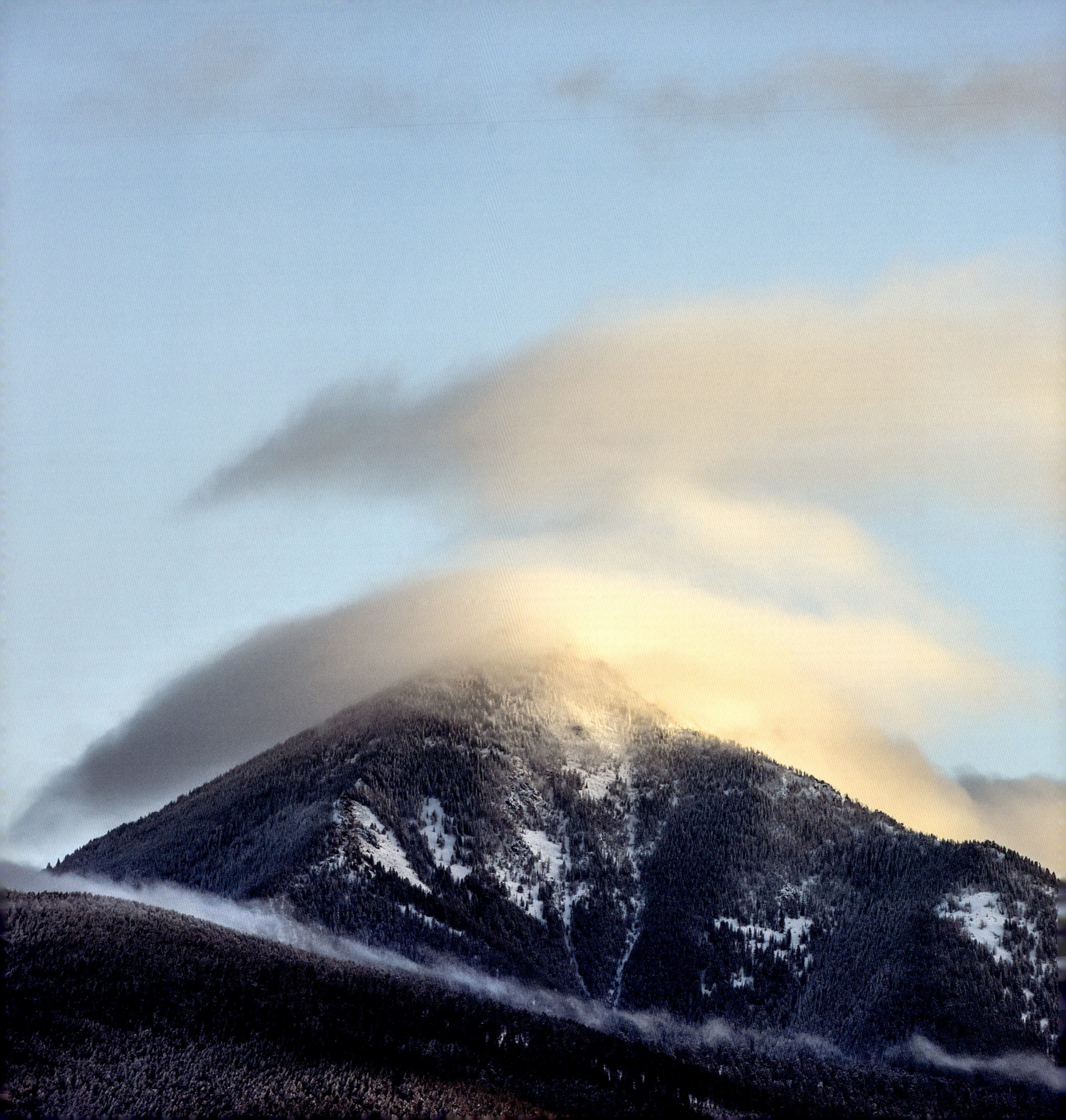

TOWNSEND SOLITAIRE

Eric Heidle

She was hooking a cheater link into the front left tire chain when she heard the sleds whine to a stop by the rig. She figured the snowmobilers could only see her Carhartted legs splayed in the snow, so she wriggled out to show them she was still alive, and as she stood they saw her dirty blonde hair and goosed their throttles admiringly.

"You need a hand?" The bigger one spit a wad to the side, just clearing his Realtree-patterned sleeve. He grinned through a beard under wraparound shades.

"Think I got it, thanks," she said as she climbed to her feet.

The riders swapped a glance. The skinny one gestured at the Big Belts rising to the west. "Where you headed?" She put a gloved hand on the door. "In."

The big guy shrugged. "Okeydokey. We'll see you up there." He gunned it and the pair raced off up the road, the sleds crapping snow in their wake.

The door hinges groaned as she stepped in and fired it up. "Like hell."

She drove another mile on the road before veering off through an unfenced pasture to get around a deep stretch. It was a good snow year and she knew she'd be skiing a few extra miles to the cabin. The overcast sky draped the Baldy peaks ahead in flat afternoon light. It had a been a few years since she'd come this way, and more than a few since she'd done it in winter. It was the long way around through Deep Creek and White Sulphur, but a fine drive all the same. Maybe an hour, Mint to Mint. Her dad hadn't had the good sense to die in summer.

She made it as far as a little corral below the wide curve she knew was usually drifted in, and it was. She rolled the truck off the road and pulled her skis and pack out of the bed. From the bench seat she took the carefully wrapped gin bottle and a worn leather flap holster and stuffed them in the top of the pack. She lashed a folded entrenching tool to its back and cinched everything up. She locked the rig and shrugged on the pack, setting her poles before clicking into the skis.

She set off across open ground, skirting the drift, headed uphill toward the forest boundary through a desert of white. The skis slicked along in the snow as she worked her way up the slope through clumps of bunchgrass and sage. She regained the road, freshly defaced with sled tracks, and skied in silence until she reached the cattle guard at the top of the hill.

Panting hard, she leaned on her poles and looked across to the line of trees. Tomorrow would be a much longer haul, and she wasn't in shape. The first tinge of evening was easing across the hills and glancing back she could see yard lights sprouting in the valley below.

She felt the flat thump in her chest before she could properly hear it. A moment later she saw a helicopter, flying well below where she stood. Its blades punched the air with a flat *thwap* as it crawled across the deepening light of hayfields, heading home to roost at the ranch she'd just driven through, one of the biggest in the state. The thing pivoted with insectile grace before it passed behind a hill and was gone.

She stamped the skis in place to kick off the balled-up snow under her boots and pushed on. The spur road, untracked and pure, gradually vanished under a fresh pillow of snow as it parted from the main route. She skied through a line of aspens and over the top strand of a buried barbed-wire gate before entering the trees. A light wind had come up and it shushed in the pines around her as she followed the road in.

She paused again at the creek, which was barely bubbling up through the fresh snow. There had once been a sign naming the gulch but it was gone now. She heard a chirp and looked across to see a little gray bird perched on a cut log by the bank. It tilted its head and gave her a moment of cockeyed regard before calling loudly and flitting off. She knew it shared a name with her town and that it survived the winters by gorging on juniper berries. It would guard them with jealousy and fight anything that tried to take them away.

⁂

The cabin was steeped in gloaming when she reached the metal gate. She tried closing it to keep the sledders out but it was drifted in hard and wouldn't budge. She passed through and went up to the cabin, which was clad in government-steel siding. A foot of hard snow covered the deck. She propped the skis in a drift, opened the combination lock on the door, and stepped inside.

Her boots echoed on the chipped wooden floor. Somehow it felt colder indoors. She set the pack on a chair and opened the old stove in the center of the room. The last residents had left kindling and a *Billings Gazette* and she got a little fire going, the pine popping as it caught in the darkening room. She unloaded the pack, unwrapping the gin bottle and setting it beside the holster on the table. She pulled out her sleeping bag and tossed it on the vinyl couch at the edge of the room. The wood bin was pretty full but she figured she'd split and haul more for the next group before skiing out on Sunday.

She held a match to the globe of the propane lantern, which hissed to life as it slowly filled the corners of the room with light. Next she lit the Coleman stove to warm a pot of stew made from an elk she'd shot last fall. Emptying the rest of the pack, she set a paperback beside the bottle along with a bladder of red wine and the rest of her rations. She eased into a chair and took the paperback in hand, riffling its pages with her thumb. Pouring a shot of wine into her plastic mug, she found the chapter about the dead man whom the author had once searched for in the blistering Arizona desert. *I look in the shade of every juniper and overhanging ledge, likely places to find a man besieged by thirst....*

The stew began to bubble on the stove and she rose to give it a stir. There was a massive steel Monarch range beside it but she hadn't even considered firing it up for such a simple meal. Its many-chambered heart would hold a lot of timber and a cook who cared to could roast a Christmas turkey in the thing. She took the pot off the stove and returned to the table, blowing on the first spoonful to cool it. She cracked the paperback again. *Out of water, I return to the truck. My brother is waiting for me and by the lost expression on his face I understand at once that he has found our man.*

It was this damn book that had given her the idea. She'd had no brother to find the old man, so she'd done that herself after not hearing from him for a week. Her father lay unmoving on top of the quilt in his back bedroom, and she'd covered her nose and mouth in the doorway. She went no further before calling the sheriff's office and sat in the kitchen until a deputy arrived. The coroner was summoned, and people went in and out. Among the last was her father, zipped in black vinyl. She'd returned to the bedroom for a last look. On the nightstand was a bottle of gin, the very last bottle, a few swallows still patiently waiting inside.

⁂

She sat now at the table and picked up the bottle. The last of the stew cooled beside the tented paperback as she twirled the bottle's contents to watch them clump and shift beneath the gaudy Beefeater logo. The most ridiculous coffin imaginable, a glass suit of clothes tailored perfectly to its wearer. She'd poured the last of the gin into a flask and left the bottle to dry out, something her father had never quite managed. When she brought the box of cremains home from the mortuary, she'd set it on the kitchen table and slit it open with his Buck knife. She meant to pour him right in but the sonofabitch was all clods and chunks and she had to go to work on him with his own knife, slicing and carving until he was a pile of dice. After that, he poured easily into the bottle one last time, assuming its shape as his own, never to emerge again.

She'd read the Ed Abbey book in her teens and remembered liking it. She'd bought it at a reading by his friend, the bear expert, at a bookstore in Bozeman. In doing so she'd shaken one of the hands that had carried Abbey's corpse to a waiting pickup bed, driven it into the desert, and buried it without permission, apology, or tombstone. It seemed like the very best grave anyone could ask for. Also, it was all she could afford.

She set the bottle upright again on the table and toasted her father with the mug. How he could drink enough of that shit to kill him was beyond her; she would have rather drunk gas. She emptied the mug and pulled on her boots to hit the outhouse before bed.

Outside, the cold was bracing and welcome. It was a clear night and Orion filled the meadow above the gate and she was about to walk down when she heard them: horned owls, hooting at each other in the trees all around the cabin. She held her breath and counted until she was sure there were at least four. They called to each other in their perfect cartoonish voices, exchanging information above the curl of sparks issuing from the cabin's stovepipe. Then she looked up and saw a dark shape, feathers spread against the icy spray of stars overhead, making no sound at all as one of them passed just beyond her reach.

⁂

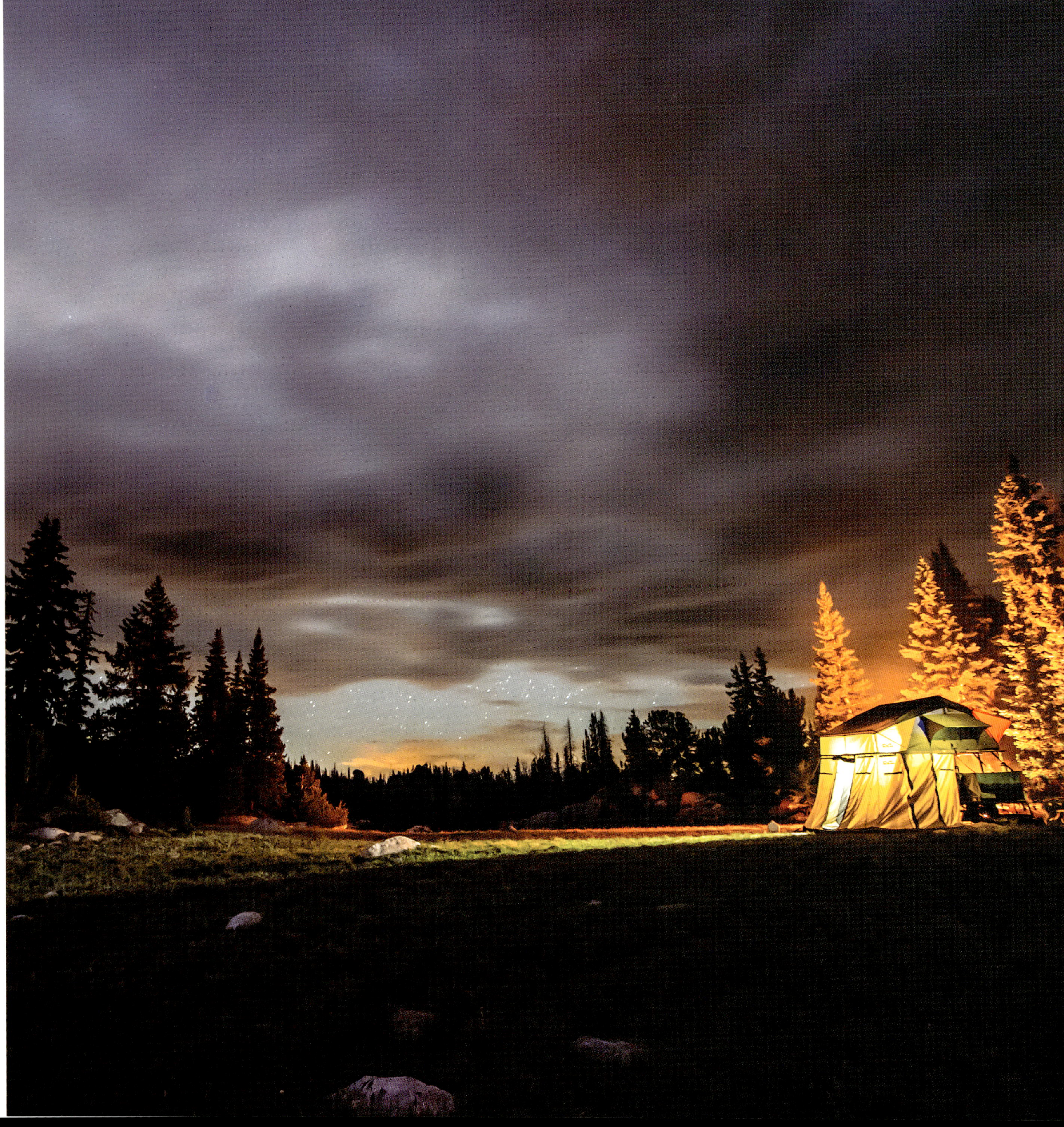

WHAT YOU DO FOR FUN

Maile Meloy

When my brother and I first started going on the Smith River in the 1980s, we had rain gear made from black plastic garbage bags. When it rained—which it did—we sat huddled on a cooler on the raft, wearing orange horseshoe-shaped life preservers buckled over our bags. There were no permits or assigned campsites then, so there were groups jockeying for position and sending kayaks ahead to get dibs. You could get to a campsite, find it full, and have much farther to go (in your garbage bag, in the rain).

When the sun came out, shoulders blistered and sunglasses fell into the deepest swimming holes. When the wind came up, it yanked tents out of the ground and rolled them away into the river. We made our aunt sing a funny love song she'd written, over and over until the adults screamed in protest. But those same protesting adults told really bad jokes and long shaggy dog stories. They also set the opposite bank of the river on fire one Fourth of July, then frantically paddled across in the dark to put it out.

Our cousins' grandmother broke her ankle and had to be carried down from a hike, but still rode in the raft for two more days without complaining. There have been bears, lightning, hay fever, hypothermia, poison oak, and trips that made us swear we would never go again. But mostly it's a mellow five-day float trip, with trout lurking under the banks. Panicky merganser ducklings flee the boats, their feet going like outboard motors, and bald eagles perch overhead, unruffled. With assigned campsites, you know how long your day will be, and there's no unexpected slog to the next free spot. There's time to hike up the canyon walls, overlooking the bends of the river, and to learn a kayak roll in a deep pool.

The group has changed over time, and you know someone's new love is a serious prospect if they're invited. The river isn't dangerous or technical, so you don't always learn what people are like under pressure. But you do learn useful, everyday things. Are they cheerful after sleeping on the ground? Before the coffee is ready? Will they take dish duty more than once? Can they share a two-person tent, and also entertain themselves? Those aren't the only criteria for choosing a mate or a friend, but they're not terrible ones to start with. The test works in reverse, too: some people say, "*This* is what you do for fun?" And once is enough.

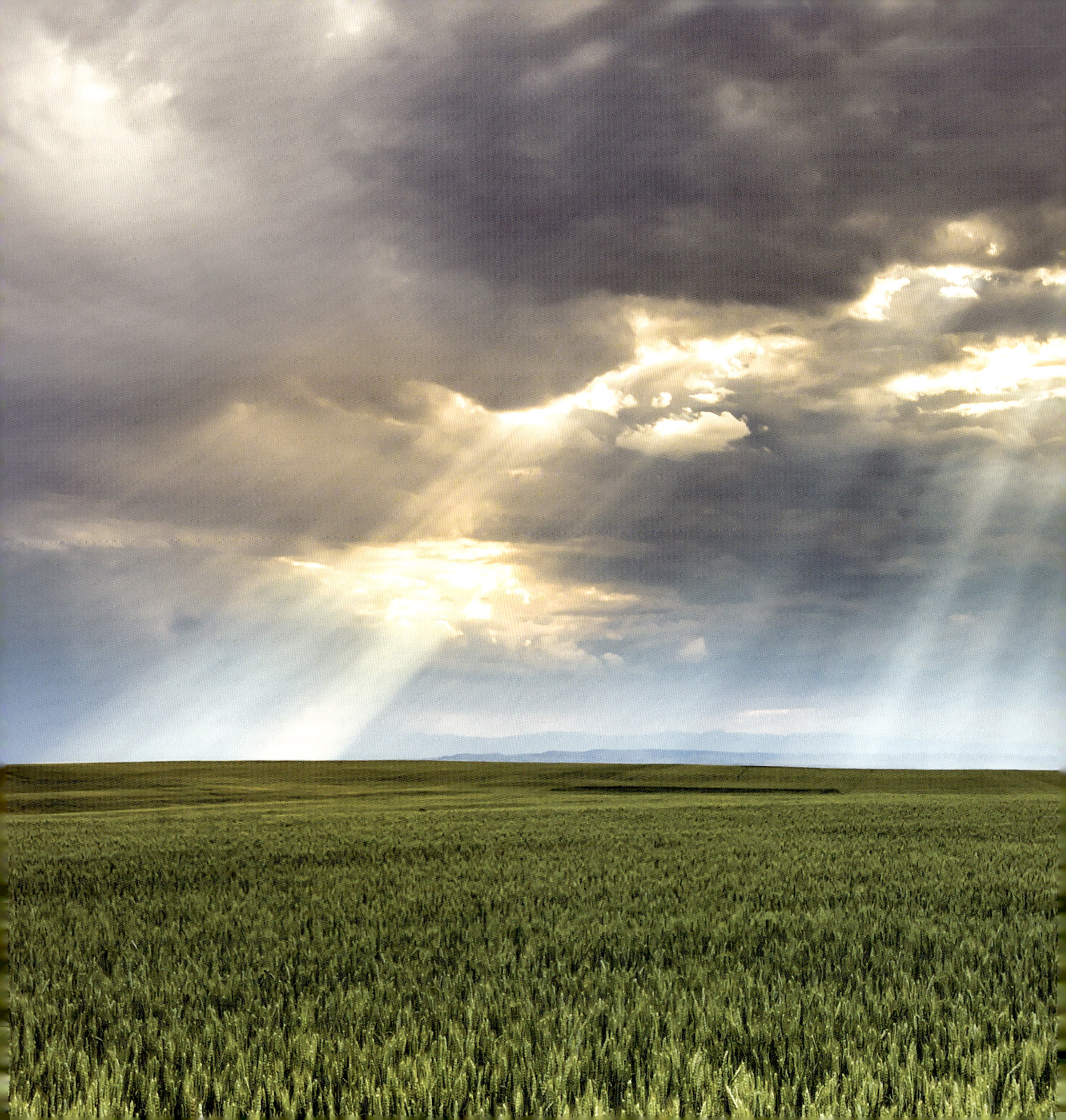

MY FATHER'S CATHEDRAL

Janet Skeslien Charles

Montana is known for its majestic mountains, but I prefer the plains: the pastel prairies, the patchwork of farmland, black-eyed Susans bordering lonely stretches of road. Growing up, I could see a hundred miles in any direction and I believed there were no limits, only endless possibilities.

Now, arriving from Paris, I gaze out the plane window and smile when I see the tidy fields of wheat as vivid as the quilts my mother stitches together. Driving down the dirt road of my mind, it is harvest time again on the Hi-Line. In the red combine, Dad barrels down the field. As I watch the header snatch up the wheat, I feel no sight is more majestic. In the pug-nosed grain truck, Mom sidles up to Dad and the arm of the auger pours the wheat into the truck. It flows quickly and abundantly. They are both covered in the dust of harvest, their brows lined with worry. Will it hail before they finish? Will the truck break down again? They won't relax until harvest is over and Dad puts the combine in the Quonset for another year. My parents danced this duet for thirty-four years and are now retired. When they meet me at the airport, I see the weight of worry has been lifted from their shoulders. I hug their wiry bodies, already looking forward to a morning walk with my mother, basking in silence broken only by the rumble of a truck or a horse's neigh. Each direction offers a kaleidoscope of colors and textures: a poppy in bloom, a robin pecking for breakfast, a deer bouncing over a barbed-wire fence.

The truth is, when I lived in Montana, I didn't appreciate all this. I looked out our windows and wondered when my life would begin. I spent more time indoors than out, more time in books than in the real world. Time and space and silence were not luxuries; I didn't even notice them on my way to school, as I did my homework, as I wrote in my journal. In Shelby, we all shopped at the same grocery store and we drank from the same well. Sharing the same past, we repeated the same stories. Old Mrs. Murdoch wasn't as mean before her husband keeled over while shoveling snow. Buck Gustafson was never the same after the war. We read the same paper, we depended on the same doctor. We looked after our own. Teachers helped students with their homework after school. When it came time for funerals, Mom and the other ladies cooked feasts so the bereaved could focus on their grief while Dad and the other men wrote checks so death would be less of a burden. We traveled on dirt roads that bordered fields, some fallow, others fertile. I knew we were tied to the land and that we were lucky. Still, I viewed the vastness as emptiness, as something missing.

As a teenager, I didn't want to live in a small town. I wanted more than one radio station to choose from. I longed to walk into school and see new faces instead of the same fifty classmates I'd known since kindergarten. Watching strangers drive past on the gray ribbon of interstate, traveling to someplace bigger and better, I felt envy. I wanted to rip my roots out of the dry earth and go with them. I wanted to be among swarms of people. I wanted things I could not name.

Daydreaming of the City of Light, I longed for the sight of real cathedrals like Notre Dame, the buttery taste of croissants, a whiff of Coco Mademoiselle perfume, the soft touch of kisses on both cheeks. While studying French at the University of Montana, I applied for a teaching position through the *Ministère de l'Éducation nationale* and was assigned to a junior high school in Paris. I was stunned when some of my students insisted they'd rather live elsewhere. They couldn't Rollerblade or run in the city because the sidewalks were too narrow and crowded, and there was no place to play soccer. These teens longed for space and quiet the same way I longed for noise.

Well, I got what I wanted. Paris is the constant clang of construction, the fervent jackhammer of upkeep, the skeletons of scaffolding surrounding old buildings as workers endlessly scrape sooty facades. Even inside, there is no longer any such thing as silence. In restaurants and cafes, at airports and hotel lobbies, and even in public bathrooms, background music or twenty-four-hour news channels play. It becomes impossible to think or reflect. Once, it was possible to flee the din, to find a corner where someone else's songs couldn't be heard. Today, state-of-the-art sound systems and flat-screen TVs will not let us escape the dictatorship of noise.

Having lived in Paris for over a decade now, I long for quiet, space, the clean scent of clover, a homemade cookie, a hug. Why the change? Is it because I'm growing older? Because all of us want what we cannot have? Am I a salmon who simply wants to swim home? Or have I finally understood that growing up in a farming community—where people look out for each other, where the land itself told me there were no limits—was a blessing? Other expats in Paris tell me they get homesick, too. Together, we reminisce about "the old country," whether we're from Connecticut or Kentucky, Minnesota or Montana. We talk about the friends and family we see no more than once a year, of the comfort food only our moms can make. Sometimes we're surprised by what we miss. For one, it's simple connections like small talk with a stranger. For another, it's eternal air conditioning in hundred-degree weather. For me, it's that barren landscape and the silence that comes with it, the solitude of the farm I so rarely see.

When I return home, it is with love and longing, needing to hear the hush of the prairie and see the calm of the trees, the silent journey of the hawk floating above me in the pasture, the breeze that brings the wheat stalks to life until the waves in the field resemble the sea. All the things I didn't notice for the first twenty years of my life.

In Montana, each morning at sunup, my mother and I walk down gravel roads. The yellow clover smells so sweet that I inhale until my ribs hurt. Mom is as constant, gentle, and warm as the sunrise. Back home, coffee in hand, she puzzles over the crossword in the paper as I return to my desk. I've spent my life staring out windows. First in the classroom, daydreaming of the time I would be on my way with plane ticket in hand, the day I'd escape church picnics and wheat fields. As a writer, I'm still looking out windows, hoping to unearth characters, settings, veins of desire. Instead of escaping life, I try to create lives and find the points that bring people together.

My father, too, has spent his professional life looking out windows, through the grimy glass of his tractor, combine, and sprayer. Helping a neighbor harvest, he moves methodically over the land at six miles per hour. The wheat field is his university, his temple, his cathedral.

This is the glory of a wheat field. It is where my father finds God. Ignoring the monotone rumble of the engine, Dad contemplates life's questions, staring out over the land as flat as paper. Looking out the window, we both reflect.

Stand in the middle of a wheat field. The heads of wheat will whisper to you. Grasshoppers you can't see will sing you their songs.

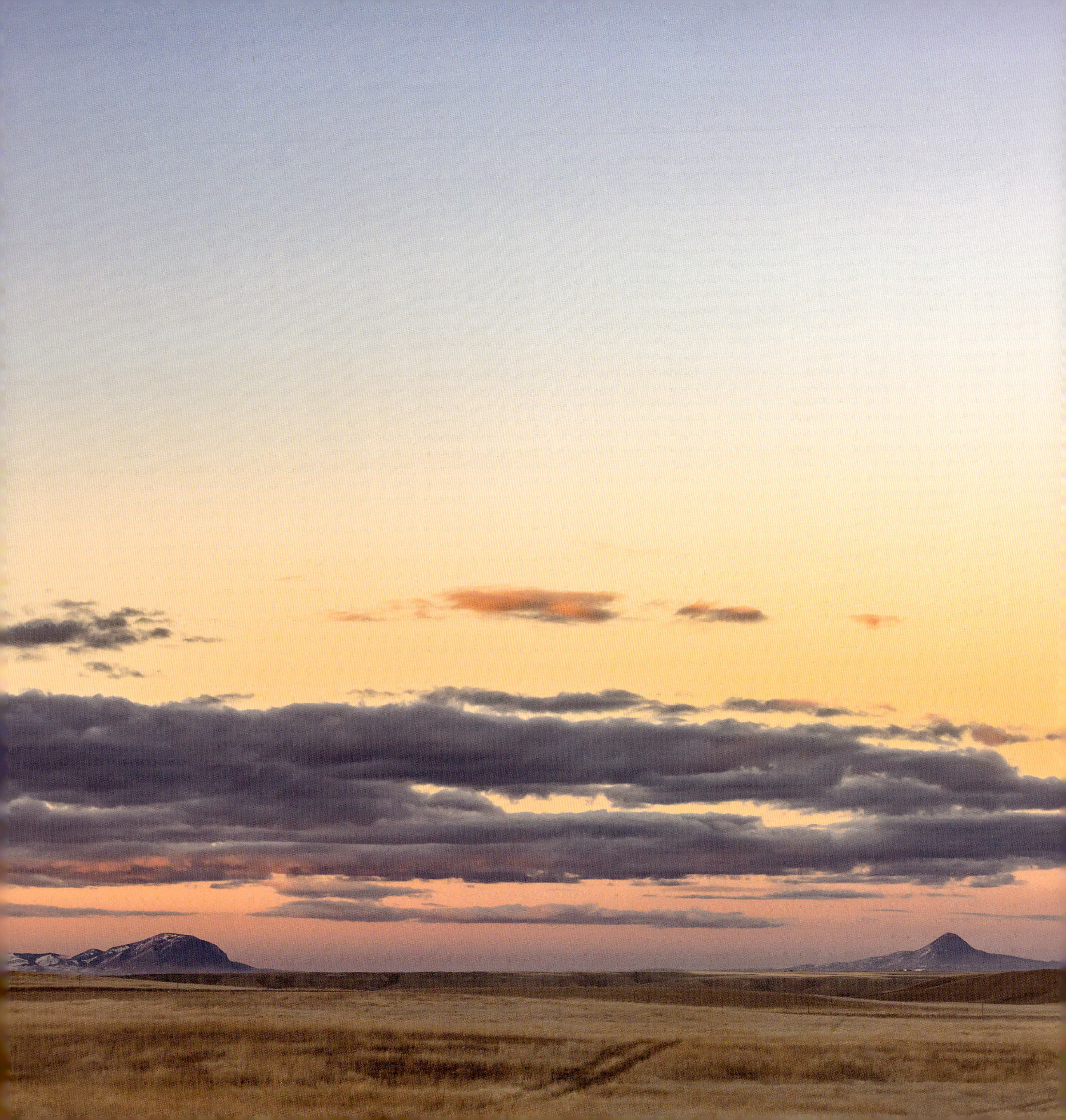

OUT THERE

James Grady

Sawtooth indigo mountains shrink in your car's rearview mirrors. The highway races away from your windshield toward a high-prairie infinite horizon strangers can't believe. They can't fathom the endless blue sky curving over their heads, holding this yellow sun over the brown and gold landscape. Those musk-scented fields might be weeds, might be wheat that keeps America from starving to death.

Visitors who drive this oceanic *Where are we?* gaze with awe at its beauty for at least the first hour. Maybe even the second. Then comes the third. The fourth. And in a tick-tock of "*Oh my God, we're trapped inside this car!*" comes the realization of why cartographers call this earth rolling under their wheels the Big Empty.

But it's not empty.

There's always the wind.

Even if the hairs on your bare arm lay still, the wind is there.

Give it a minute or two.

Maybe it'll be a summer breeze barely noticed by locals or blessed by them on a 101-degree August Tuesday following that snow dusting first o' July.

Maybe a throbbing energy that scurries autumn leaves over cracked sidewalks.

Maybe it's a blizzard of white roaring toward you faster than you can flee, like the steer with its legs trapped in deep snow as wolves circle nearer in Charlie Russell's painting *Last of the Five Thousand*. He cowboyed with my grandfather.

Perhaps the wind you feel will be that lifesaving force Russell yearned for in his painting's alternate title, *A Chinook*, a wondrous warm melting brushing across this winter-cloaked vastness like your soulmate's sigh.

The mountains disappearing in your rearview might have framed Butte, where the Richest Hill on Earth is now a mile-long, quarter-mile-deep-and-rising lake of poison. Immigrants from Ireland, Italy, Sweden, Lebanon, and China built a proud middle-class cultural legacy there that also includes the lynching from a downtown railroad trestle of a union organizer whom Dashiell Hammett, the father of *noir* art, refused to murder for a big-bucks corporate contract.

Or you could have started in Bozeman, a twenty-first-century university town with coffee shops, ski resorts, and the mansions of expats for whom Hollywood is often not a dream but a primary residence. In the long shadows of the nearby Crazy Mountains live 1970s feminist hero Dorothy Bradley and centuries-spanning prose star Tom McGuane.

Maybe when you left Bozeman or Butte for the Big Empty, your car went through capital city Helena, home turf for nature photographer Bess Wong, twenty-first-century literary magician Maile Meloy and her rock-star brother Colin, and the launch pad for Australian expat short-story writer Yvonne Seng. Helena is the state's political center, where a comfortable middle class has replaced the civic culture once dominated by a triumvirate of the Roman Catholic church, hardworking hordes of state bureaucrats, and old money. That power triangle faded with tech replacing tailings as our source of gold.

Or maybe your highway rollout started in the mountains around Missoula, another skiing and university town, this one clinging to the rebellious Sixties with Brooklyn-bearded heirs to those Beatles longhairs of yore. The university football team is named for the grizzly bear, once king of the prairies. Chief Joseph's fleeing families and warriors rode through Missoula unchallenged. Now its city sidewalks are scarred by the shadows of novelists like James Lee Burke, James Crumley, Gwen Florio, and Keir Graff.

The Ox is still there. The Oxford means diner food, booze, maybe cards. An Oxford counter stool was the preferred seat of the late Mike Mansfield, the US Senate Majority Leader from out here who seldom talked, hated being in the historic photographs, avoided taking credit, has only *PVT—US MARINE CORPS* on his headstone instead of the fact that he led and won the Senate battle for 1964's Civil Rights Act.

Everywhere you look in those Western mountains rise pine trees. There are running rivers made legendary by fly fisherman, professor, and legendary author Norman Maclean. Sky-piercing crags with valley towns like the one where poet Richard Hugo lamented your last good kiss.

The Missoula-out route winds you up over picture-postcard Rogers Pass, where the last thing you want your windshield to follow through these long-drop mountains is the back end of a flatbed truck loaded with bouncing logs.

Those safety chains will hold—right?

You'll roll through a midpoint mountain crossroads town called Lincoln, famous for its pit-stop cafes and being the hideout for the Unabomber. When the mountains in your mirror start to shrink and you're still on a narrow *only two lanes* highway, don't worry: the interstate is coming up.

Of course, if you left the mountains via a Butte-Bozeman-Helena route, you got a four-lane divided highway all the way through the maroon stone V of Wolf Creek Canyon.

Either way, now your windshield fills with as-far-as-the-eyes-can-see.

But this *now* is starting to look like *not* the Montana pictured on come-hither websites.

Sure, cows munch grass inside fences near the roads—bigger than they used to be, thanks to 4-H programs teaching farm kids how to breed ever-better animals for this rolling earth where the buffalo roamed. Before buffaloes came dinosaurs, which hardscrabble ex-Marine Montana paleontologist Jack Horner realized were like birds. Horner's epiphany is a less emotional confirmation of evolution than a 4-H girl's sobs as the county fair livestock judges hand her the grand prize for the Bessy she bottle-fed, pampered, and raised to win that treasured blue ribbon and the auction's top bid from the slaughterhouses.

You can't have a cowboy without cows.

Look at them as you drive by. Those black ones are angus, right? And the reddish-brown ones with white furred faces, you're pretty sure they're Herefords.

Heifers. Bulls. *Whatever*.

If you're lucky and know how to look, you'll spot a corral of horses fit for saddles. Mares. Stallions. Geldings. Mustangs. Arabians. Quarter horses. They're black and brown, Picasso-worthy Appaloosas and pintos with swirls of colors, even a few horses of blue.

Horses helped the first settlers work this open country: the Blackfoot and Crow and the lesser known Gros Ventre who moved here from the Midwest a while back. *Yeah*, Chief Joseph rode this turf, and you hear the hoofbeats of the Cheyenne and Sioux, other tribes, too.

Fur trappers brought French and Canadian *patois* into these winds. After buffalo hunters cleared away those easily shot critters, the cows took their place. With them came seasonal and day-laborer cowboys for shape-ups and roundups, many of whom like my grandfather hung up their spurs for the winter and took "town jobs" like dealing poker in saloons.

Not every cowpoke can become a great painter.

Following the cowboys and the sheepherders—including Basque refugees—came the influx of scrappy dreamers who evolved into business entrepreneurs and became the economic and cultural glue for these gold-and-brown chessboard fields.

Today we call them farmers.

Yesterday, well . . .

Honyockers. Sodbusters. Homesteaders.

Families gambling on hopes and dreams fueled by back-East marketing campaigns comparing virgin Montana plains to places like Iowa, where corn grew as high as an elephant's eye in a climate bright with rainbows. Such Madison Avenue advertising campaigns were bankrolled by railroad tycoons who needed passengers to ship in and cargo to ship out, even if their railroad company was a federal-government welfare beneficiary that got fortunes of timber, minerals, water, and land free for building the tracks of their business.

What helped make this America great was the Homestead Act of 1862, which after a 10-dollar filing fee awarded you 160 acres, provided you "proved up" your new home within five years. Subsequent Congressional generosity upped the grant to 320 acres.

Thousands of brave human beings came west for America's promises.

My other grandfather was a homesteader.

The first few years of the twentieth-century homesteading boom were merciful. Decent weather, though a tad dry, and the never-tilled prairie soil plowed up well. Homesteaders lived in shacks of found wood, tar paper, and prairie sod. Don't ask about plumbing, how deep you had to dig, or far you had to wagon for personal-use water.

Then came brutal winters that trapped those sodbuster shacks like a steer in snow.

Then came the endemic droughts that had been hiding and giggling.

Then came biblical clouds of grasshoppers that attacked crops and children.

Between 1919 and 1925, twenty thousand homesteads were foreclosed, according to K. Ross Toole, the state's eminent historian, and eleven thousand farms "blew away." Half of those pioneers lost their farms. Madness was common in those who fled. And stayed.

And that was *before* the Dust Bowl of the 1930s, when the deep plowing by homesteaders' horses broke the earth so badly that those winds raised sky-high walls of dirt that rolled like tidal waves across these prairies.

The stubborn courage of surviving honyockers, combined with savvy government scientists' help during the Depression, altered Montana agriculture with eco-smart conservation methods that included strip farming and crop rotation. That science-led savvy made farming viable in Montana. And that New Deal with "bubble up" federal bailouts offered WPA jobs in public-works projects like building small-town Montana courthouses.

To picture how we evolved out there, consider how Montanans make hay.

Back in my grandfathers' era, pitchforks dotted the farmland with haystacks.

After we won World War II, most farmers used twine to bind this crop into sixty-pound, child-sized rectangles of *itch* called hay bales. Lucky high-schoolers toughed out summer pocket change by lifting and thrusting—"bucking"—thousands of hay bales onto the back of a flatbed truck that might be chugging down the rows with no driver behind its lashed-in-place steering wheel.

Now you drive past sophisticated agricultural domains where post-Sputnik machines spin hay into truck-sized, straw-colored spirals. The jockeyed tractors and harvest combines of Elvis Presley's era have been upgraded to enclosed, air-conditioned, and GPS-directed earth crawlers that sometimes barely break the earth as they get their job done.

Praising the farmers is not to slight the ranchers. But in this sprawl of geography called the Golden Triangle, there are more visible farmers than ranchers, even though Montana cows way, *way* outnumber the state's whole herd of humans.

Look where you are.

Out of the purple mountain majesties, on the endless fruited plains.

You're going north now.

Through Great Falls to take a picture of the tumbling waterfall that stymied two federal government investigators named Lewis and Clark. This is the big city for the northern Big Empty: 59,000 folks, literary stars like Jamie Ford and Eric Heidle, plus Montana's first major newspaper that in the 1950s wasn't secretly owned by corporate heirs of the Copper Kings. An air force base helps fuel the bustle of Great Falls. Jet fighters streak the sky. A giant smelter smokestack once dominated this city's horizon. That smokestack's bricks have long since been busted up, but in every direction you turn are distant mountains.

Especially the Rocky Mountains, that blue sawtooth, often snow-capped ridge some forty miles west from the interstate you're now driving north.

Off to your left, a wondrous mesa rises nine hundred feet up from the prairie.

Crown Butte, scores of square miles of never-cultivated wild prairie on its flat top, slides past your car windows as you drive through rolling "settled" fields.

Those endless plains.

After a couple hours, that's all most strangers see.

As you roll north on the four-lane divided highway of Interstate 15, hiding in vast fields are canals that even many of the state's native-born souls don't know exist.

In fact, this swath of semiarid Montana has more miles of canals than Venice, Italy.

You'll probably spot farm reservoirs. Ponds. Ditches that gave name to the whiskey-and-water drink ordered nowhere except Montana.

But out there somewhere beyond the interstate also shimmer miracles like Freezeout Lake, a seasonal venue for three hundred thousand snow geese and ten thousand tundra swans who each year wing off the lake and into Facebook posts of tourists from Europe and Japan.

Out here loves birds.

Brown sparrows. A robin perched on a barbed-wire fence post. High in the blue sky fly vast V's of black-headed Canada geese, no visas needed as they honk their way toward the warm weather behind you. There go ducks, green-headed male mallards and more cautiously feathered females. Maybe you'll spot a ring-necked pheasant with his green hood and red-jowled face, prancing the fields as he listens for the shotguns of autumn.

If you follow the white-on-green road signs to a rest stop, then turn your engine off and let the day settle, you might hear the distinctive seven-beat musical twitter of a meadowlark.

True luck is a silent swoop and the shadow of a golden eagle by your shoes.

Owls are out here, wherever they decide to "who."

Who you are is driving out of the mountains, into the Big Empty, up through the Golden Triangle toward Canada, the other half of the seasonal commute for geese.

While you don't see most of those birds and maybe don't see any deer and antelope playing, or loping coyotes (out here pronounced: "*Ki*-oats"), what you mostly notice is you don't see people.

Hardly any other cars on this four-lane tan highway.

Small towns of gray, ten-story-tall grain elevators, lonely cafes, and emergency gas.

Yet, also out there off the interstate, on the bend of a two-lane blacktop road named for wondrous author Ivan Doig sits a town called Depuyer—a mashup of French for *buffalo grease*. Depuyer shelters a gourmet barbecue restaurant with Austin-Greenwich Village décor. Further up the road in Conrad—not named for *Heart of Darkness* author Joseph Conrad—people say there's a fabulous homegrown, unfranchised coffee café.

You decide to keep going toward Canada, toward something your GPS calls the Hi-Line. That sounds like a good place to get off, to leave homeboy author A. B. Guthrie's "thousand hills" you're just learning to see for a little civilization.

Plus you want a closer look at three blue humps ruling the northern horizon.

Anywhere else, they'd be mountains. Here, they're the Sweet Grass Hills.

East Butte is the boring one: it just looks like a strung-out rock pile as tall as small planes like to fly. Gold Butte—the middle one—rises above the prairie like a proud volcano. West Butte is the cool one, a cobalt blue 9 lounging on its back like a waiting lover.

You decide to pull off into a coming-up town called Shelby.

The GPS says it's less than a half an hour north of Conrad.

Out there, time is the measure of all journeys.

Something's different about the land you see up ahead through your windshield.

A line of hills that looks like a row of teeth—the gullied tops are dark purple, shale maybe, turning golden as the earth fans down.

River breaks.

Not the famous Missouri River Breaks—they're way behind you now. You're headed to the river called Marias.

Maria was a cousin of that government investigator Meriwether Lewis.

Dead Man's Curve is coming up on the two-lane blacktop highway to the left of the interstate you drive. Alongside that curved blacktop from yesterday stands a *cryin' tires, bustin' glass* memorial of four small, white crosses. Today's freeway pavement under your wheels is straight, wide, and empty as you top a hill . . .

. . . *whoosh* down a steep half-mile slope to the bridge across the cousin's gray river that cuts its own valley through this land. Rattlesnakes bask there. Trees flank that water. The eastward flow of the Marias made it easier for Lewis and Clark to report back to DC.

An army of robots locks onto you when you top the hill on the river's north bank.

Off to your distant left, rising almost three hundred feet into the air, are more than one hundred cylindrical white towers, each with three spinning blades over one hundred feet long.

Windmills.

Of course! *Finally!* Only as the twentieth century died did science and business unite out here to exploit the one dependable, renewable resource on these plains—that wind.

The wind that rocks your car cruising this highway in our land of the free.

Sunlight glistens on silvery razor-wire and chain-link fences caging a huge field left of the highway just before the Shelby exit. A prison. A for-profit prison. A Wall Street–owned corral of men on the receiving end of the low-bid payout for the care and custody of those who get convicted.

Turn away from that and put on your right-turn blinker.

Drive down the exit ramp.

Down to the crossroads.

Down to a town called Shelby—named for a railroad man.

Now this town is the junction for the two-lane US Highway 2 and Interstate 15.

Odds are, what fills your windshield first are miles of railroad boxcars on multiple tracks. Some boxcars sport logos of yore like Burlington Northern Santa Fe. Most of the boxcars' corporate names chant *China, China, China.*

If you turn left after you exit the freeway, the two-lane blacktop of US 2 leads you past the windmills. In about half an hour, you'll be in Cut Bank, a town chronicled fictionally by its daughter Deirdre McNamer. Beyond those western city limits comes the Blackfeet Reservation that birthed poet and novelist James Welch, a founding father of the Native American Renaissance literary movement.

If you follow US 2 through the reservation town of Browning, the Rocky Mountains take you in again and you can drive through the glories of Glacier Park. In cowboy days, the park was home to one hundred fifty glaciers; now only twenty-six shrunken hills of ice remain, melting, melting.

If you turn right on US 2 after you exit the interstate, you roll into Shelby.

Imagine your yesterdays as the road curves onto a Main Street with its own ghosts.

This town is a national legend, a mud-streets burg that in 1923 bankrupted itself trying to buy publicity by hosting the heavyweight boxing championship in which Jack Dempsey beat Tommy Gibbons. That absurd disaster nearly killed the town.

By the time Our Boys came back from beating World War II's Nazis and imperious dictators, this nearly half-mile-long paved Main Street bustled with seven bars, called "joints." There were two locally owned banks. Two independent town newspapers and a local radio station.

Three dress shops and two men's stores, plus department store J. C. Penney and a competitor called Anthony's. A dime store full of toys. Two jewelers. Two car dealerships. An ice cream parlor called the White House and a widow-run bookstore. A bakery for heavenly smelling fresh bread, sticky cinnamon buns, chocolate donuts. There was a hardware store and one of the town's two lumberyards. There were electricians and a radio shop, its dusty window full of tubes, wires, and a novelty water-glass bobbing dodo bird.

Just off Main Street stood the two-story brick box telephone company, from which county linemen were dispatched and into which, precisely on time, marched women and teenage girls, all wearing mandatory dresses, ladylike stockings, and proper makeup so they could sit behind locked doors facing switchboards as "operators."

Main Street held two drugstores where the pharmacists knew their patients and the second-floor office of the town's former mayor and frontier doctor who, until the early 1970s, performed illegal abortions for desperate women who came from as far away as St. Paul.

There was a post office and two hotels competing with a half dozen nearby motels. A bus depot. A revolver's worth of restaurants vying with two out-of-town roadhouses or "supper clubs." A parking-meter pole with a battered black-and-white metal sign reading *TAXI* for the only way johns were allowed to patronize the police-protected, county doctors–inspected, red stucco two-story brothel just outside of city limits that was staffed by *of course voluntarily* imported employees.

The town had more than a handful of churches.

Chimes in the Methodist bell tower rang every Sunday morning. They still do.

Until the big Main Street fire and the five-story-tall trackside grain elevator burst one block over, right before you reached city hall on the east end of the commercial strip stood one of two major chain supermarkets for the town that also had a thriving mom-and-pop vittles store. High-schoolers got jobs as box boys carrying groceries to shoppers' cars.

Smack in the middle of all the action rose Main Street's tallest building, the Roxy movie theater, employing heartthrob high-school girls and one gawky boy while projecting cinematic dreams into local hearts and minds.

One earthshaking night, back when *Vietnam* was just entering Shelby's vocabulary, the Roxy—that only a few years earlier had staged one of America's last vaudeville shows with a ventriloquist, people then called midgets, steamer trunks, and magic—showed a Western movie starring real-life war hero Audie Murphy as a cowboy gunslinger riding back to save his old hometown . . . of Shelby, Montana.

The theater erupted because the town shown on the screen was gentle green and tree-filled, a squeaky clean oasis of civilization with white picket fences and no wind.

To paraphrase the great American author of his generation Bruce Springsteen, those souls in the Roxy's audience that night found themselves caught between flesh and fantasy.

Aren't we all.

And yeah, with its boxing and cowboy past, being a terminal for smugglers along the Bootlegger Trail during Prohibition as well as a hub for gandy dancers (sledgehammer-swinging crews who maintained the railroad tracks), wildcatters (who worked the rigs of oil derricks), ego-soaked hometown drunks, and two or three brawlers who never shook the crazies, Shelby was a tough town.

Blink of an eye. Like the night an outraged citizen stormed into the Alibi on Main Street to kill the dogcatcher. Shot but didn't kill him. The bullet passed through the dogcatcher and killed the guy on the next stool. My cousin Max, the bartender, ducked.

Folks expected that kind of thing mostly across the railroad tracks in the north side bars, one with a walled "bullpen" out back, the other known as the Bucket of Blood.

Drive around that side of town.

Pigeons coo under the viaduct spanning the railroad tracks.

Seagulls glide above the town dump.

Drive just out of town past the now-gone drive-in movie theater where I shot a man when I was about eleven. Accidentally. We used his jackknife to cut bullet fragments out of his leg. No law—or more importantly, my Dad—ever knew.

A one-minute drive north of there, the gung-ho Fabulous Fifties Chamber of Commerce created a federally-recognized international airport.

Because everybody knew things were only going to get better.

All that was then.

All this is your now.

A Springsteen Main Street with whitewashed windows and vacant stores.

Parking is easy. Most of the retail shops disappeared or got swallowed by a big-box store just west of the crossroads. There are fewer restaurants than fingers on your hand, though many bars remain, including a famous literary launchpad called the Tap Room.

Sunny summer evenings, sitting on the bench out front of the Tap might be a genial oil and gas company president-*cum*-farmer, a former student-body president of the big pink high school built with President Eisenhower's beat-the-Commies-and-save-America strategy of publicly educating everybody equally in everything from science to Shakespeare.

Ike's strategy worked. Shelby's schools turned out hundreds of solid citizens, including a few multi-millionaires like the stayed-in-Shelby national trucking tycoon and the left-town cargo airline czar who flies back for visits in his World War II fighter plane, plus legendary bar rocker Russ Nasset, my Chicago education-biz star sister Jane, author Sidner Larson, that paleontologist Jack Horner, and biologist Leroy Hood, who pioneered key advances in sequencing something called DNA.

That big pink high school's giant gym used to fill past legal capacity with thousands of basketball fans and produced phenomena like college star and NBA pro Larry Krystkowiak.

Now that high school building also holds the middle school. The football team that once got forty-three turnouts now can only field enough players for the eight-man game.

For Sale signs linger in front of so, so many houses.

Somehow, the private prison on the edge of town didn't deliver its promised prosperity—at least not to Shelby. Federal grants also haven't seemed to boost the whole town much.

But so far, it's survived even our Armageddon, at which you can still tremble just east of town, in open country chronicled from Paris by its former farm girl Janet Skeslien Charles.

That End of the World apparition is near two roadside signs.

The first sign celebrates the area's gushers of the 1920s: "*The oily bird gets the woim!*"

The second sign testifies to the nearby Baker Massacre, when American soldiers gunned down more than two hundred members of a peaceful Piegan community, most of them women and children. A US soldier shot Chief Heavy Runner as he waved a signed peace treaty.

Waiting in the weeds just north of that two-lane blacktop highway, flanked by those signs, lies doomsday.

An ICBM site inside a chain-link fence, one of hundreds of such US Air Force underground lairs in Montana, ready since the Sixties to launch mushroom-cloud missiles whenever Dr. Strangelove pushed the button. You can park by the missile site on summer nights. Watch shimmers of northern lights color the star-shot sky while the buzz of mosquitoes keeps your car's windows rolled up tight.

Back in town on sunny summer evenings, sitting on the bench in front of the Tap Room, what that genial, zen-eyed Baby Boomer hometown success sometimes sees is *nobody*.

Nobody cruising past on this street once filled with his generation's teenagers "dragging Main," car radios dialed in to scratchy AM rock 'n' roll from mystical far-off Oklahoma City as they drove around looking for the road to who they wanted to be.

Now on that Tap Room bench, sit long enough, you're bound to see somebody.

Of course, lots of them are *going* in the street while *being* in their screens.

That's just the way it is.

What's most important to see on the streets of Shelby is that yesterday's ghosts and today's ghost makers see you driving through their town. They hope you see them. *Really* see them. Loved or loathed, they're worth your look and listen.

Sometimes they're everyday heroes of our American Dream.

The always laughing bartender-owner of the Tap Room who tells a mind-blown and body-scarred Vietnam veteran that *damn it*, he's gotta eat his *here-it-is* breakfast if he wants to sit on his safe stool to nurse cups of coffee until other volunteer regulars make sure this lost soul gets back *best as can be* to his peeling-white-paint home.

The county librarian who creates a Halloween haunted house to delight local children and introduce them to our civilization's sanctuary of dreams and visions.

The niece with her own busy life who makes sure her near-ninety aunt in the assisted living facility gets to church and to the weekdays' ten a.m. coffee klatch at the Main Street café that closes after lunch. Of course, the aunt is usually driven to coffee by her, *yup*, older cousin who lives by herself up on the hill near the cemetery.

Your drive through Shelby might get caught up in the annual Four-County Marias Fair and Rodeo parade with fire trucks blaring sirens and gray-haired veterans marching past in military cadence, led by the color guard's snapping American flag. There are flatbed-truck floats for a few businesses and community groups. Giant glistening rumbles of farm machinery. A convertible carries a sashed high-school beauty or an honored grand marshal. They smile and wave. Two handfuls of shy children shuffle past your eyes. Shriners crammed into tiny zipping go-karts toss candy to other kids watching the parade. A posse of cowboys riding horses always comes last, after the marchers at the end of the parade because, well, you know.

The whole show takes about twenty-one minutes.

Then the parade is over.

Folks go on about their way.

You drive out of town.

As the wind *out there* caries the lonesome whistle of a going-*gone* train.

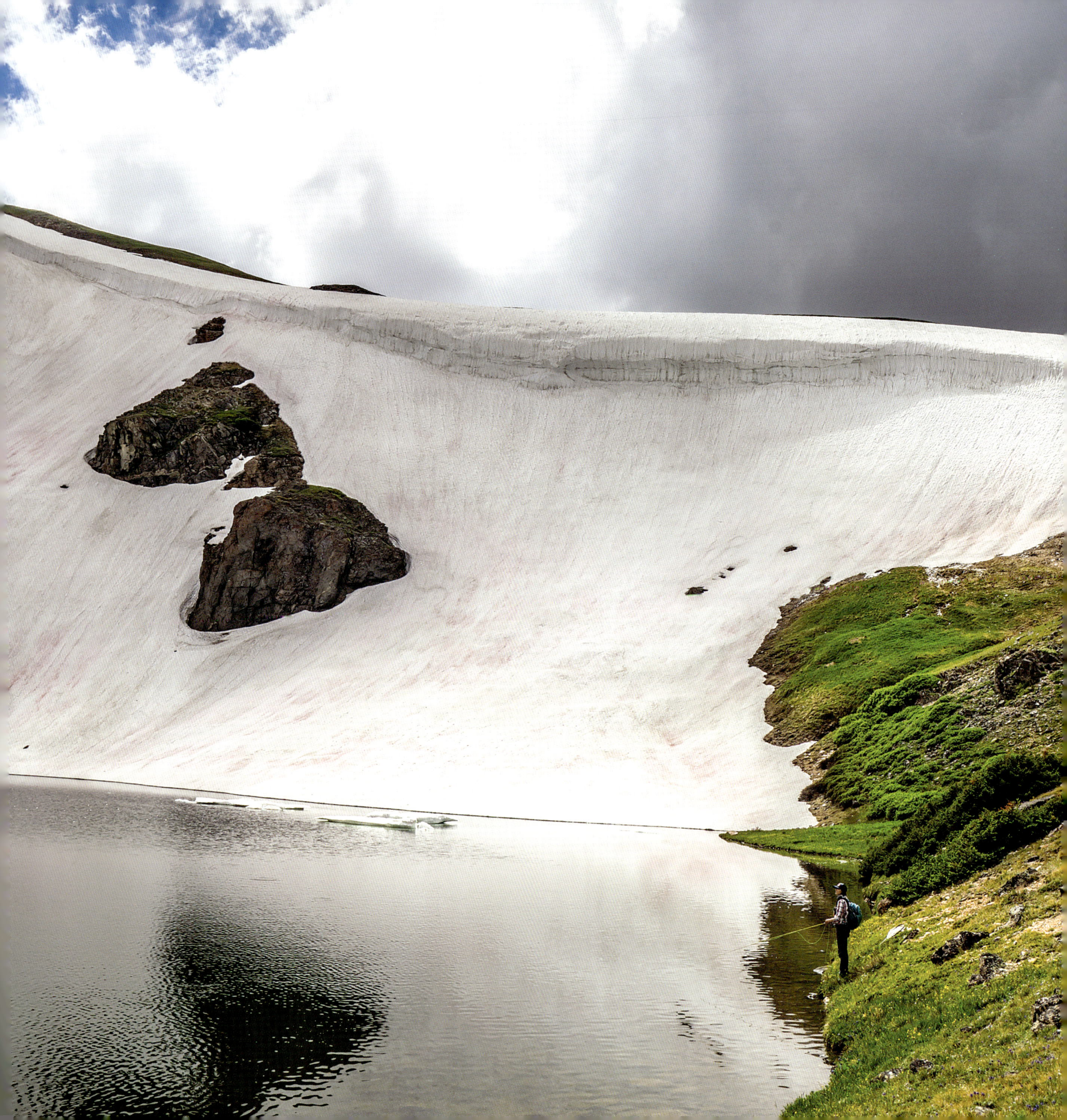

A FINE SPRING DAY

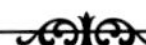

Allen Morris Jones

He had just turned sixteen and was living outside Great Falls with his mother, who was still a young woman, still someone who liked to watch movies and go to bars and laugh. He'd been growing fast and carried his new height awkwardly, all wrists and ankles and Adam's apple. But underneath this lanky adolescence was a hard kernel of observation and judgment passing that no one, it seemed, had yet discovered he had.

He came in for breakfast to find his mother at the sink, wearing her flannel nightgown and a blue down hunting jacket. Her boyfriend Jerry sat with his long legs stretched out under the kitchen table, drinking beer in bare feet and frayed jeans and a white T-shirt.

"Charlie," he said, toasting the boy, "welcome to another fine day in America."

Jerry claimed to be Blackfeet although Charlie had his doubts. Dark hair, but the mustache suggested Italy. This morning, Jerry's hair still held the lines of last night's comb and his eyes took a few seconds to focus as they settled on the boy.

Charlie found cereal and milk, then sat down across from him.

"Jerry here thinks Oly's some kind of breakfast food," his mother said.

Jerry put both elbows on the table and pushed his eyeglasses up with the back of the hand that held the beer. When he wasn't drinking, Jerry worked as a drywaller and always had money to spend. He'd taken to buying Charlie hunting magazines on his way up to the house. His hands and forearms were the thickest Charlie had ever seen: bowling-pin slabs of muscle and vein and ligament. When he turned a beer can in his hands, it seemed a delicate motion for such muscles.

"Your mother's pissed at me, Charlie," he said. "Know why?"

His mother went to the refrigerator and pulled out a beer for herself, spraying foam as she cracked it open. "Charlie's smarter than you, Jerry," she said, shaking off her hand. "Don't talk down to him."

"I'm a free spirit. I live like I want to." Jerry sat back and pulled a penknife from his pocket. "Makin' my own life," he said, trimming a fingernail. "Old Indian trick."

"Your uncle Frank called," his mother said. "He wants to go fishing today. Said he found you a new place."

Charlie walked his bowl to the sink. "Did he say what time he'd be here?"

"Nine-thirty."

Jerry stared at his beer, rolling it back and forth in his palms.

"But I wouldn't mind it if you stayed home today, Charlie," his mother said.

Charlie ignored her and opened the door to the garage, where he kept his fishing gear.

Jerry said his name and he turned back.

"Catch a big one, my man," he said. "It's later than you think."

He sat on the porch steps, canvas bag with waders and a creel of spoons at his feet, spinning rod over the bag. His uncle's Dodge truck, heavy as a boxcar, worked its way up the graveled drive to their house, switchbacking from empty lot to empty lot, tracing the contours of a subdivision that never quite panned out. Frank parked below the steps, engine clattering. Charlie threw his gear in the bed and climbed into the cab, breathing the familiar odors of diesel fuel and cheap cologne and animal hides.

"Where we going?"

"I found us a place."

Frank smoothed his mustache and looked toward the house. He was ten years older than Charlie's mother, with hair going grey at the temples and a stomach wadding out over his belt. Charlie liked to walk to his taxidermy shop after school, to sit on a bench against the wall and sometimes help flesh out the fresh skins. Trophies cycled through the door, cold and stiff, to be disassembled and slowly pieced back together. Glass eyes set into foam, wet skin sewn down from the crest of the neck, faded noses painted black. It had given Frank an early power in Charlie's eyes, this resurrection of animals.

His mother opened the front door and walked down the steps toward them, feet loose in a pair of unlaced Sorels. "Morning, Frank." She laid her forearms on the open window, glancing down at the truck's floor, at the dashboard. "Where are you boys going fishing?"

"Got us a good place. You don't know it."

"Where would that be?"

"Up by Pine Butte. Up in there."

"I know about your good places, Frank. Don't get caught."

"Annie." He shook his head.

"I mean it, Frank. Stay out of trouble."

He put his hand on her shoulder and leaned close. "Oh, sweetheart. You should be working at that yourself."

Frank had a church that he went to in Great Falls, and something always seemed to go out of him when he noted the beer cans piled into the back of their little yellow pickup and the broken windows in the garage door. It was probably true that he saw Charlie and his mother as problems to be solved.

She raised a hand as they pulled away. Jerry stood in the doorway behind her, staring at her back.

"This place, Charlie," Frank said, "this place has got rainbows like *this*." He took his hands off the steering wheel and spread them apart. "And they're trying to spawn right now. They can't, but they try. They're gonna be stacked up against that dam like cordwood."

"That doesn't sound like Pishkun."

"Pishkun." Frank shook his head and took his pack of cigarettes off the dashboard, pulling one out with his lips. "I got us a couple jars of eggs, enough to fill up the freezer with fish. Your mom won't know what hit her." He lit his cigarette with the truck's lighter and reached over to smack Charlie's leg a couple of quick times.

His mother had never worried about him much before. Things always happened for the best, was her view, and she'd told him often that luck was on their side.

"How old are you now, Charlie?" Frank slowed and turned north onto the highway, away from Great Falls.

Charlie had turned sixteen three days before, but he didn't want his uncle to feel embarrassed about missing his birthday. He liked Frank—he liked fishing and hunting with him—and he didn't want that to change.

"Sixteen and a half."

"That's a good age. Maybe the best age."

"How old are you?"

"Too old. It ain't the years it's the miles. Isn't that what they say?"

"You're not that old," Charlie said.

"You get to a certain age and you think you got no more choices. Probably you don't. But then I look at somebody young like you, Charlie. You got all kinds."

"Like what?"

Frank nodded. "Sometimes you can't see it."

They left the haze of Great Falls behind, finally turning off at Choteau. Ear Mountain rose thirty miles to the west, its bent back hinging the Front, north and south. High sheets of cirrus clouds blew fast toward them over the mountains, curling at their leading edges as they hit the plains.

"What do you want to do when you grow up? Maybe that's a place to start."

"A writer."

"Like a newspaper writer?"

"Stories."

Frank drove quietly for a while, biting his thumbnail. Then he said, "What about a vet? Your dad's a vet."

"We don't talk much." Charlie reached up to grab the pack of cigarettes, but when Frank didn't react, he put them back. "Are you going bear hunting this spring?"

"Don't think so."

"Why not?"

"I'm sick of skinning them, to be honest."

"They look too much like people. You told me that once before."

"That's just it." He lifted his hand off the steering wheel and flexed his fingers. "They got those paws, you know."

The road turned to gravel, then to bare dirt, muddy in the swales below the largest drifts. Frank stopped to put the hubs in. They rolled down their windows and rested their arms on the doors. The air was cold and smelled like new grass.

Frank ground out a half-finished cigarette and lit another, bending down over the steering wheel to look up at the peaks, whistling tunelessly through his teeth. He'd always said that he liked hunting best, but next to hunting he liked fishing, and when he was going fishing the world was a fine place for him. The road became steep, and they turned off it to churn up a bare, untracked hillside.

Charlie stepped out to open a gate at the top of the ridge. Stapled to one of the fence posts was an orange and black "No Trespassing" sign of the sort you might buy at any hardware store. From up here, there was a view of the whole countryside, including the pond where he guessed they would be fishing: a plate of water set flat and blue inside a thousand square miles of rolling dead grass and unwashed boulders and festering patches of snow. Above the lake, the snow gradually increased until, on the highest slopes, the mountain was all rotting cornices and old avalanches.

They dropped into the ravine below the lake and parked. It was steep country—steep enough for the dam to have become the horizon—and Frank's truck would be hidden from anyone coming onto the pond from above. Frank stepped out, stretched, and walked up to the front bumper to take a leak. Charlie shrugged into his jacket and reached back for his bag.

"You won't need your waders," Frank said, looking at him. "And we'll just be taking my one fly rod."

"Fly rod?"

Frank zipped up and walked back to peer over the side of the truck into the open bag. "You might want that creel, though."

⁂

They eased up over the crest of the dam, stretching their necks until they could just see into the water. Judging from the gradual slope of its shores, the lake wasn't naturally deep, but the bottom had been excavated. Piles of gravel and clay lay humped in a ring around the banks like mine tailings. A raft of ice floated in the middle, necklaced by the ripples of rising fish.

"Who owns this ground?" Charlie whispered.

Frank stood beside him, breathing hard. "Becker," he said, after a moment. "Something Becker." He stood up straight and put his hands on his belly. "Bill or Bob or Buck. Used to be George Rainy had it but he sold out about five years ago for sixty bucks an acre." He shook his head. "Sixty bucks."

They stood above the water, letting their eyes adjust to the glare. Then Charlie began to see the fish: long, dark slivers coasting in pods among the rocks. Even in the lightly broken chop of the breeze, it was possible to make out the fins as they cut through the surface, the backs rolling briefly into the air, black as glass, thick as salmon.

Frank grinned. "Do you see them?"

Charlie nodded. "Big."

They backed away from the dam and Frank unscrewed the lid from his jar of eggs. "They'll come for miles," he said.

Charlie watched as Frank pulled the rod from its case and pieced together three antique lengths of bamboo, then pulled the reel from his vest and screwed it onto the butt of the rod. Age had tarnished the metal into the color of old ice, but it was clean, and the line spooled smoothly when he stripped it through the guides.

"Your grandpa left this to me," Frank said. "Hardly ever fish with it anymore. But on this fine morning . . ." He filled his chest with air and looked at the sky, the mountains, the water. "It's just what that old doctor ordered. You haven't fly-fished before, right?"

Charlie shook his head.

"That's OK," Frank said, letting him pinch the line to feel its diameter. "See, you've got to have you a line light enough to float down slow, but it's got to be heavy enough to get out there a ways. Let me test the water, then I'll pass the rod off to you. Now watch."

Frank crouched on the flat of the dam and reached into the jar of eggs, threading the first one onto the bare hook before flicking another one out into the pond. It floated undisturbed, a bright punctuation in the murky water. He flicked another egg, then another, until four or five were floating in the water at any one time. Within a few minutes, the eggs seemed to be bouncing as they went to the bottom, jigging to the currents of unseen fish. And then the fish were striking at the eggs as soon as they hit the water. It was how Charlie imagined tuna to feed in the Pacific: a whirlpool of eyes and tails and white stomachs.

Frank looked back at him, and although Charlie expected him to smile or make a joke, he didn't; he was solemn and wide-eyed and tense. He lifted the rod and made one or two false casts off to the side before sending the line out over the water, laying the egg precisely in the middle of the feeding knot of fish. Charlie breathed, and then breathed again. Frank tensed through his shoulder and lifted his arm. The fragile-looking rod jumped and sawed and bent itself into a horseshoe. Frank walked down the dam, following the fish.

"That's how you do it!" he yelled, his voice booming out over the quiet water.

The fish jumped only once, a loose-boned breaching that smacked against the water like a hand across a cheek. Frank reeled, let the fish take the line, then reeled again until it lay exhausted and rolling on the surface a few yards from the bank. Frank stepped in after it, even in his jeans, and pivoted from his hips to sling it back onto the bank. It landed with a hollow thump, as long as any trout Charlie had ever seen, but chunky, too. How big? Six pounds? Seven? It could have easily gone seven pounds. It flopped once, and then again. Frank stepped up and grabbed it behind its gills, his large hands not quite large enough to reach all the way around. He rapped its head on the rocks, then raised the leader to his mouth, clipping it with his big teeth.

"Fish you've caught for yourself taste better," he said, sliding the trout into the back of his vest. The fan of its tail protruded. "Remember that. Now it's your turn." He handed Charlie the rod. "Put on a new hook and give it a try."

A few minutes later, he stood beside his uncle, the length of bamboo trembling in his hands.

"Cast along the dam first for practice," Frank said.

They stood parallel to the water, facing the opposite hillside. Charlie noticed for the first time that the dam had tire tracks on it, winding out past the dam and then through the sagebrush flats.

"Keep your wrist stiff," Frank said, grabbing his forearm, "and act like you're pounding nails. Pick it up, throw it down. Pick it up, give that line some time to get out behind you, pound it down. But do it pretty hard. And keep your wrist stiff."

The first casts were fine. Charlie kept his arm loose and let Frank show him the motions. But when Frank took his hand away, the next cast draped the line around Charlie's shoulders. And the one after that caught on the grass and accordioned into Charlie's back.

He gave the rod back to Frank. "Do it again."

"Watch close, then we'll get you set up." Frank walked down the dam to undisturbed water, not bothering to hide, not bothering to chum. He cast and let the egg drift to the bottom, then he cast again. "See that there? Pounding nails. And watch the line when it goes back."

On the third cast, a fish struck at the egg, and Frank's reel hummed.

"There it is," he said, holding his thumb heavy over the line. He glanced up at the sky, at the mountains. "Yessir," he said, "fine, fine day."

This new fish was smaller than the first, and he beached it quickly, hitting it on the rocks before sliding it into his vest.

"Your turn again," he said.

Three or four hours passed and Frank caught two more fish, each of them over four pounds. Finally he stopped fishing to stand behind Charlie while he cast. "Don't worry about watching the line once it's in the water," he said. "They'll take that egg and just suck it on down. It's not like fly-fishing with flies. Just get it out there."

Charlie stepped off to the side to fish over fresh water, casting in one long, rolling loop. The egg dropped lightly on the surface and floated there for a moment before it began to sink. He gripped the rod handle hard, poised and tense. Everything felt right, but still the egg sank undisturbed. He was lifting his rod for another cast when color bloomed off the bottom. A dull orange roll as brief and sharp as a flashbulb. Then the line's slack was burning through his fist, collapsing his stomach and drawing the moisture from his mouth. Frank walked up and laid his hand on Charlie's shoulder.

The fish ran fast, parallel to the dam at first but then away from it, deeper, and deeper still. The world had acquired a new center, a pivot around which the lake wobbled like a loose tire. Behind him, the plains began their great surge to the Mississippi. In front of him, the Rockies flared away from the plains in splintered detonations of stone. The fish was the heart of the lake and the lake was the heart of the plain and the plain was the heart of world, outward and outward in spinning revolutions that slung him hard against his own rod. The fish dove deep, and the line hitched as it hit against the bottom.

"God a-mighty," he said, and grinned back at his uncle.

Frank had taken his hand off Charlie's shoulder and was looking up the hill. Charlie followed his eyes.

A blue Ford truck stood parked on the rim a quarter mile above them, the afternoon light starring off its windshield, or perhaps a pair of binoculars. As they watched, it began to move down the hill toward them, picking up speed to plow through the first, high drifts of snow. Pastured horses followed behind, head to tail.

Frank reached up for the tip of his rod. "Swing your line over here, Charlie."

"I've about got him," Charlie said, although it wasn't true. He reeled frantically, pulling hard against a fish that was suddenly much heavier. He was already expecting the hook to pull away, already anticipating the sudden, stomach-emptying slackening of line.

Frank had a pair of fingernail clippers from his pocket and was reaching for the line. "We got to get going, bud."

"Hold on, I can get it."

"We got to leave, I said."

"Will you just hold on?" Charlie swung the rod away from him.

There was a pause, a long ten seconds, but then Frank was stepping forward and reaching for the line again, no longer asking. Charlie moved away, keeping the rod tip high, reeling hard, the butt of the rod seated against his stomach. He heard the crunch of Frank's steps behind him and moved away again. The Ford was closer now, the sound of its motor and the whine of its transmission steadying. Then the engine shut off and a door slammed.

Charlie's fish was less than twenty yards away from the bank. He clamped his fingers around the line and raised the rod above his head, backing down the other side of the dam, away from the water, away from Frank.

"That's it, then," he heard Frank say. "Shit."

Charlie slipped on the gravel, falling hard on his elbow but keeping the rod high. He slipped again. The fish was still there, still heavy on the line. Charlie slid fifteen or twenty feet in a few long, cascading steps. He was almost at the bottom of the ravine before the smooth texture of the pulling changed into a rough flopping. He dropped the rod and sprinted back up to the water, glancing briefly at the truck at the end of the dam and the small man in the red woolen jacket walking toward his uncle. Frank stood with his back to Charlie, straight and still, hands in his pockets. The fish lay exhausted on the gravel. Hook-jawed and wide as an open book.

Charlie pried his fingers under the gills, biting at his line even as he stumbled back over the dam, back toward the truck. The line fell loose, and he ran without impediment, holding the struggling fish at his shoulder, its tail flapping against his thighs and its weight cramping his arm.

He threw the fish on the floorboard and sat over it, breathing hard. The fish's sides were mottled with the dark, burning colors of an ocean reef. Its head lay on the slope of the gearbox but its tail folded against the door panel. He picked at the blades of dead grass stuck to its sides and brushed at the leaves crumpled across one eye. Its gills convulsed and flashed, then stilled. It was so unlike the pale wild trout he'd caught before, those minnows with their oversized eyes and tiny, pinched mouths. This was something else, something he'd never imagined.

The fish had been motionless for a long time when Frank finally came back over the dam, his vest hanging loose and empty over one shoulder. The man in the woolen jacket walked beside him, and although his uncle was much the larger of the two, there was no doubt who was in charge. Charlie stared down at his fish.

The two men stood talking in low voices at the front bumper of the truck. Frank laid his hand on the hood and listened, nodding and walking a few steps away to light a cigarette and study the mountains. The other man put his hands in his pockets and looked at Frank's tires for a moment, thinking. Then he walked back to Charlie.

"What's your name?" he asked in a Canadian accent. He was a short man, skin-weathered and thin. He wore thick glasses low on a short nose. His eyes were gray and cold.

Charlie told him, and stuck his hand out through the window.

The man considered it for a moment before deciding to shake. "Bill Becker. Do you know where I got these fish, Charlie?"

"I was wondering."

"British Columbia. Do you know what it takes to bring these fish down from Canada?"

"I don't."

"Did *you* bring these fish down from Canada?"

"Guess I didn't."

"So what did you do to deserve these fish, Charlie?"

"Nothing."

Becker put his hand on the side-view mirror and leaned in, his face inches away. "Goddamned right. *Nothing*."

Charlie stared past him, up to the snow patches and the flat top of the dam. There were still so many fish in that lake.

"Are you going to come back up in here?"

Charlie shook his head.

"Do I have your word? As a man?"

"I guess you do."

"Well, then. That's okay then. Give me that fish and we'll call it good." He opened the truck door.

Charlie lifted his legs, leaving it to the man to reach down for his fish. It slid out onto the ground. Becker stepped back, surprised by its size.

"How can anybody own a fish?" Charlie asked suddenly, unaware until then that he was going to say anything at all.

As they pulled away, Charlie reached through his window to adjust the side-view mirror so he could watch Becker carry the fish toward the dam. He saw him stop and swing it back and forth to finally toss it, enormous and spinning, into the willows.

Frank drove with both hands tight on the wheel. "You know, seems like buying a bunch of ground like this, buying a bunch of ground and not putting cows on it, letting this pasture go to waste, seems like that's more of a crime than taking a few fish." He shifted gears. "What'd he want to talk to you about?"

"What?"

Frank breathed heavily through his nostrils.

"He asked me if I thought I owned these fish. He asked me if I thought these fish were mine."

"What'd you say?"

"I said no sir."

"Was there anything else?"

Charlie thought about it. "No."

"So why'd you run, boy?"

Charlie started to say something about his mother, about staying out of trouble, but Frank shook his head. His face was flat and hard. "Ah, horseshit. Don't give me that. Don't try to tell me that." He lit a cigarette and shook his head, and that was all.

They didn't talk again that day. Not through Choteau, not outside Great Falls, not even when they pulled into his driveway. Frank sat silent while Charlie took his gear from the bed of the truck, nodding when Charlie lifted his hand.

Then he pulled away. And although they went fishing again after that, there was a new absence of trust to everything they did, or a presence of distrust, and it was never the same.

He found his mother sitting alone at the kitchen table, still in her nightgown and down jacket, smaller than she had been that morning. Her hand was curled around a half-empty bottle of wine. The only wine glass on the table was filled with cigarette butts. She glanced up when Charlie walked in, then looked away.

The right side of her face was a bloom of red, from swollen eyebrow to lip. A thin trickle of blood had dried at the corner of her mouth. She had been crying, although she wasn't now. Charlie thought of Jerry's bowling-pin arms and felt sick. He swallowed. His throat worked against nausea, then worked again.

"How was your fishing?" his mother asked.

He sat down next to her, opening his hand on the table.

"I'm okay, Charlie." She tried to smile, but it was all she could do to stretch her lips tight against her teeth, to grimace.

"When did he do this?"

She shook her head and took a drink from the bottle. "Goddamnit. I fall in love like other people fold their clothes. Just one man after another. It's no damn good for anybody."

"Where is he?"

"Who knows, who cares." She took another drink, and Charlie knew that her day would end like it had begun, drinking at the kitchen table. "But hey, Charlie . . . ? Promise me you won't fall in love. Hey Charlie?"

He shook his head.

"Promise me." She was very serious now, moving the wine bottle to the side to lean forward.

"All right."

"That's good. That's a good boy. Thank you." She took another drink, and set the bottle down on the table, hard and off-center. She grabbed at it. "Do you want some wine?"

He started to stand up, but she caught him by the arm. She was strong when she wanted to be and her fingers dug into his skin.

"Sit down, Charlie," she said. "Just sit." She let go of his arm and put her head in her hands. "Just sit."

Lately, if his writing has been going well, if he has a certain distance from the world, he can walk home from his office and see everyone still. The flash of shame that leads—hammer against knee—to Frank's dark eyes, the clenched muscles in his cheeks as they pulled up to the house. His mother crying that night on the front steps.

At this late age, he finds himself wanting very little. He limps from a car accident three years ago, and his glasses fog even on warm spring days like this one. After the third cigarette, he's breathing hard enough to pause over the idea of his heart, his lungs. The burnt shell of his ribs. Five blocks, and regret spreads like oil across a pan. It's become true for Charlie, as it becomes true for everyone, that he could have done more. But he didn't. And regret floats out of the depths a hundred times a day and drops again.

His mother died ten years ago, still a young woman as these things go: tired and broke and alone. He had seen her for the last time in a gas station in Missoula where she'd been working the register. It was snowing outside, and he stood holding his wallet and a Pepsi. He told her that he was taking night classes at the University. She'd gotten another divorce, she said, and was leaving soon for a good secretarial job at the mine in Big Timber. He put on his gloves, standing there while she walked around the counter. She hugged him at the waist and stepped back, briefly cupping his cheek in her palm.

"Did our luck run out?" she asked. "I guess our luck might've run out, hey Charlie?"

He thinks about his mother, and Frank, and Jerry. And it occurs to him as an irony that the only advice that stayed with him, the only lingering wisdom from that day of common wisdom, came from Bill Becker.

"How can anybody own a fish?" Charlie had said.

Becker had looked at him sharply. But then he relaxed, smiled, and reached through the window to shake Charlie's hand again. He said that while it was true that he had bought these fish, paid for and delivered, it was also true that he didn't own them.

"But," he said clearly, enunciating, biting at the words until each syllable stood between them, blunt as boards: "But some things own you."

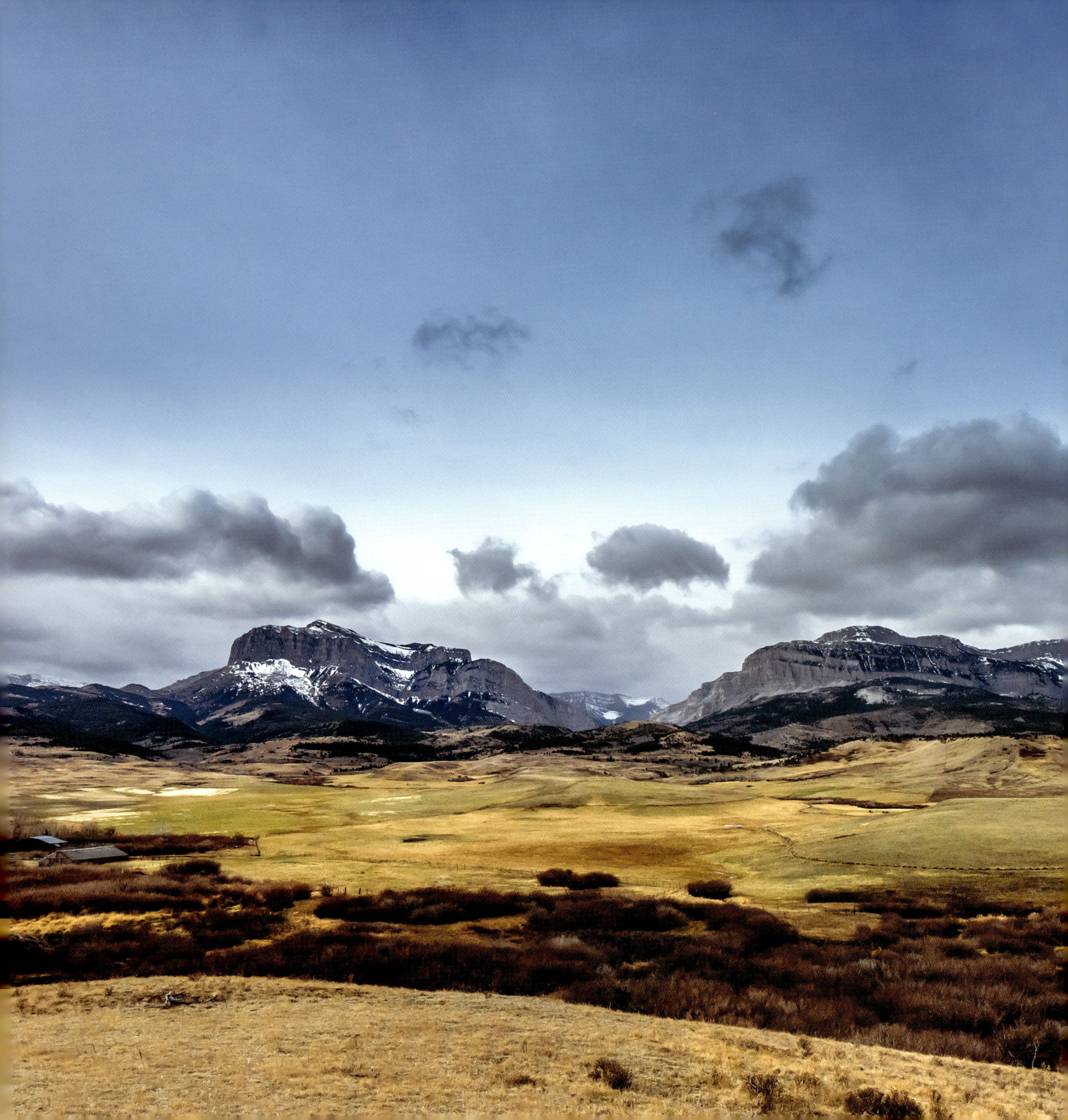

FINDING HOME

Gwen Florio

My journey to Montana started in a darkened Delaware living room and took forty-five years. I could have walked here faster.

It began when I was five, the summer my father spent several weeks in Meadow Lake, Saskatchewan, then one hundred miles from the nearest paved road, doing battle with ducks.

The ducks were deviling the farmers of Saskatchewan, descending in ravenous hordes upon fields of cut wheat and barley, where they stripped the shocks left to cure. "When they were done, there was nothing left in those fields but feathers," Dad said. The farmers' proposal? A duck massacre.

Dad was part of a team of US and Canadian wildlife biologists intent upon saving ducks from slaughter, so that come fall, the troublesome waterfowl could take to the continent's great flyways and head south toward … slaughter. The ducks were goners either way, but probably far fewer would be killed by US hunters.

The biologists' solution involved setting off explosives to scare away the ducks. Rainy days proved a problem until the biologists realized condoms worked perfectly to keep the charges dry, a discovery that spurred mass purchases at area drugstores. "Having a party?" was one deadpan response.

Back home from Meadow Lake, Dad announced a surprise, one that had to wait until dark. We knew what that meant. When he wasn't raising eyebrows on the streets of Moose Jaw or scaring the bejesus out of ducks, Dad—a talented photographer who grew up on a farm amid Connecticut's hardwood forests and found his calling in Delaware's tidal marshes—had prowled this thrillingly unfamiliar landscape with his camera.

Slide presentations were a regular part of our childhood, most of them featuring local wildlife and waterfowl. We were expected to know the names of every plant, animal, and bird in each photo. At the *whoosh-click* that accompanied the drop of a new slide from the carousel, my brother and I, and later my sister, vied to be first as we yelled out our answers.

Merganser! Bufflehead! Green-winged teal!

We were less certain as he tried to trip us up with a run of wildflowers.

Butter and eggs. Skunk cabbage. Shadbush.

But these new images startled me into silence. A tumbledown homesteader's cabin with golden cottonwoods arching over its silvery, splintered boards. Rows of grain stretching into infinity. And, over all of it, an unending sky of a blue I'd only seen on the rarest

October day. More than anything, I was struck by the boundless emptiness, unimaginable in a place like Delaware, which at the time packed about half a million people into roughly two thousand square miles. Dad explained that Saskatchewan had twice as many people in one hundred times the space. How was that possible? What would it be like to live in a place where you could shout as loud as you liked without disturbing anyone, or run as far as you could without ever reaching the horizon?

The images lodged insistently in my mind, along with the unfamiliar vocabulary that accompanied them. *Slough. Butte. Coulee.*

I pulled our atlas, half my height, onto the floor and opened it to Canada, savoring the region's evocative names. *Moose Jaw* was the town where the biologists bunked. *Makwa. Lac la Biche.* My gaze inevitably wandered south of the forty-ninth parallel and I leafed to the corresponding pages, picking up new names from the rare dots on the map. *Hungry Horse. Cut Bank. Marias Pass.* Using the mileage graph in the corner of the map, I calculated distances, double-checking the numbers and marveling at the impossible expanses between each town.

In addition to the images, Dad brought back tangible things. Moose antlers, shed in the winter and bleached by time, to hang over a barn door. And for my mother, a heavy moose-hide coat, extravagantly fringed and beaded with flowers of red, orange, blue, and green. He held it close to my face and urged me to inhale the scent of woodsmoke that clung to it, explaining that it was cured with brains and a smudge fire in the traditional Cree manner.

Cree?

My parents had bought us an encyclopedia, the tactile Google of its time, and I dove into it, acquiring more new words. *Assiniboine. Blackfeet. Métis.*

In Delaware, tribes were a matter of archaeology, like the skeleton preserved under glass at the museum in Dover. Supposedly a member of the Lenni Lenape, the remains had been wrenched from their resting place for the edification of white children. But in the West, I read, some tribes still lived on their ancestral lands, while others had been resettled elsewhere, all working against outsize odds to maintain the traditions linking them to their ancestors.

From maps and the encyclopedia I turned to books, the more adventurous the better, then deemed "boy books" and usually set in the West. Through them I traveled the Oregon Trail, splashed across the Rio Grande, and snowshoed traplines in Alaska, exploring a limitless world.

This would have been in the languid summers when I was too young for a job, and before parents relentlessly organized their kids' lives. I rode my horse early in the morning while it was still cool, cantering bareback along the solid ground skirting the marsh before squadrons of mosquitoes rose up on their daily mission to suck dry every warm-blooded creature in a ten-mile radius.

After I rubbed down the horse and turned him out, the rest of the day was for reading. I claimed the wooden swing on the screened back porch. Beyond the wire mesh, the air hummed and buzzed with voracious swarms, not just mosquitoes, but greenhead flies whose bite revealed the mosquitoes as mere amateurs, and also wasps, bumblebees and, every seventeen years, the hypnotic rise-and-fall drone of cicadas.

I tuned it all out and read of quieter places marked by the eerie bugling of an elk, a coyote's lonely song, a mountain lion's unearthly scream.

Call of the Wild. Tikta'liktak. Lone Cowboy.

I read these books at home, careful not to bring them to school or leave them lying around where my friends might see them. School taught me the language of Barbies and Nancy Drew, a necessary verbal shield. Lowering that shield brought severe consequences, as I learned one careless day when I announced a plan to convince my dad to save the brain of his annual deer, so I could use it to tan the hide the Indian way. The silence at the lunch table was absolute. (Wisely, he refused.)

Years of subterfuge, pretending even to myself that what I loved didn't matter. After all, how could you love a place you'd never seen, or things you'd never experienced?

With each year of school, the West receded a little farther. I grew up.

I spent twenty years shuttling between newspaper jobs in Baltimore and Philadelphia and South Jersey, only a couple of hours from the marshlands and forests I'd roamed in my childhood, my occasional weekend visits home doing nothing to relieve a constant itchy, constrained feeling, like clothing too tight at the neck and wrist.

So many things to blame, from bad marriage to worse divorce and a moribund career. In the midst of it all, a friend urged me to read "this book about fly-fishing"—a subject about which I knew little and cared less. "Read it for the writing," she said, and there she had me. Yearning to distill the same elixir I'd imbibed for years from books, I'd started writing fiction, furtive attempts that involved wastebaskets full of crumpled pages desecrated by tortured sentences. A break to read another book, even one about fishing, offered a welcome distraction. Was Norman Maclean responsible for fixing my gaze on Montana? Maybe. For sure, I wouldn't have been the first to have that response. But from *A River Runs through It*, I moved on to other Big Sky classics.

Winter Wheat. Fools Crow. This House of Sky.

This at a time when tall buildings cut my own view of sky into small gray squares. Concrete crowded out grass and regimented trees served as landscaping ornaments. Philadelphia's very air pushed back at me, heavy, wet, and choking, the city exhaling exhaust, rotting garbage, stale piss. I longed for the scent of sagebrush described so evocatively in all those books. Whatever the hell it smelled like, it had to be better than this.

My stack of Montana books mocked me with descriptions of places I'd never live, vivid with sentences I was incapable of writing. My computer screen sat blank but for wistful headings like, "Short Story Number Five." Or ten. Or twenty. Who was I kidding?

I rationalized a reality check, a trip to prove the foolishness of my fantasies and help me make peace with adulthood. I picked up the phone and called my brother, my partner in too-infrequent outdoor adventures. "Let's go camping in Montana," I told him.

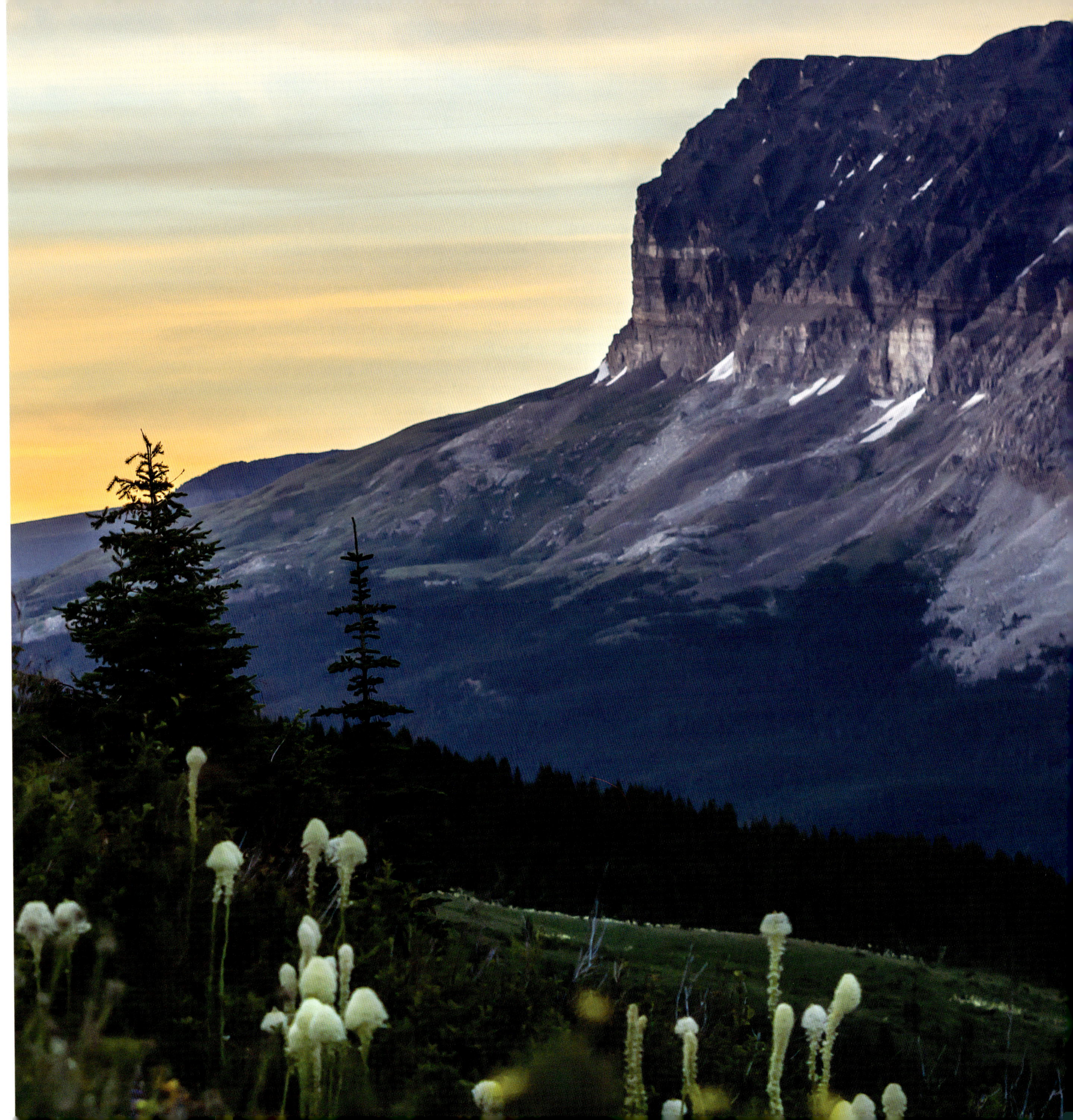

SILENCE ITSELF

Sterling HolyWhiteMountain

When I think about land, I think about the drive out of Browning toward Spring Hill, which I bet is the highest point on Highway 2 east of the Rockies. I'm going out with those luminous peaks at my back, and there is this beautiful moment—one might even call it transcendent, which it is, on the right afternoon—when I'm on top of the world, and the asphalt and barbed wire, the white crosses signifying highway death, the huddled dumb cattle, the stark radio towers, the distant country houses with their rough long driveways, and the approaching semitrucks and ranch rigs all evaporate. And what is left is the great blue sky, broken by the kind of clouds that haunted Maynard Dixon the whole of his life: sky and cloud above the vast, unfurling plains, brown-dry in fall and summer, briefly green in spring, white-patched or simply white in winter, surely as they were seen and felt by Blackfoot and other plains people for millennia. Each time I drive this stretch of highway, I wait in quiet hope for that moment. Sometimes I get lucky; usually I don't. Like all good and beautiful things there is no predicting it or calling it forth; the moment arrives and departs of its own accord. When it does come, though, I feel that freedom which has become, with the relentless increase of humanity and noise, more and more rare for people in this country. I get a spacious, lonely sense of the land, and I know this is how the earth always was, for all of us—until suddenly it wasn't. When I say *us*, I mean everyone: Indians, non-Indians, the ghosts between. I don't subscribe to the great romance of the vanishing—or returning—Native American, though. Romance is for Americans who don't know anything and for Indians who don't like facts. There is no going back to the buffalo days for the same reason there's no going back to that afternoon on Birch Creek many years ago, when my dad tried to teach me and my sister how to fish. Time and its ineluctable rush-trickle-rush. The one constant, through the arrival of the horse and the rifle, metal pots and knives and sewing needles; through smallpox and whooping cough and forced starvation; through Supreme Court decisions and treaties later broken and federal Indian policy and the travesty of forced allotment and tribal constitutions and the termination era and blood quantum laws and so-called self-determination; through loss of tradition and language and the extraordinary knowledge of the natural world it would take millennia to reattain—the one constant, for all parties involved, has been land.

Land ceded, land lost. Land acquired, land stolen. That vast territory of the northwestern plains once dominated by the old Blackfoot, where we hunted, held ceremony, made war and peace, and partook of the bounty of the earth as we saw fit, now fractionated, treatied, reserved for ourselves, acquired by others.

The water and the berries and the roots and the buffalo, those miraculous resources that sustained us since a time beyond memory, that we thought would never end. The earth's bounty. The great, half-told story of North America, the story that brings a hush to almost any dinner-table conversation, is the story of the land and its acquisition by the countries now known as Canada, Mexico, and the United States of America. Land. That resource both taken for granted and also just taken. Nothing is more valuable, more precious, or more essential. All things proceed from the land.

It is difficult for Americans to talk about Indian issues because of the implications. We can discuss the horrors of slavery and the possibility of reparations; we can discuss the plight of immigrants and the problem of refugees; and we can discuss the rights of LGBTQ people to marry and raise children. These extraordinary conversations fall under the rubric of justice and the possibility of better lives for more Americans. But what of Indian issues? What about the people who never wanted to be American citizens in the first place? The people whose land is the ground upon which Americans struggle for American justice?

Because unjust histories demand more than silence, we do try. We discuss state governments taking Indian children from Indian homes and adopting them out to white families in the 1950s, '60s, and '70s. But that brings us so close to assimilation and termination policy. Or we discuss the unprecedented and rapid death of indigenous languages around the globe, and consider the implications of such a loss both for tribal people and for humanity. But that brings us so close to the horrors of the boarding school system. And, if we are feeling brave, we talk about the recent conflicts in Montana over tribal water rights and the question of why tribal governments control water on their reservations. But that also brings us dangerously close to the heart of the matter, because then we must discuss the foundation of those tribal water compacts, the Winters Doctrine of 1908, a decision that established our understanding of the rights reserved by tribes during the treaty era. How deeply uncomfortable these moments can be, for liberals and conservatives alike, when suddenly the issue at hand is not merely a social matter but one that lays bare the origins of the country itself. These moments when casual or even fierce opinions are superseded by the most powerful agreements humans have ever put down in ink, those long, broad pieces of paper that act as the legal foundation of the country itself. How terrifying it must be, what kind of inchoate demons from the far past must arrive suddenly in the collective American dream, when we begin to discuss ownership of the land. Who can be where. Who can use what. Who shall call this place their own. The very ground under our feet.

America's struggle with race, ongoing since the country's inception, is related to this unease with origins. Notice how often we discuss racism but do not discuss the historical origins of racism itself, the ways European ideas of race were used to build the country. I believe we avoid this kind of historicity because it troubles the American sense of self too greatly. Because we cannot discuss race without discussing the half-conscious need for Americans to justify their dominion here. Because we must go back to eugenics, to Manifest Destiny, to phrenology, to European feudalism, to the idea of royal blood, to the encomienda system, the El Requerimiento, the Reconquista, and surely further still. And because we must discuss the long and terrible history of Christian conquest not just here but around the globe, that religion's deep, monotheistic fear of that which is not itself. These are all ways of saying the word *justify*.

So much intellectual and spiritual work must be done before the colonization of a people takes place, before the destruction of their food sources, before the theft of their children, before the suppression of their language and religion, before the acquisition of their land and resources. Before you feel OK with all of this. Americans often don't want to talk about Indian issues because then they must talk about themselves and the suppositions on which their identity is built, which necessarily means we must discuss those cultivated amber waves, those protected purple mountains, those domesticated and ever-fruitful plains. Regardless of the progress made and the beauty achieved—there has been much of both—we must discuss how we got to here. To quote Faulkner: "The past is never dead. It's not even past."

I have no sense of what Indians and Indian land mean to conservationists. I do know this: the idea of conservation is an American idea. It issued from the same well as all other American things both dark and beautiful, like Indian removal, so-called westward expansion, the transcontinental railroad, Indian massacres, lynchings, baseball/football/basketball, New York City, country, blues, jazz, the Civil Rights movement, Hollywood, termination policy, reality TV, the Twin Towers, etcetera, etcetera, and this incredible idea of freedom that runs through it all. I am not saying Native people had or have no sense of conservation, but this idea of sectioning off land for certain purposes—for preservation, for enjoyment, for wildlife, for beauty—this is not an Indian idea. And yet, because conservationists are some of the only people standing between the great, grinding machinery that threatens the beautiful places of the earth, and therefore all of us and our humanity, I must be in favor. I must participate willingly and fully, knowing full well that, if it came down to a question of returning even a small part of traditional indigenous lands, or the full restoration of sovereignty to tribes, it is unlikely we would remain allies. Political collaboration is easy to imagine when both parties exist wholly within a system and are bound together by a common goal. It is another story entirely when the two parties in question are negotiating for control of the land itself.

Growing up, I woke each morning and saw the mountains from the window in the bedroom I shared with my younger brother and sister. I have lived much of my life near those peaks, and even when I am not there I find myself in their shadow. There is a term in our language, āattṫŭppṗisskō', that refers to a place where one feels a kind of spirit or presence. There is no place I have ever been like the one we now call Glacier Park. There is certainly a presence there. It is something the old people talked about when they talked about the mountains. Beyond the grandeur and beauty, there is something else that draws people to those peaks and their singular, late-evening silhouettes. It is the same thing that drew us there for thousands of years to fast, to wait for visions, to find answers to questions, to mourn. The mountains are much more than a place where our traditional medicines grow, where serviceberries and chokecherries ripen in the late summer; many of our sacred places are there, too. We no longer have control of these sites because of that curious combination of American rapacity and conservationism, two sides of the same colonial coin, as is the case with many of our national parks. It is in the same way an angel might alight after a massacre—despite the massacre, I am nonetheless thankful for the angel. A protected space is better than no space.

The Blackfoot people lost the mountains because of mining interests; America got our mountains due to the establishment of the National Parks system. And so, each summer, visitors can feel the smallness of their lives in relief against the striking vistas and stunning lakes, taking home memories of what is for many a life-changing experience. As for us, we drive the highways cut into the valleys, sit in parking lots and laugh at each other, occasionally work at entrance stations, ride horses on the ridges of the high plains and view the mountains from a great distance. We know unequivocally they belong to us. We know the dealing was not fair. We know it is one thing to relinquish your heart on paper and another entirely to hold that place in your heart forever, passing that knowledge on to those who come after you like the most precious of possessions.

But there is more to land than what was taken and what was given under duress. There is also the land we still have. One of those places is Ghost Ridge, where the bodies of almost half a thousand Blackfeet were stacked during the winter of 1883, left there until the ground thawed enough in spring to bury them. The bodies of our starved dead, laid out in a cruel simulacrum of our traditional way of dealing with our departed relatives: wrapped in blankets, their faces forever to the sky. I have no clear memory of the first time someone pointed out that place to me. I simply remember being a boy on the passenger side of a truck's bench seat, with whichever relative was driving—an uncle, an auntie, an older cousin—telling me about it.

When we say nothing means more to Indians than land, that is not a complete picture. Land means everything to everyone, even if they don't know it. So it is better to say nothing means more to Indians than our relationship to the land, and the ways in which we gain, individually, generation after generation, that relationship. Moments like the one in which the meaning of Ghost Ridge was revealed to me show how that connection comes to be: not through reading academic articles stating land is essential to our individual and collective identities, not by watching well-intentioned but poorly executed documentaries directed by non-Indians, not even by personal ownership, but by hearing stories while on the land itself. These stories about the land, told by the people of the land—that is how things continue. And this is why the first job of colonial governments has always been to remove indigenous people from their traditional places. Make sure the land becomes memory and story. Keep it that way long enough and it becomes merely another factoid in the larger myth of settlement. An entry in an archived diary. A few lines on a weather-blasted sign at a pullout along an empty highway. A true relationship to the land requires cultural history, transferred knowledge, and personal and collective experience. All things that threaten colonial mythology.

Thus, one of land's meanings to Indian people is loss. The distance between what was and what is. Who we were and who we are. It is impossible to grasp that transition and the resulting gap without understanding the loss of our traditional territory. Such knowledge is one of the fundamental things that separates us from Americans and, in a real way, America. For citizens of the US, there is always the promise of somewhere else to go, a new job and salary, other things to own. For us, there is always something to look back toward, always the question of when and how what was taken will be reacquired. Anyone familiar with Indian Country knows this; the conversation is as common as coffee, breathing, love. There are some who have given up. But there are many who have not. There are many who know you cannot talk about this land without talking about our history. There are many who know what they want and are willing to live for it, knowing they will not see the fruition of that desire—but perhaps their children, their grandchildren, their great-grandchildren will. And there are many Indians who understand that our need for restoration—of land, of sacred sites, of sovereignty—stands in the way of the great American project. So, I must ask, what kind of dream is America, if this is what it takes to shape that dream into a reality? And how great can that dream be, if it cannot make room for us? One of the things land means to Indian people is desire.

These days, for work and for pleasure, to make connections with our northern kin and to do my small part in saving our language, I often drive north from our reservation into Canada, my destination one of the three Blackfoot reserves in Alberta. When I was younger, I liked going to Canada because it meant seeing new places and doing new things with my family and friends. Now when I drive north, I am supremely aware that no matter where I am, from Heart Butte on the south end of the Blackfeet Reservation, all the way north to the center of downtown Calgary, I am on Blackfoot land. Siksikḱaitsitṫŭpṗisksa"ḱo'. Anyone who has driven that long stretch of highway knows the spaciousness, the power, the silence at dusk that evokes longing and beauty in one's heart. I know as much as anyone what the colonial governments of North America tell us, and I value the power of our treaties. I know them for what they are: agreements that remain sacred, despite the failure of certain parties to hold up their end of the deal. But I also know that vast silence of the northern plains to be larger than all governments, all words on paper, all pain, all loss. I know it to be the same silence, evoked by the windswept land itself, the old Blackfoot heard and breathed and lived and loved and fought and died in. The same silence that received our voices in lamentation and prayer and celebration, that enveloped equally our newly arrived and our recently departed—and still does. It is the land, and the quiet upon the land, that underpins this great continuity.

The past cannot be retrieved—and maybe that is not what we want, not all old things are beautiful. But at the right moments, if we listen with the right kind of ears, see with the right kind of eyes, and are given the space to do so, we might gain a sense of something larger: a sense of the vast silence that belongs to no one but which we all need, out of which we all come and into which we all return. There is no way to quantify the value of this silence, so closely related to beauty that often we cannot tell them apart. And both are nowhere more available than the places where beauty has more to do with what we haven't done than what we have. We can protect that silence, Indians and non-Indians alike, we can work together to keep sanity in our lives, and we can do so without pretending we are truly together.

And perhaps for now that is enough.

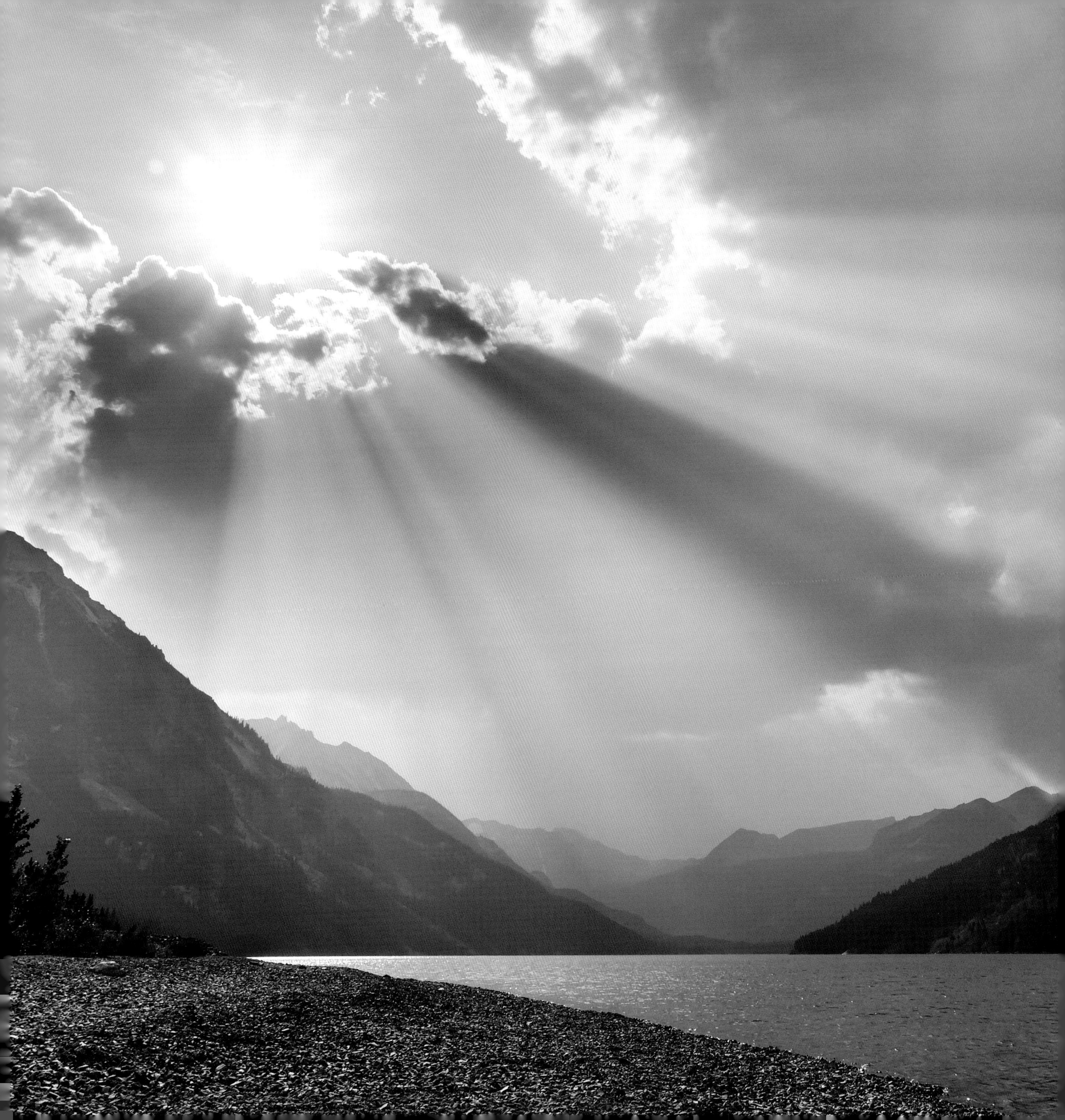

SURRENDER

Christine Carbo

"Catch any?" the bearded man asks.

"A few," I answer as I walk up the narrow, dusty trail from the river, heading for my tiny campsite at the top of the knoll. He and his friend have parked their truck near my white Subaru, its windshield and bumper plastered with the innards of a thousand dead bugs. I have just returned to Montana after driving my daughter Paige to LA for her first year of college at a private school where she has earned a hefty scholarship. The trip—a bona fide road trip—seemed like a good way for us to spend some quality time together before saying goodbye. We played the Red Hot Chili Peppers' *Road Trippin'* and sang *we got snacks and supplies* as we headed out. We camped near Bozeman the first night, near Zion the second, and drove into LA the following evening. We moved her into the dorms by late afternoon on Friday after picking up the things we'd ordered at Bed Bath & Beyond.

I said goodbye to her on Sunday morning, a teary-eyed but quick parting because she had a convocation at nine a.m. I was initially thankful a swift farewell had been forced upon us, thinking that would make it less painful, but the hurriedness seemed to make it sting even harder. My vision was blurred by tears as I rolled onto Interstate 405. I knew I should pull over, but instead just kept stubbornly wiping my eyes. I was glad to be on the road and let the sorrow of saying goodbye to my only child wash over me as the landscape flashed by. I had no idea how her departure would affect me in the long run. All I knew was that other emotions, not just about her leaving, cluttered the grief of her exit, like dirt mixed into flash-flood waters.

Paige made me promise I wouldn't camp solo on the return trip. I told her I wouldn't while I was on the road, and I didn't. I had taught her there were certain things that women didn't do alone without great care. I had walked that line like so many other mothers of daughters, trying to teach her to be fearless and strong and not beaten down by the damaging messages of society. "Don't be afraid to speak up in class," I told her when she was starting school. Now, years later, years that passed so quickly I feel as though I've only watched a brief photo-essay of her life with eighteen years spooled into a collage of memories, I've heard myself say, "Don't stare at your phone when you cross a dark parking lot to your car, Honey. Look up and observe your surroundings, especially now that you're in LA. And don't forget to put that mini pepper spray on your keychain."

Los Angeles. So different from Montana. Montana seems safer, where our biggest fears come from surprising a grizzly sow on a bend in the trail or getting buried in an avalanche while skiing the backcountry. Now that I'm home, I've decided to spend my remaining days off camping. When I crossed into Montana, just seeing green forests again loosened the grip of loneliness. I was in my home state, where mountains, cliffs, plains, lakes, and waterfalls provided a sense of comfort and regeneration. I also wanted to get outside because, in addition to my grief at Paige's departure, the slight but persistent feeling that I was also saying adios to my own youth had been sticking to me like cellophane. I had just turned fifty, and while others declared they didn't *feel* fifty, I felt every minute of it, and I wondered if that made me weak, not as strong as those who chirped, *I don't* feel *old. I still feel thirty-five!* Retirement from the Forest Service loomed around the corner, and it suddenly seemed as if my career, my child, and my routines were only stilts propping me up from a flood of insignificance. Driving through the barren, sun-scorched Southwest had done very little to ease the ominous sensation that the rest of my life, that my presence on earth, could be completely, utterly irrelevant.

My pup tent is pitched among the cool pines near the North Fork of the Flathead River, which winds its way down from Canada and borders the west side of Glacier National Park. I'm away from the view of any passing vehicles, and my cooler sits at the base of a large Ponderosa pine. My dad always used to say that the pines provide air-conditioning in the summer and natural warmth in the winter.

"Gonna have 'em for dinner?" the bearded one asks, coming a few steps closer. He looks mid-forties and wears faded, baggy jeans that hang low on his bony hips. The other one, maybe in his late thirties, seems quieter but is more filled out and has a healthier complexion. He's wearing Carhartts, a camouflage Jack Daniel's ballcap, a navy T-shirt, and I can see cords of muscle snaking down his arms.

"Catch and release," I say.

"Oh," says Beard, chuckling like I've said something funny. "You're a *rule* follower."

He turns and mumbles something to Ballcap. All I hear is, "... afford them waders ... afford to follow the rules, too." The way he says it, the way he strokes his stringy facial hair and cackles, makes me feel as though a row of dominoes is falling one by one.

For the first time in a long time, I question my decision to camp by myself. Working as a district wildlife biologist who's surveyed wildlife from lynx to pileated woodpeckers, I've come across many women who spend time alone in the woods, and nearly all of them have experienced head trips while spending the night in a tent, conjuring the most violent headlines they've read over the years: the middle-aged next-door neighbor raped, the young mother left for dead behind the mall, the teenage girl found in the trunk, the woman's body discarded on the side of the highway. Statistically speaking, the woods are safer than most homes, and even though I know I'm more than capable of taking care of myself, a pinprick of unease needles my spine when Beard chortles at something Ballcap says.

But I ignore it. I have a gun under my driver's seat and capsaicin spray in my fishing vest, and I've encountered all types of people: those who don't respect authority; those who take fish in release-only areas; those who kill elk, deer, and bear in the off-season; those who feed wild animals; those who make camping uncomfortable for everyone else around them; those who make catcalls at young women passing by ... and many more who don't do any of these things. I put it down to the other reasons I'm feeling vulnerable.

I turn away from the men and force myself to go about my business.

Twenty-four years ago, I went backpacking in Glacier National Park with my ex-husband, from whom I've been divorced for more than fifteen years. We made plans to leave our car on the west side of the Continental Divide and hitchhike to Many Glacier on the east side. We intended to hike past Swiftcurrent Lake, around the north end of Lake Josephine, and partway up Piegan Pass to camp in Cataract Creek Valley. I had insisted we get a backcountry permit, but my ex wasn't a rule-follower and brushed the idea aside. "Are you kidding? We live in a state with less than a million people. Just because we're in Glacier doesn't mean I want to spend the night in a campground with a bunch of assholes."

Our plans were derailed when he got delayed at work and, after hitchhiking from St. Mary's to Many Glacier, it was already six in the evening when we arrived. With the sun sinking behind the mountains, I figured there was no point in hitting the trail; we'd only make a few miles at best. "Best just to camp at the Swiftcurrent campground and start in the morning, don't you think?" I asked him. "Why carry heavy packs if we're practically going to do a through-hike anyway?"

He disagreed. At twenty-six, I was still doing what girls learned to do long ago: smile, be polite, avoid conflict. So I went along with it. We began our hike with the lowering sunlight smoldering across the ridges, lighting the mountaintops in an orange glow.

As we made our way through the darkening woods around Lake Josephine, clearings offered views of the daunting spires of the Divide; Angel Wing, Mount Gould, and the Garden Wall reared up and dominated the horizon. When we eventually reached the far end of the lake, twilight had clotted around us. Bushy, prickly foliage grabbed our legs, and the pungent smell of dying bear grass, thimbleberry bushes, and wet soil rose up from the cooling earth. As our eyes adjusted, we came upon a muddy seep—and there, in the mire, like admonitions for breaking the park rules, were large bear tracks with the points of long, sharp claws perfectly and forbiddingly cast in the dark mud.

I was furious. Here we were, without a campsite in an area with fresh signs of bear, all so we could get a two-mile start on a trek we should have begun hours earlier. I pictured a sow with major anger issues erupting from the thick alders at any moment, ready to sink her sharp teeth into our delicate, unprotected flesh.

I didn't complain.

We got out the flashlights and pressed on. Finally, we made it to a clearing by a small beach as darkness blanketed us. There was no designated campsite, only a small, open-sided log shelter, a place for the ferryboat passengers to keep out of the sun while waiting to be picked up. We set up our tent beside it, planning to break camp before the boat started its first graceful glide across Lake Josephine's silky waters.

All night I lay awake, brooding over the fact that we were camping without a permit, angry at myself for going along with whatever my new husband dictated, and fearful of the grizzly whose tracks we'd seen. And then the noises began—lots of them, louder than I'd ever heard before while camping. I know the nighttime woods are not always quiet places: breezes make the scrawny lodgepole pines creak as they rub against one another, crickets chirp, chipmunks scurry through the underbrush, fish rise and gently break the surface of the lake water. But this was different. Larger animals sounded like Mack trucks as they barreled through the tangled alders. Loud splashes echoed across the lake as if some two-armed creature were picking up hefty rocks and tossing them into the deepest part. The moon wasn't full, but it may as well have been, as the animals

suggestions about my attire. "When you gonna show those long legs of yours in a skirt?" he'd ask. He bugged me constantly to go for a drink after work, and when I said no, he brought up the fact that he was close friends with our superior, the forest supervisor, and that he *might* just have to tell him that I'm not a very "cooperative" coworker—"not really a team-player"—the next time they were out. Of course, he said this with a wink, as though he was just joking around. One day, worn down by his nagging, I politely gave in.

We met at a local bar after work. He was already there when I arrived and had obviously downed a few. When I got to the table, he stood up and hugged me. I courteously returned it, letting go quickly and catching a whiff of his acrid booze breath. His clothes smelled earthy and sour, like he'd sweated quite a bit during the day.

He had several vodka drinks to my one beer and insisted I order another. I explained that I was only staying for one and that I couldn't stay long because my husband was waiting for me so we could go to dinner. Ron ignored this and ordered another beer for me even though I was only halfway through the one in my hands. When I felt I'd stayed long enough to not feel rude about leaving, I told him I needed to be on my way. He mocked me, calling me a stick-in-the-mud, but finally relented. He insisted on walking me to my car. When we reached it, I thanked him for the conversation and told him I'd see him at work.

He spread his arms—a come-to-papa gesture—and leaned into me for a hug. I reciprocated stiffly, bending at the hips to give him a rigid, arms-only hug. As I started to pull away, he pulled me in tighter and smashed his lips onto mine. I jerked my head to the side and pushed him away, but not before I felt his tongue drag across my cheek, wet and slippery like a slug. He smiled at me, a drunk, lopsided smile, his face looking like it was only a rough, sloppy sketch drawn on for the evening. As I drove home I had to grip the steering wheel tightly to prevent my hands from shaking.

There was no sense in telling anyone at work, I thought. It wasn't as though I'd been raped, and it was my fault for saying yes to him and meeting him for drinks in the first place. And, of course, he was drunk, so he just wasn't thinking. Everyone loved him; he was fun, he was jolly, he was just old-school, having grown up on James Bond movies. No, I simply carried it around with me like an extra load—annoying, bothersome, but not the biggest of my burdens.

Until another coworker, a younger female wildlife surveyor with even less seniority than me, complained about him. She told me he came every night to the place where she tended bar to make some extra money, waiting until she got off work and walking her to her car. One time, he insisted on a hug, then groped her and shoved his tongue into her mouth.

As a state worker, I was legally bound to do something, if not by reporting what she'd told me then at least making sure she knew how to file her own complaint. In the process, I ended up reporting my experiences, too. My coworkers did not support me. They refused to join routine meetings that I attended or to participate in any projects I worked on. They wore black armbands to the meetings they couldn't avoid to miss, making a statement that that those who'd come forward—and there were at least four more after us—were only on a witch hunt. Many coworkers, including other women, wouldn't speak to me. The backlash shook me more than the actual incidents, more even than the feel of his wet tongue on my cheek—to learn that speaking openly about harassment would bring down an avalanche like those that crush the tamaracks trying so hard to survive on steep mountain slopes.

Now, even after all the focus on the #MeToo movement, I still feel slightly guilty about the whole thing. After all, I didn't face violence at Ron's hand. This wasn't the kind of story that warranted public notoriety and universal scorn. These were just muddled, everyday encounters, sadly commonplace and difficult to describe, but certainly warranting some form of condemnation.

The great thing about where I work, even though it is male-dominated, is that I can always go into nature, to rugged places where the façade of civilization is stripped away with an act as simple as getting your boots and socks wet when the temperature is dropping, a place where the shadow of vulnerability follows all of us, not just women.

In the North Fork, lying in a newer, lighter tent—a Double Rainbow Tarptent I bought recently—I can't sleep. I can hear the stream, relaxed and chatty like an old friend, but I can also hear the two men, their voices clear in the still night. They're talking by the campfire they made, another illegal move.

Any Montanan will tell you that August is fire season. And although we've been fortunate so far this year, the forests are bone dry: the soil hard and dusty, the surrounding underbrush like tissue paper, the broad leaves of thimbleberry bushes brown and curling like arthritic fingers, the bear grass pallid yellow, and the once-bright, reddish-orange Indian paintbrush bowing limply and faded like lipstick at the end of the evening. I picture a glowing spark from their fire rising, drifting innocently into the trees, and igniting a blaze in a bed of desiccated pine needles on the forest floor. I feel that same spark somewhere inside myself, but I'm not sure whether it wants to flare into a furious inferno or simply fade into a pinprick of dull heat. I want to unzip my tent, march over, and tell them to put out their fire, but I already said something they disregarded. When they were lighting the fire and I told them it wasn't allowed, Beard said, "Yeah, yeah, Smokey Bear, we know you like them rules, but we ain't gonna let it get out of control." Then he winked at me as if that made everything good. I told them then that I work for the Forest Service and that I'd appreciate it if they followed the rules. I knew I sounded like a cranky mother, like the dreaded crone.

"You working now?" The younger one had finally spoken, and I couldn't tell if he was challenging me or simply curious.

"As long as I'm in these woods, I'm working," I lied.

"Okay, okay," Beard said with an exasperated groan. "We'll put it out."

They made a lame show of stomping it out, but every time I glanced over, I could see smoke and rising flames. By the time I made it into my tent, I could hear the pop and crackle of a full-blown campfire.

The words "rule-follower" now stick to me like a fever. So what if I'm a conscientious person? I can't get comfortable in my sleeping bag. Zipped up, I feel caught and claustrophobic. Unzipped, I feel unprotected. Eventually, my muscles slacken and my body feels heavier as I focus on the snapping of their fire, the gentle sough of the wind in the trees, and the babbling of the river. I have almost drifted off when I hear the words, "You're kidding, right? Smokey Bear over there?" Mumble, mumble. ". . . kind of hot."

"She's older, man."

"Not that much."

Words too faint to hear, and then: "Uptight, too."

Anxiety rises inside me and my body goes tense as a steel spring.

The other guy laughs. "Shhh." Something, something. "… come after you with that can of bear spray."

"Sheee-it." I hear a spitting sound and imagine a string of brown tobacco juice splattering on a grayish-green or wine-colored river rock, the kind of rock formed by the great, clashing forces that created the Divide millions and millions of years ago.

"Prolly sound asleep." More mumbling. "… just the thing to unwind those tight wires."

The other guy laughs again, a high-pitched, silly giggle that still manages to sound menacing. Inside my flimsy tent, I know they are talking about me, but I can't tell if they're taunting me on purpose.

⟡

Eighteen years ago, exactly on Paige's due date, I went pheasant hunting with my ex-husband. After all, the doctor had said I was probably going to give birth a few days late. My husband insisted we go, and because I had a deep, irrational fear of being left behind, I asked my gynecologist if she thought it would be okay. She said, "Sure, just don't overdo it. Make sure you rest appropriately."

But, my ex-husband didn't *do* "rest," and I had not yet learned how to *do* the word "no." Hunting was another one of his passions. We'd wake up at 6 a.m., hit the coulees by sunrise and hunt until sundown, barely stopping to eat the food we'd brought. I didn't yet understand that his innocent obsessions were signs of an addictive personality. On that particular day, wearing men's hunting pants that could fit around my swollen belly, I'd already logged many miles with him, humping up and down over the rising and falling ridges of the Sage Creek Hutterite colony near the Sweet Grass Hills.

I liked the Hutterite colony. Despite its anachronistic ways, it seemed to belong among the golden fields and gently sloping hills, unlike the slowly dying town of Chester that was built for prosperity by the railroad but slowly buckling under the weight of neglect. I liked the Sweet Grass Hills, too. They weren't magnificent like the mountains I was used to, but they intrigued me—how they sprouted out of flat, endless fields the color of camel hair, creating their own defiant cluster in the middle of nowhere. I wanted to ditch the whole hunting effort and go find the ancient teepee rings I'd heard about, but there was no point in suggesting it. I knew the drill. We were hunting, and nothing would interfere with that.

As the sun set in soft, pinkish-orange hues, we walked up a large coulee that grew wider and wider, then forked. He insisted I take one side while he took the other. After all, it made no sense to hunt birds from the same side of the ravine, even though it was getting dark and I was very pregnant.

As we moved further apart, I could no longer see or hear him, and he didn't answer when I yelled his name. Cows grazing in the twilight mooed softly, and the wheat stubble crunched under my thick-soled boots. When the cramps came, I went down on one knee, breathing deeply like I was in a yoga class. I inhaled a mixture of the wheat field's fecund soil and the fusty smell of dried mud from the coulee's stagnant streambed and felt what seemed like strong fingers raking across my tight belly. Braxton Hicks contractions, I thought. But what if they weren't? What if it was time?

I thought of the ominous bear tracks we saw on our hike in Glacier Park years earlier. There were no grizzlies around these parts, but I did not want to have my baby on a Hutterite colony in eastern Montana, as much as I liked the place.

Thankfully, I did not have her out on the windswept prairie. I breathed until the cramps and the anger subsided, then turned and hiked back to the car in the fading light. I made it out at dark. He came out ten minutes behind me and we headed back to our little motel in Chester. Everything was fine. It was no one's fault but my own that I hadn't learned to say no yet.

In the morning, pale sunlight fans over the mountains but the sun is still behind the ridge. My tent sits in the cold shade, the brush around me wet with dew. The wind has picked up, twitching the sides of my tent, and it is quite cold for August. I pull my Smartwool socks higher up on my calves, slide on my trail-runners, and step outside the tent. The heady smell of damp pine hits me along with the smoldering campfire of my neighbors.

I look over at their campsite. Empty bottles lie strewn around their fire, which is still aglow with burning embers beneath the remains of charred logs. Swirls of smoke rise and scatter in the strengthening breeze. On a boulder sits a half-eaten bag of chips. I shake my head at the stupidity of leaving open food so close to the tents. I had lain awake until 3 a.m., worrying about what they'd said, tossing and turning and unable to find a comfortable position that didn't leave my back feeling exposed. My ears strained to track their movements every time one of them shuffled over to grab another beer from the cooler or take a piss at the edge of their campsite. I had hoped I'd hear one of them turn off the music they began playing around midnight, stumble down to the river, and return to drizzle water over the sizzling coals, but it never happened. Worse, I wondered if one or both of them would stumble over to my tent in the darkness—and, emboldened by alcohol, begin unzipping the flimsy structure's entry flap. Somehow, I eventually drifted off to the sound of jokes, more laughter, and a soundtrack of country rap and rock 'n' roll.

I walk up the path to use the outhouse and when I return, I check on my car. Everything is just as I left it when I locked up before going to sleep. Of course, everything is fine. Silly woman. But something inside me aches, and I'm not sure if it's the dull blade of anger or the pinch of loneliness. I fold my arms across my chest and face the ridge towering over me, bathing me in deep pools of frigid morning air.

I dig my keys out of my pack and hit the unlock button, sending an electronic chirp into the quiet morning. I grab a large, empty milk jug from the back and walk down to the river, where I dunk the jug into the icy water and fill it to the brim. Rainbow trout are rising, making tiny rings that fade as they expand. Resisting the urge to grab my rod, I carry the jug back up, march over to the fire, and begin dousing the embers.

"Hey," someone says behind me.

I turn to see Beard, his brow furrowed in confusion, anger, or disbelief. His hair is a ratty mess and he's got his hands on his fly, like he just stepped out to take a piss when he noticed me. "What are you doing?" he asks.

"Making sure these coals don't catch in this breeze." I lift my chin to indicate the stirring wind. "You should've put this out before you went to sleep."

"Want to get it going for coffee, anyway. This is our campsite."

"You're really not supposed to have a fire at all," I tell him. "Like I told you, fire danger is really high right now."

He laughs, that same cackle that makes me feel like something inside me has shifted in the wrong direction. He's standing about ten feet away from me, close enough to see that his teeth are stained, but far enough away that I don't feel threatened. Ballcap, no longer wearing one and his hair matted from sleep, pokes his head out of their tent.

I had intended to camp for two nights, but I realize now that I'm going to pack up and leave before the sun reaches the bottom of the canyon. Despite the fact that I am declaring or *reclaiming* myself out here, I am the one who will surrender. There's no point in staying and feeling uneasy around these two men. I will find a different place to camp or simply go home. Old lessons don't die easily.

"We're just going to get it started up again," he says matter-of-factly.

"You can do that after I leave. But like I said, the wind's picking up." I march over to my tent and start breaking it down. My jaw clenches as I yank each stake out of the ground. I can't think straight and feel like I'm on the verge of some kind of outburst, but I don't feel safe unleashing my rage. My mind feels like their fire pit: charred fragments of self-doubt and burning embers of anger at the human race. I am pissed off about being pissed off in a place that usually brings me peace.

By the time I get my car packed, they are working together to relight the fire. They've laid down new kindling over a crumpled piece of paper, and Beard is hunched over it, blowing steadily at the glowing embers. When he looks over his shoulder and glares at me as I finish loading my car, I want to lift my hand and flip him off.

I almost do. I really almost do. I actually find my hand in a tightly balled, white-knuckled fist right in front of my chest like some alien appendage that doesn't even belong to me.

I'm so close. All I have to do is lift that one finger. *But for what?* I think. *What will it gain me?*

Suddenly, the fact that I am contemplating the gesture instead of simply making it hits me like a lightning bolt. The absurdity of overthinking this pathetic act of defiance in a place where animals tear flesh and kill for food—in a country where each day, whether bitterly cold or soothingly warm, begins with its own glory and its own overpowering purpose—strikes me as funny. I begin to giggle at the insignificance of myself and these stupid men.

Beard stands up, and both men turn to face me. They stare at me oddly for a moment, then look down to inspect themselves as if they've forgotten to zip up their flies. I shake my head, laughing out loud at them, at myself—at my own restraint and conscientiousness before nature this grand. I picture the delicate rings in the water expanding and fading. *Just ripples*, I think.

"What?" the older one demands. They both look at me like I've gone crazy.

My fist unfolds and I put my fingers over my mouth to rein my giggles back in. I take a deep breath and look at the Livingston Range again. After all, it's a gorgeous view. I take it in. I point up, where the sun spreads across the peaks, painting them in a wash of gold. Both men turn to look. I hop in my car while they're hopefully surrendering to it and drive away.

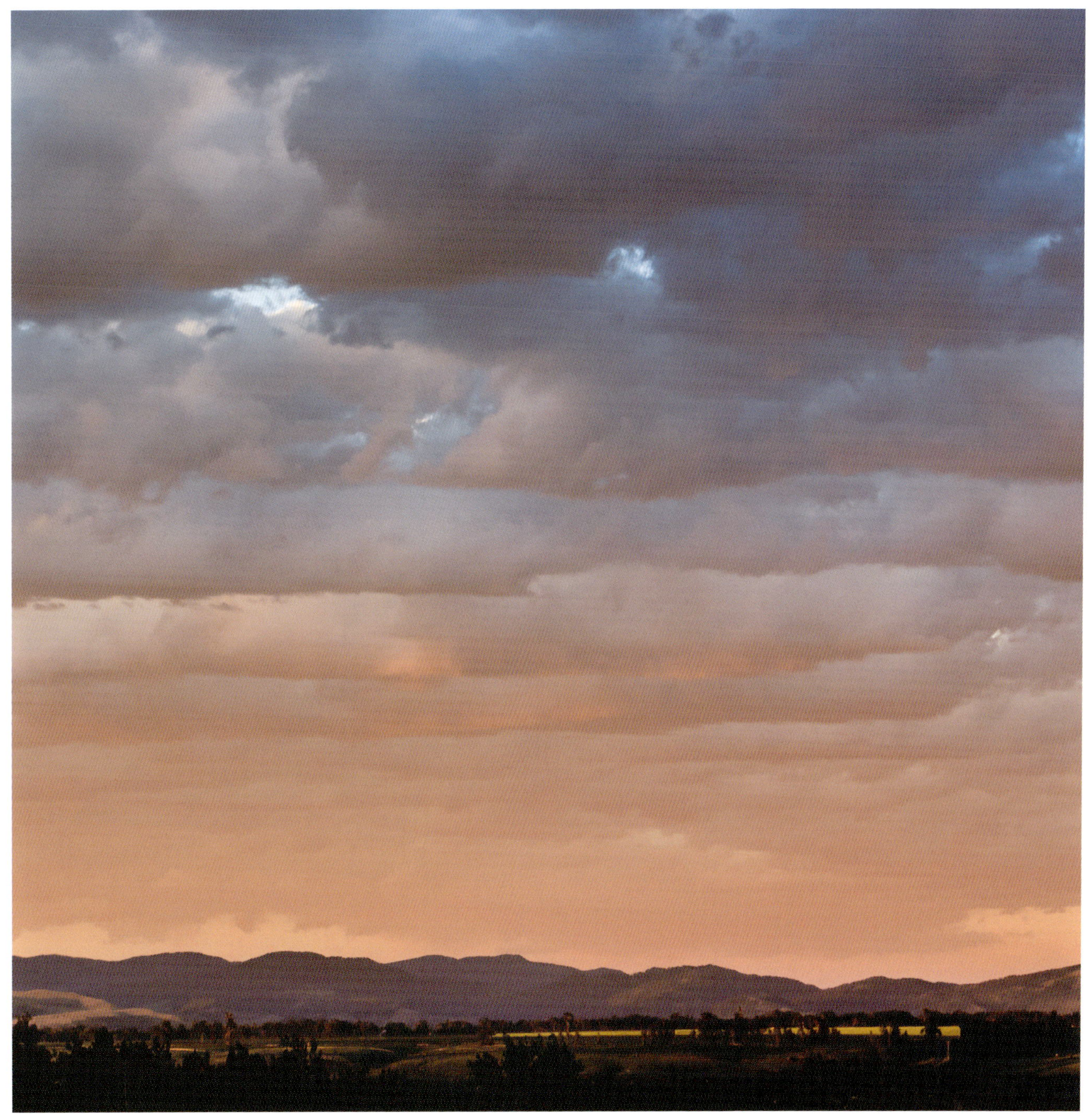

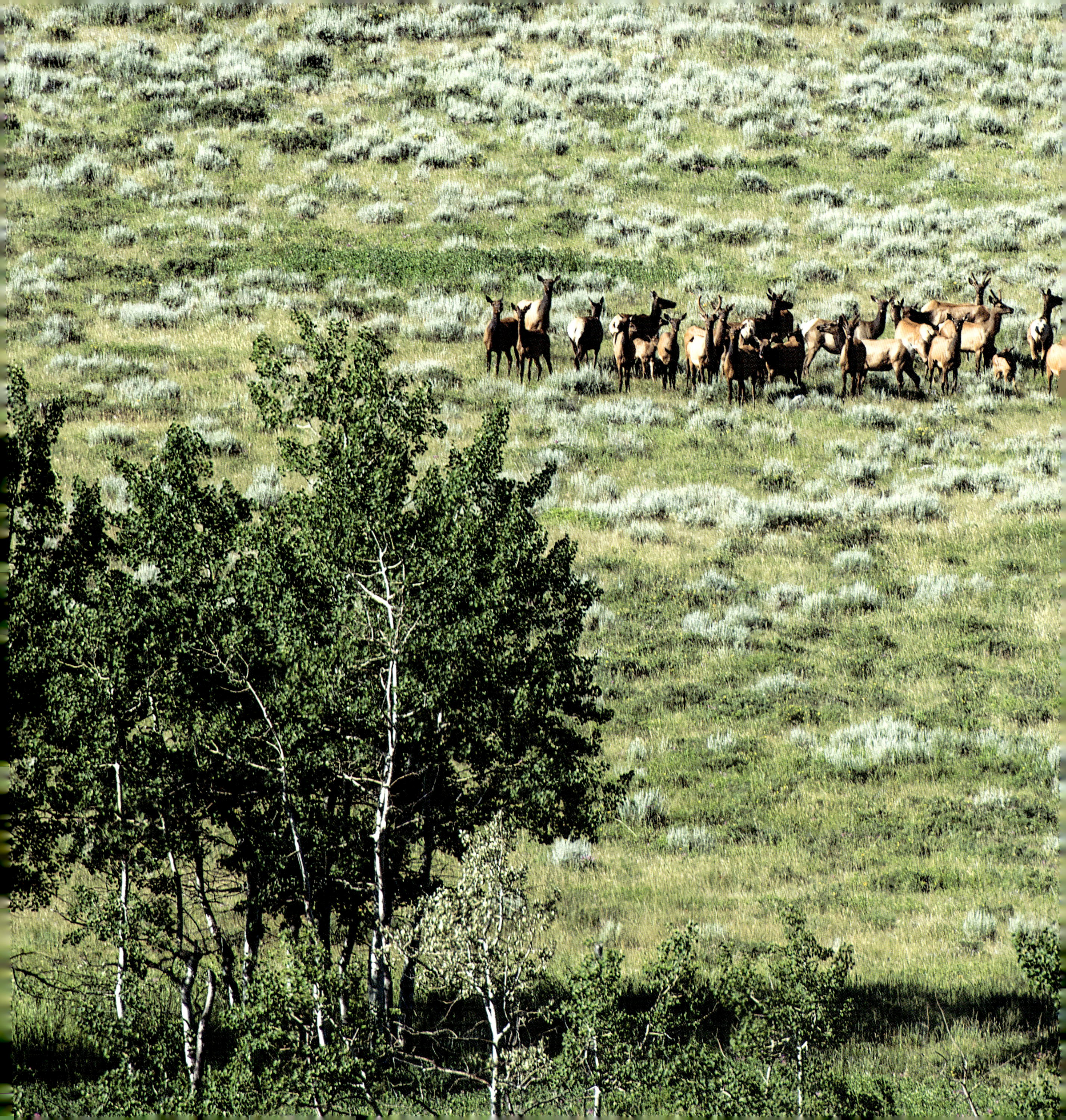

THE BEAST IN ME

Maxim Loskutoff

In the summer of 2012, the same year scientists fully decoded the genome of the bonobo, the last great ape, my partner and I were stalked by a female grizzly bear. We first saw her high above us in a field of huckleberry bushes as we hiked along Grinnell Lake on the east side of Glacier National Park, only a mile from where we, along with a large wedding party from Wisconsin, had disembarked from the ferry across Lake Josephine.

The sky above us was clear blue, in striking contrast to the emerald, silt-colored water below. It was the perfect distance to see a grizzly: close enough to make out the rolling power of her gait and the light gold fur on her back, and far enough away for us to feel safe. She stopped and raised her head. It seemed she was looking back into my eyes—a strange moment of communion—though I knew her eyesight was so poor she could barely see the berries around her feet. Instead, she was tracking our scent on the breeze. We watched her for several minutes, remarking on her beauty, then continued up the trail into a stand of stunted, high-altitude pine, the trunks just tall enough to obscure our vision. When we emerged, the bear had traversed and descended along our path and was now only a hundred yards away. A football field. A quick sprint. (Grizzles are as fast as racehorses, a fact I couldn't connect to the great furry mound above us.) Several things happened in my mind at once: I realized the bear was following us, I realized she wanted to eat us, and I realized that I was an animal.

It was a strange epiphany, especially after a lifetime spent mostly in Montana. To be human today is to deny our animal nature, though it's always there, as the earth remains round beneath our feet even when it feels flat. I had always been an animal, and would always be one, but it wasn't until I was prey, my own fur standing on end and certain base-level decisions being made in milliseconds (in a part of my mind that often takes ten minutes to choose toothpaste in the grocery store), that the meat-and-bone reality settled over me. I was smaller and slower than the bear. My claws were no match for hers. And almost every part of me was edible.

My partner looked at me. I looked at her. The appropriate responses to a grizzly attack, ones I'd been taught since I was a boy, clamored in my mind: stand your ground, use bear spray, play dead, *never run*. We turned and sprinted back into the trees the way we'd come.

In the pounding of our footsteps, below the wild panic, I remember a distinct thrill of pleasure. Not in a suicidal sense (I was desperate to reach the safety in numbers of the Wisconsinites, and certainly didn't want to feel

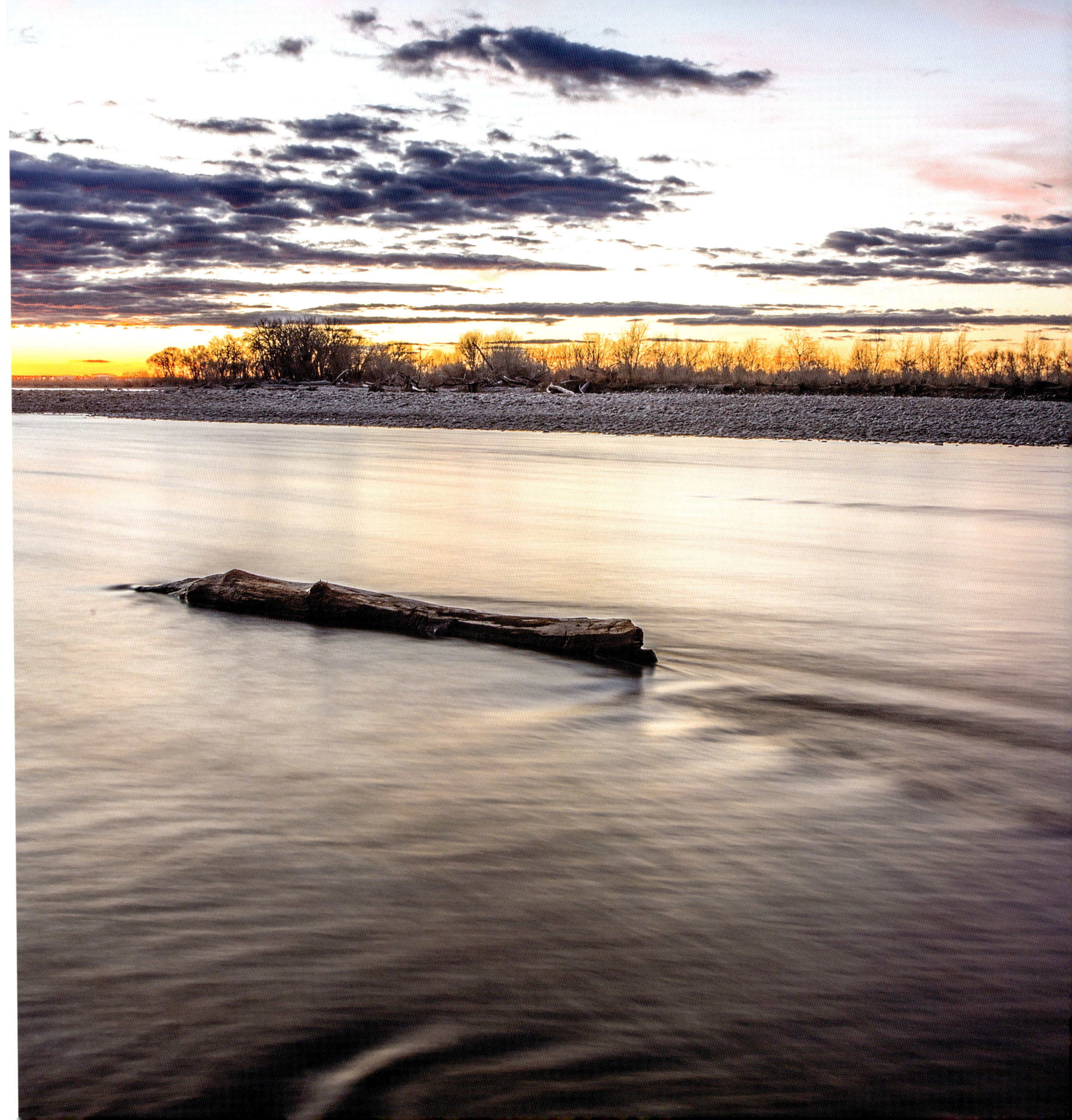

FOURTEEN WAYS OF LOOKING AT THE CLARK FORK

Caroline Patterson

I do not know which to prefer,
The beauty of inflections
Or the beauty of innuendoes,
The blackbird whistling
Or just after.

–Wallace Stevens,
"Thirteen Ways of Looking at a Blackbird"

I

As it flows five hundred miles west from Montana's Silver Bow Creek to Idaho's Lake Pend Oreille, the Clark Fork is many rivers. Called at various times *In mis sou let ka*, the *Spet-lum*, the Southern Branch of the Flathead, and the Missoula River, the Clark Fork is ponderous as it divides the naked hills around Warm Springs. Furious as it squeezes through the Alberton Gorge. Swift and mysterious as it cuts between high banks at Superior. But the part of the river I know best is the watery vein that flows through Missoula. Broad, slow, and brown in spring, green in late summer, the Clark Fork is a river I have always thought of as civic.

II

It is May, and I am walking the south bank of the Clark Fork. As I follow the trail past the old Milwaukee Station to McCormick Park, I look across the river at downtown—at the gray, mysterious Wilma Building, a catacomb of apartments and theaters where Marian Anderson once sang and Houdini escaped from a locked trunk; at the brick bank buildings and hotels and the ramshackle houses that comprised Missoula's first red-light district. I have looked at this downtown for thirty-nine years and the sight still fills me with longing for new dresses at the Mercantile, for lunches at the linen-covered tables of the Florence Hotel, for the childhood those names conjure.

III

Imagine him, a young father at the crack of a new century, in search of a new home where the water is clear and the air is clean, where his frail, five-year-old son will thrive. The train churns west across hot prairies and over the Continental Divide into Butte where, he reports, "the smoke nuisance is no worse than ordinary Chicago smoke, but it is bare and unsightly."

He continues on to Missoula, situated in a wide valley surrounded by mountains and divided by rivers drunk with snowmelt. As he steps off the train that giddy day in May, he knows he has found the place.

"My dear sweet wife. My darling Cad," my great-grandfather, John Edward Patterson, wrote to his wife on May 6, 1900, "Missoula is the place you can expect to settle .... Missoula is a beautiful town. The business portion is very well built, several nice 4-story brick buildings with elevators, steam heat, etc., and the residences are pretty.... There are plenty of lovely drives along the river for us and Johnnie and waa [the child my great-grandmother was carrying]."

IV

If rivers tell stories—and who's to say they don't?—the Clark Fork would gather around a campfire with the other tributaries of the Columbia and tell a tale something like this: nearly seventy million years ago, there was a lake stretching from Drummond to Dillon until the first Rocky Mountains rose up to divide its waters into streams and lakes and rivers.

What came next and many years later, the Clark Fork would say in a hushed voice, was ice. Thick masses of ice inched down the broad Purcell Valley of British Columbia to dam my waters, which swelled and became Lake Missoula. Back then, if men were around, they could have swum from Trapper's Peak to Mount Jumbo in waters deep as the Andaman Sea.

Then the dam broke. And in the five days it took to empty the lake, my drainage carried more water than all the rivers of the world combined, continues the Clark Fork. Imagine the screaming wall of water churning west at nearly sixty miles an hour, scrubbing canyon walls bare in the Clark Fork and Flathead rivers, sculpting Rainbow Lake out of solid bedrock and clawing out stream beds in southeastern Washington. The lake filled and drained at least thirty-six times, each time engraving my story in the earth and necklacing Mount Jumbo with a new shoreline.

V

As a child, I turned my back on the river. So did my father and his father and his father before him. In 1904, my great-grandfather built our prairie-style brown house with its back to the river and its face to the street, the opposite of how people build homes today. This difference has everything to do with what people deem precious: in a sparsely populated town newly scratched into the dirt, my great-grandfather chose to look at other humans. Perhaps it was habit—he had just left the crowded streets of Chicago—or an instinctive huddling for warmth against the wilderness. Perhaps he needed assurance, right out his window, that he wasn't alone.

Nevertheless, when he wrote to his son about his prospective home, he sold the Clark Fork River as its principal attraction. "My dear boy," he wrote on June 28, 1900. "Right near where you are going to live when you come is a nice river. Won't we have fun fishing, though? And we can throw stones in the water, and when we get tired doing that we will hitch up the horse and take a buggy ride."

VI

"A river is a road that moves," wrote philosopher Blaise Pascal. And up this river—that the Salish crossed to dig bitterroots, and the Pend d'Oreille plied with birchbark canoes and fished with hemp nets strung bank to bank—came the curious, the disaffected, the rebellious, and the desperate. It was a highway of wonder, an interstate of grief.

There was Meriwether Lewis. On July 3, 1806, Lewis attempted to cross the river at a "rapid and difficult part of it crouded (sic) with several small Islands and willow bars which were now overflown." His raft sank and he had to swim to shore—soaking his chronometer, he noted with irritation. In 1809, David Thompson, the man the Salish called Koo-Koo-Sint, or Man Who Looks at Stars, established the "Saleesh House" trading post above present-day Thompson Falls and mapped the area from the "brown knowl" of Mount Jumbo.

Settlers arrived in the 1850s and chasing after the settlers came the railroad, snaking alongside the Clark Fork in canyons so narrow the locals joked that dogs had to wag their tails up and down. Huge camps of railroad workers—with thousands of Chinese and many fewer white men—crawled east and west until they met at Gold Creek in 1883.

There were also fugitives. The Lees escaped from Utah after Grandpa Lee was executed for leading the September 1857 massacre of non-Mormon immigrants. Settling on Trout Creek, a tributary of the Clark Fork west of Missoula, they were a tough bunch. The grandmother had been partially scalped, the women carried six-shooters, and one of the family members was a preacher who married and buried them and shot them if they got out of line.

My great-grandfather was the most unlikely pioneer of them all. A sturdy, industrious Scotsman who wore round-rimmed glasses and wool suits, he set up a law practice in the old Florence Hotel and was neither particularly unhappy nor particularly bold. "I am delighted with Missoula," he wrote in his formal script on May 11, 1900. "Even if it seems as if all the nice pleasant sociable fellows I meet go to cockfights, etc."

VII

The possibilities of the place infected my great-grandfather with an uncharacteristic zeal. "My darling wife and boy," he wrote on June 4, 1900. "There are great opportunities here for raising fruit, principally apples.... A person for $1500 can put out an orchard that in six years will begin to pay from $2000 a year. To tell you what apples and pears will do here, you'd think I was daffy."

His exuberance builds as he concludes the letter. "I'll make enough money here in a few years so both of you and Grandma and Kate and Abby will have more than they no [sic] how to spend. This is the place for the whole crowd to come and *cut out* all worrying."

VIII

My great-grandfather planned to build on five acres west of Missoula in a subdivision now called Orchard Homes. "It is beautiful there and will make us just the home we want right close to town," he wrote to his wife. "I wasn't going to tell you, but as you are going to come soon anyway, I thought it best to tell you now. I never was as much in love with anything except you and my boy as I am with that five acres." My great-grandmother would have none of it. A city girl, she did not want to move to the frontier to live on the outskirts of a fledgling town. She did not want to be a farmer, rancher, or even a gardener. She liked neighbors, grocery markets, and being able to walk to church, thank you very much. So instead, my great-grandfather bought land in town. After he won a lawsuit against the

Northern Pacific Railroad in 1903, he built our two-story Foursquare house with an ample porch and a fireplace on an inside wall, rather than the more expensive outside wall, because my great-grandmother wouldn't spend a night in a house with a mortgage.

IX

Eight years after my great-grandfather arrived in Missoula, it rained for thirty-three days and thirty-three nights and the town held its breath as the Clark Fork rose to the twelve-foot mark on the post of the old mill. Wagon bridges washed out, the Milltown Dam nearly overflowed, and the Northern Pacific railroad tracks flooded, stranding the Missoula baseball team in Helena. The Higgins Street Bridge collapsed on June 6, 1908, and businessmen who, like my great-grandfather, walked across the river to their offices that morning were unable to return home. To deliver the Sunday *Missoulian* on June 7, carriers shot an arrow attached to a rope from one side of the bridge to the other, then hauled papers across the river.

I'm sure the flood's religious symbolism was not lost on my grandfather, for whom it seemed the water's fury wanted to carry his new home away and wash the land clean of anything man-made. "Everything imaginable almost came down the Missoula river yesterday," began a *Missoulian* story wittily subtitled, "Houses that Pass in the Day," "including many houses, three railroad stations, and one section house."

When the sun finally came out on June 8, its heat was dizzying—especially for one reporter. In "Flood Waters Fall Fast and Old Sol Reigns Again," the writer proclaimed: "Yesterday was the first of the long series of days that will see the spirit of Missoula arise and correct the wrong done by the might of the waters. Western pluck has brought Missoula through the time of storm and stress. Western energy will restore her to conditions that will be so much better than those of a week ago that, a year hence, people will rise up to call the high water of 1908 blessed."

X

As a child, when I stood in the alley behind our house and looked down the bluff at the ditch bordering the river, this is what I saw: dirt-clouded bottles, tin cans, old stoves, car seats punctuated with rusty springs like errant corkscrews, and an old refrigerator. Across the river was an ice house where, for a quarter, the proprietor would allow a truckload of garbage to be dumped into the river. Further east was another garbage dump. The university and the local hospital discharged untreated sewage into the river.

The river disgusted me. The water was gray and oily and occasionally ran red as blood. The fish we caught were sickly and sluggish. Once, to my mother's horror, I actually swam in the river and afterward developed a terrible itch. The river was something we turned away from, something we dumped our waste in, something we hated.

The Salish, who dug bitterroots and battled the Blackfeet on its banks, called it the River of Awe.

XI

They came to Butte in the mid-1800s, men scratching and burrowing into the Silver Bow Creek Valley for gold, silver, and copper. They came first by tens, then by hundreds, then by thousands, drawn west like bees to pollen. After honeycombing the ground with their tunnels, they opened up the earth and swallowed whole towns with their hunger and when they were done, they washed their sins away with the waters of nearby rivers.

But the sins did not vanish. The men mostly disappeared but their waste lived on and seeped into the earth, into the hidden waters of the aquifer. Silver Bow Creek, where the Salish had fished for bull trout, was declared officially dead. The next 110 miles of the Clark Fork, where cutthroat, brown, and rainbow trout once thrived, were scoured by heavy metals which gathered at the Milltown Dam like sand in the bottom of a giant sink. And those metals lay submerged until February 1996, when the rising waters of the Clark Fork tipped over the dam and headed west, those ghosts of excess—the arsenic, copper, zinc, and cadmium inheritance of our fathers—killing thousands of fish in their wake.

Now the men move on to the Cabinet Mountains, and to the headwaters of the Blackfoot River, where they want to build more mines, dig holes in the earth larger than ever before, swallowing trees and meadows and whole mountainsides, and when they are done they will slake their thirst with river water, and the rivers know the metals will come rushing down again. And again.

XII

When I was a child, I was told I could play in the yard or the neighborhood, and even walk downtown, but I was never, ever to play by the river. This wasn't just because of the danger of drowning. The Milwaukee Railroad ran alongside the river, bringing with it a world apart from my protected existence. A world of loud metal booms and smoke as the trains carried lumber and coal and silk from west to east. A world of hoboes, those men who slipped around the edges of things and scrawled mysterious symbols (cat's paws, some called them) so the others knew to show up at my great-grandmother's door for a loaf of bread or one of my great-grandfather's old overcoats. I still like to picture these wilder versions of him riding the rails out of town.

The railroad was a world of heat and dust and desire for what lay beyond the green hills surrounding our valley. At night as I lay in my high, white bed in my brown, square house, I listened to the shift and crash of the freight trains as the railroad shunted the cars. When they were coupling cars, I imagined the explosions of metal on metal were gunfights and that, at any moment, I could look out my window and see a man blowing the smoke from his pistol as another man writhed on the ground. This, I thought, was what happened when you met the outside world: someone got killed.

The tracks have long since been pulled up, the railroad station has been converted to a national hunting club, and old-fashioned lights now line paths crowded by joggers and dogs with lolling tongues and windmilling tails. While these paths have opened up the riverfront for me, I almost yearn for that old sense of danger and foreboding. We have tamed our urban riverbanks into a land of bark-covered paths, but we have lost that sense of mystery, of life on the periphery, the hoboes drifting here and there, the trains whinnying their way out of town. The morning I found several empty bottles of Olde English malt liquor near a blackened fire circle in Hellgate Canyon, I was oddly comforted.

XIII

I walk along the river in fall, winter, spring, and summer. It is where I go to watch the clouds roll into our valley, it is where I go to watch them roll out. A friend once compared this walk to the Lincoln Memorial in Washington, DC—this is where we go to touch the heart of the town.

It is high spring. The sun is bright, the air is soft, and all is a riot of color and sound and smell. The river is brown and muscular and fast, and as it crawls up the banks and spills out of the ditches, it even sounds dangerous. It floods the island in the middle of the river where, I once heard, society matrons proposed putting a whorehouse so they could keep track of who rowed out to it. "There is a whole island in the river," my great-grandfather wrote to his son in May 1900, "by the bridge within 200 feet of my office and the deer was on the island eating grass. A lot of men and boys tried to catch and lasso it and nearly did, but it got away from them by swimming down the river."

From the tangle of budding mountain alder and willow comes the high staccato of chickadees, the braying of blackbirds, the liquid arpeggios of robins. Pink blossoms flock the stray apple tree in front of the *Missoulian* and I wonder who planted it and why they left. There is the sweet smell of wet earth and of cottonwoods with their leaves curled in sticky syrup.

As I walk, I feel inextricably linked to this place that filled my great-grandfather with such uncharacteristic longing and excitement that he had to reassure himself and his worried wife he was constant in his affections: "If I could only go to sleep with you (and Johnnie) in my arms and sooth [sic] little waa to sleep how happy we would both be. Don't think for a moment I don't miss you just because I am in a new place with new scenes, they don't take your place for a minute."

But of course they did take her place for a minute—and why wouldn't they? Here he was, in a place that was nothing but possibility, with earth, river, mountain, and sky all clay he could mold in the shape of his dreams. Isn't that what happened to all of our grandfathers? At first, before the Indians were deciminated and forcibly moved from their lands to reservations and the rivers were ruined and the air darkened with smoke, wasn't the West all about their dreams of what could be? And was this sense of possibility destroyed in the end because it was simply too beautiful to exist?

An osprey flies straight down the river, dipping down and down, threading water and sky. As I stand on the bank four generations later, with a baby of my own, I wonder if my great-grandfather would sorrow for what his generation did to the river and if he would still bring an ailing child to a country where the water is laden with heavy metals. I wonder what happened to the innocent and high hopes he brought to this raw country where he settled forever: "My dear sweet wife, I am so anxious to make a nice home for you so we can all live together and have all we want and not have to worry." Great-grandfather, I want to say as I stand on the brink of life with a new child, this river—with its beauty and its danger—is the mystery between us.

XIV

Just as my great-grandfather once did, I walk across the Higgins Street Bridge each day to my office. On a bitter December morning, I stop in the middle and stand at the railing to study the river. The metal-colored water is clotted with rafts of white ice that mirror the clouds in the gray sky. The ice moves swiftly, purposely, as do the pedestrians crossing the bridge: it is ten degrees and everyone moves quickly in the cold.

More than two decades on, my children are grown—another generation reared. In that time, the Milltown Dam has been removed, in 2008, releasing a century's worth of heavy metals and toxins into the Clark Fork, killing numerous fish downstream as they flowed to the ocean. After a $120 million cleanup, the river that was once the nation's largest Superfund site is now civic in a whole new way. Each summer, the river blooms with a "tube hatch" of floaters in black, white and yellow inner tubes, rubber rafts, even inflatable swans. On hot summer weekends, the craft are so dense you can barely see water between the floaters. There are kayakers, paddleboarders, boogie boarders, and river surfers, not to mention the fly fishermen lining the banks casting for expanding populations of brown and rainbow trout. Each summer, I float the river with my daughter, a lively young woman, and my son, an athletic, intelligent young man. I do it to cool off, to laugh as I rush through sets of ripples, and to celebrate the fact that this river is now clean enough to swim in. To celebrate the fact that the water is now clear and moves freely, much like the river my great-grandfather described to his son, where they could throw stones in the water and the family could "*cut out* all worrying."

As the crowds jog up and down footpaths lining both riverbanks, pushing strollers and walking dogs, or speed by on bicycles and clattering skateboards, or huff and puff through yet another 5K or 10K, I long for a river less discovered. But it is there. If I travel east or west, where the banks are steeper, the sloughs and side channels more tangled, and farther away from the sounds of cars and people, I can still feel the quiet ways, the ancient stories, and the wildness of this wide, green river muscling its way west.

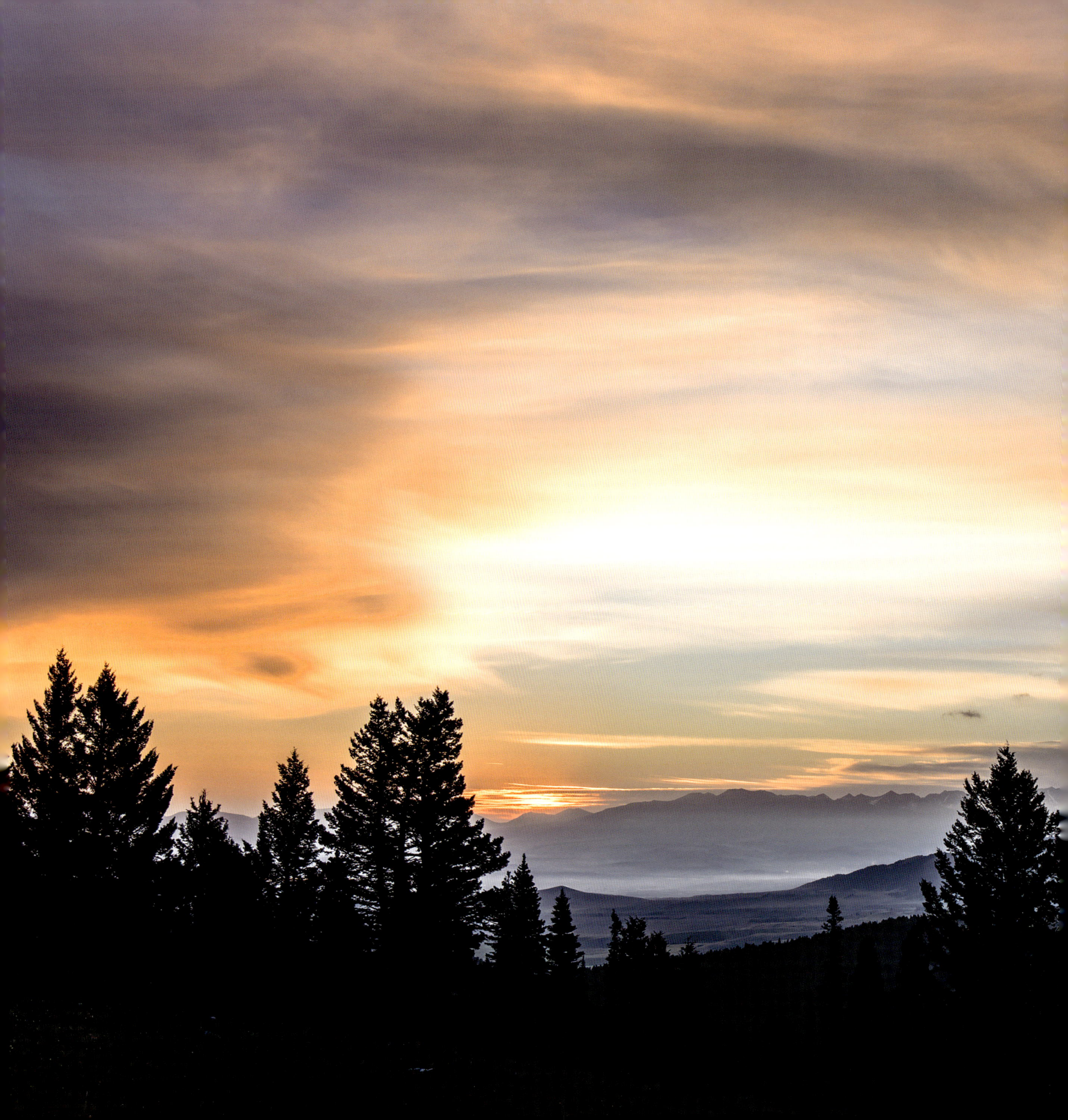

THE ARK OF THE YAAK

Rick Bass

The lowest part of Montana, the Yaak Valley, is also the newest, the last place to be released from the clutches of the Ice Age. This most northwestern valley is a garden of sorts, with more diversity and—once upon a time—bounty than anywhere else in the state. The Yaak is so young in the world that sometimes it seems like only the second or third day in the garden. The older I get, the less it surprises me when I see an old story playing itself out yet again, in roughly the same fashion, as if the taut spin and centrifugal force of the world dictates that the raw material of all stories—stone, sky, fire, river—be lathed again and again into a retelling of all first stories, with only a few minor modifications in each new iteration.

The Yaak River empties into the Kootenai, the largest tributary to the Columbia, near Troy at an elevation of only 1,888 feet. Almost everyone who's visited the Yaak country bordering Idaho and British Columbia—roughly a million acres, ninety-seven percent of it national forest—uses the word *magical*, an abstraction that's as immeasurable as it is overused to describe too much else in the world. Still, it's the word people use, whether they've lived there since birth or have only just arrived. I've spent a fair bit of time wondering why that word comes up: How do we define a thing that depends on being undefinable, unknown, immeasurable?

Perhaps what we call *magic* in the Yaak is not magic, but instead a remnant of the way the world once was—a world we then might not have thought of as magic but normal, as expected as the rising and setting of the sun. Not taken for granted or underappreciated, but still, no more magical than the ebb and flow of the tides or the sound of sandhill cranes grating south in the fall and croaking back north in the spring. No more magical than snowmelt filling rivers, or bull elk whipping saplings on grassy ridges and in lodgepole shadowlands.

What I mean to suggest is everything is still in the Yaak. That which was once familiar to us—with everything present and nothing extinct—is how the Yaak still is. It's one of the only places in the world where this condition of fullness still exists. It was once normal to us but now is rare: What else can we do but call it *magic?*

Grizzly bears, wolves, wolverines, lynx, great gray owls—there seems no end to the Yaak bestiary. It's a place where every living thing struggles to pin down that million acres, as Doug Peacock puts it, with the weight of their four paws. As if the Yaak is a map that would otherwise blow away.

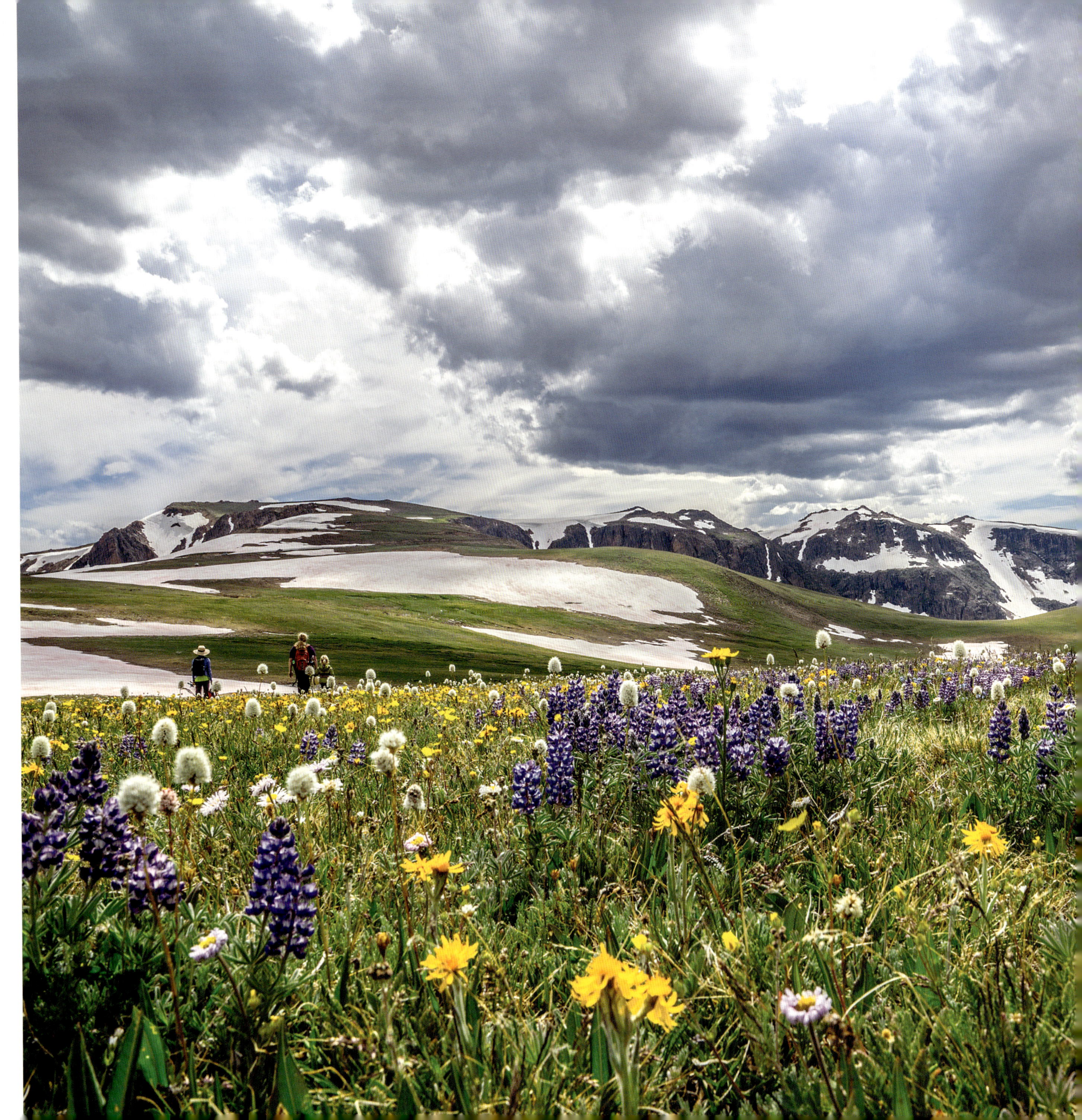

WATER LEVELS

Keir Graff

Todd was halfway between the motel office and the car when he realized they hadn't given him the key. If you could call a dirty snack bar that dispensed towels and cans of beer to pool guests an *office*.

Turning around, he went back through the door, squeezing past an avocado-shaped, sunburned man whose intricate homemade tattoo disappeared into his faded cotton board shorts. The clerk behind the counter seemed preoccupied by his broken-spined, water-swollen paperback, forcing Todd to rap on the counter. Below the glass, a museum-worthy collection of off-brand candy lay petrified in dusty wrappers.

The clerk looked up. "Need something?"

"You forgot the key," said Todd mildly.

The clerk smiled, dragging a horny thumbnail through one muttonchop sideburn. "No, I didn't."

"Well, I don't have it, and you didn't give it to me," replied Todd, regretting his reasonable tone and thinking he should have led with I Don't Have Time for This. Grace would have. Service workers who raised their eyebrows at her often found themselves staring down the barrel of I Want to Speak with Your Supervisor.

"There's no key, is what I'm saying," said the clerk, clearly anxious to return to his novel.

"What kind of rental cabin doesn't come with a key?" asked Todd, now too befuddled to play either mild or hot. "How do we get in?"

This the clerk found funny enough to close his paperback, which had the unlikely title *Black Cherry Blues*, marking his place with a book of matches. He unfolded his beanstalk limbs and moved closer as if to impart a confidence.

"Don't worry, you'll get in and get out just fine," he said.

Unable to make sense of this and unwilling to carry the interrogation further, Todd returned to the car and directed Grace, who was behind the wheel, to their cabin using a poorly photocopied and obviously reused map. He thought it best to omit the absence of a key until he could assess the situation in person. Also, he didn't want Grace to storm into the office while he was present.

In the back seat, their daughters Morgan and Marissa, ages fifteen and thirteen, gazed impassively out the windows, Bluetooth noise-canceling headphones streaming god knows what to their ears.

The cabin, three hundred yards back down the dusty road, was called Bearpaw. As the girls lugged the bags up to the warped plywood porch with all the enthusiasm of rock-haulers in a Soviet gulag, Todd and Grace stared at the doorknob. It was a cheap, interior doorknob of the kind Todd had purchased at Home Depot for the girls' rooms at home. No deadbolt, no slot for a key.

"We'll just see about this," announced Grace, climbing behind the wheel of their rented Nissan Pathfinder just as Morgan pulled the last bag out of the back. The hatch door slowly closed as the vehicle rooster-tailed back up to the office.

The girls, their headphones still canceling all external noise, seemed unaware of the imbroglio yet remained careful to thump the bags hard on each step.

Todd turned the handle and went inside the cabin. He inventoried the collegiate furniture, the naked light bulbs, and the uncurtained, unscreened windows (which were anyway painted shut). The kitchenette they'd been anticipating—hadn't the website promised one?—consisted of a microwave, a Mr. Coffee, and a dorm fridge, meaning their cooler of store-bought game meat would remain uncooked.

In the bathroom, a scrawled message was taped to the speckled vanity mirror over a yellowing sink: *Please DO NOT drink water. It is not potable.*

Curious, he turned the tap handles and examined the warm but anemic trickle. Other than the slight sulfurous odor that seemed to permeate the whole area around the hot springs, there was no obvious anomaly—but who knew what heavy metals or brain-eating microbes swarmed within?

The girls were standing side by side in the underlit main room, disdaining the couch. Caryatids of resentment. They hadn't spoken more than a hundred words between them since the cell service had gone out as the rental descended into the Grasshopper Valley.

Todd could see that a few efforts had been made to dress up the cabin: there was a bear mount displaying the promised paws, and on the plank floor tracks had been painted to piquant effect, as though a cartoon bear had stumbled through a painter's tray and ambled its way around the lodging. Which, to the right guest, could seem as ominous as it was charming.

Gravel spanged off the wheel wells as Grace slid to a stop in front of the cabin. The interior, thought Todd, should certainly take her mind off the lack of security.

For the past several years, Todd Harrow had been preoccupied with two fears: that his life was not worth living, and that the world would soon end. He was not a candidate for suicide, however: his desire to see his daughters grow up and to find out how each season would end for the Chicago Cubs were generally reasons enough to continue driving the Eisenhower Expressway from Downers Grove to the Loop, where he worked as a financial adviser recommending products for a global investment firm.

The job was fine, the money was fine, but he had become increasingly preoccupied by the meaninglessness of the tasks that filled his days and in some sense had become his real work. By his reckoning, he had spent more time troubleshooting the family's electronics, safeguarding the family's substantial computer network against hackers and viruses, and dealing with the decade-long fallout of a particularly bad case of identity theft than he had, say, pulling boozy pranks on friends. Taking spontaneous road trips with no destination in mind. Making love to Grace, who had lately stiffened at every affectionate touch as though she feared the back of his hand brushing her arm meant he was going to lobby for sex later that night. Which it usually did.

The end of the world seemed, too, to be regularly brought forward on the schedule. Given scientists' dire prognostications of the effects of climate change, usually buried on page fifteen of the *Chicago Tribune* so the front page could be devoted to more urgent concerns such as the latest congressional hearing, it seemed likely that by the time the girls were considering careers and families of their own, the planet was going to be engulfed in deadly weather, beset by food and water shortages, and presided over authoritarian strongmen who continued to shift attention from the real peril by continuing to create imaginary crises.

In such a scenario, the quick annihilation of nuclear war almost seemed preferable.

What troubled Todd even more was his realization that, increasingly, his irritation at the thousand small indignities of modern life—summed up by the young man he'd recently seen having a shouted FaceTime conversation while scattering pedestrians on the sidewalk with an electric scooter—had begun to seem more and more equivalent to the end of the world. Awash in a sea of irritations, overtired and overstimulated, everything felt equally important.

And yet the more he tried to do something different, the more he found himself imprisoned by his unvarying routine: his inability to turn in early and rise refreshed, his habitual third cocktail while he watched Netflix shows he couldn't remember the next day, his venting about work even though Grace hated it.

Todd had been well aware of the Montana Office of Tourism's assault on Chicago because it was impossible to avert his gaze from the nature porn flashing itself on buses, billboards, and buildings. There had even been fiberglass sculptures of large, horned and antlered animals installed on top of subway stations with hooves poised over the heads of Chicagoans forced to commute in the urine-soaked subways. He had thought idly of what it would be like to stand in that scenery but it was Grace who had announced the family was going on vacation.

"Can you believe this shit?" she huffed as she stomped back into the cabin. "When I asked him what happens if our stuff gets stolen, he said, 'Oh, we've never had a problem with that!'"

To her credit, Grace recovered more quickly than the rest of her family. Despite her own disappointment with the dire circumstances—and overruling a voice vote from the girls to "leave now and, like, find a real hotel?"—she stood firm. There were no other hotels within fifty miles. There was no Internet connection with which to book one. And, she reasoned, wasn't the whole point of this vacation to get away?

Never mind the fact that she was the one who'd decided they needed to get away. Once Grace determined a course of action, she proceeded to its execution with Germanic resolve.

Todd sided with the girls but knew better than to undermine Grace in front of them. Getting her to retreat from this mistaken vacation would take tact and timing. "If we can't lock the door, what should we do with our stuff?" demanded Morgan.

"The clerk suggested we lock it in the car," said Grace curtly.

Todd contemplated the two canvas bags full of electronics they'd lugged from Chicago: laptops, tablets, game system, headphones, white-noise machines (in case they couldn't sleep in the silence), plus the full complement of cables, chargers, backup batteries, and portable hard drives. Somehow, years ago and without his consent—and based on a sexist assumption?—he had been assigned IT responsibilities for the family.

"Maybe we can just leave it here," he suggested. "After all, they've never had a problem with that."

Grace's sudden conversion had much to do with the fact that she had picked the resort—and it was a resort in the same way a yard sale was a shopping center—and that she had, in the face of their indifference, planned the entire vacation. *The Pioneer Mountains!* she'd chirped, as though the image of covered wagons might set fire to their imaginations.

That night, after eating steaks in the restaurant while the steaks they'd brought slowly spoiled in their lukewarm cooler, they went to the pool. Morgan and Marissa, who had spent an inordinate amount of time putting on swimsuits, flip-flops, and cover-ups, did an immediate about-face upon seeing the facilities and began walking back down the dusty road to Bearpaw.

"Girls!" scolded Grace, taking off after them in what would be an ultimately unsuccessful intervention.

Todd opened the gate and entered the pool area. In the larger of the two reservoirs, several families with an indeterminate number of chubby children floated like apples in water that smelled of rotten eggs and was filmed with dead insects and other organic matter. The battle among the children to acquire and pilot a single inflatable shark was earnest and predatory. All the adults and some of the children seemed to be drinking beer.

He climbed down into the smaller pool, where steam was already rising into the chilly Montana evening. The water level in both pools was extremely low, and as he entered the scalding water Todd had a fleeting memory of being given a bath as a tiny boy, only a few inches of water in the bathtub so he wouldn't drown.

A man whose bear-like pelt climbed his back and stopped at his head before cascading down his chest was crouched under the water spout. The effect reminded Todd of water grass in a steady current.

Todd crouched until his entire body was covered with the simmering water and watched as a curly chest hair—he hoped—floated by.

Grace stalked down the steps and into the pool, her shower sandals slapping the slick concrete steps. She looked good in her sensible one-piece J. Crew suit, and Todd wished their bedroom in the cabin had a door.

She splashed down next to him, fuming, then glared at him when he accidentally brushed her arm.

"What's wrong with the girls?" she asked. "When they were little, they ate dirt in the yard."

"They're teenagers, give them twenty years," he offered lamely, flashing forward as he said it to bread lines, power shortages, freak storms.

"You'd think we brought them out here to die," continued Grace without acknowledging him.

"Maybe we should go back to Missoula tomorrow," he said. "Or at least find some place with a nicer pool. It's their vacation, too."

She looked at him like a general calculating which member of her staff had plotted to betray her. "You do realize we came here for you."

⟡

The next day, after a restaurant breakfast during which the girls' hostility was assuaged by feeding Cheerios to a squirrel who frequented the dining room and was known by name to the waitress, they went hiking.

"Sawtooth Lake," said Grace, consulting her itinerary. "It sounds picturesque."

Behind her, the girls exchanged a look that spoke multitudes despite their utter lack of expression. Todd knew himself for a Judas because, when Morgan caught his eye, his own expression was equally blank and complicit.

Their phones' GPS was useless and they couldn't find the trailhead. After several wrong turns, they were rescued by a local who, driving toward them, stopped and flagged them down.

"You look lost," said the white-haired, aggressively maternal driver before giving them directions, rolling up her window, and motoring on.

"Good people here," said Grace as Todd wondered how anyone in a car could "look lost."

The trail began as a series of switchbacks through Christmas-tree-sized conifers that seemed to be growing back after a somewhat recent forest fire. Todd had pictured majestic pines but this part of the forest seemed jumbled and unattractive. The most interesting part was pondering whether a tangle of delicately balanced weather-bleached logs would suddenly give way, crushing them all less than a mile into their outdoors experience.

"This sucks," said Marissa.

"So this pack is heavy?" said Morgan, preamble to a complaint Todd tuned out, imagining that he was now the one wearing noise-canceling headphones.

Eventually they moved out of the burn area and into a boulder-tumbled canyon green with bushes and shaded by taller trees, with a creek—an actual babbling brook—running alongside the trail. The cloudy and raw July day soon turned just plain cold and all four of them shivered in their thin sweatshirts. Marissa had worn shorts and her legs were red and goose-bumped.

Todd listened to his own ragged breathing and felt the chill air chafing his knuckles as he wondered why Grace refused to elaborate on her comment last night in the pool. She had seemed tired, as though the warm water was leaching out the stiffness of her resolve.

Tiny white beads of what looked like Styrofoam pellets began dropping from the sky at random intervals.

This at least prompted the girls to take out their phones and record videos of themselves *hiking* in the *snow* in *July*—which, of course, they would be unable to post, send, or share until they returned to *civilization*. Todd and Grace used the opportunity to put some distance between themselves and their daughters.

The snow had stopped by the time they finally reached the lake—small and moderately picturesque beneath the promised jagged ridge—but the cold had intensified. They found the foundation of a cabin and hunkered against the logs while they ate the buffalo jerky, string cheese, trail mix, and crackers they'd bought in Missoula. Todd thought it was impossible to tell whether the cabin was an abandoned ruin or simply unfinished.

Grace had read in a guidebook at the restaurant that the remains of a crashed plane could be seen in the water at the end of the lake. The girls had no interest in finding it, and even Grace conceded the weather was against them.

"I'm going," said Todd, surprising everyone, including himself.

Was it because he wanted a break from his family or because he wanted a story to tell at work, back in Chicago? Or was it because of some dim notion he needed to find what Grace had brought him to Montana to discover?

He caught her eye and she seemed about to speak. For a moment he thought she was going to say, "Well, I'll come, too." But before he could decide whether he really wanted her to join him—he thought he did—she pursed her lips and gave a short nod, as if his impulsive solo was one more thing she'd planned and could then cross off her list.

While Grace and the girls headed back down the trail to wait in the car, he worked his way around the lake, not entirely certain he was on the right trail but reasoning as long as he could see water he couldn't get lost. At the far end, rivulets of water and a stream coursed down from the snowfield above, irrigating a spongy, lush green meadow. After crossing the stream on a rocking log, he zigzagged through the grass, completely soaking one New Balance sneaker and muddying the other.

Finally, he stood at the base of a rocky cliff, peering at the water and looking for the wreckage. The bright cloudy sky and the flat gray water made it impossible to see below the surface, so he climbed higher, scraping his numb hands on the rocks. Thirty yards up, the water remained opaque.

The windswept, rocky gray bowl surrounding the lake wasn't worthy of a bus or subway ad, but it was peaceful. If he weren't freezing his goddamn nuts off, thought Todd, he might sit down on a flat rock for a while. Take the time to imagine what it would be like to die in a place like that, your plane dropping out of the clouds, the cliff wall suddenly filling the windshield, the startling realization you would never again have another thought before you were dead.

Climbing down, he slipped, caught himself, and nearly tore off a fingernail in the process. He had the finger in his mouth and tasted hot blood when he saw the twisted metal of the plane on the shoreline, not far from where he stood. Maybe it was underwater in spring, he reasoned, and the lake's levels fell as summer progressed.

The aircraft looked smaller than he had expected, the sheathing of the fuselage impossibly thin, hardly the protection needed to fly through over mountains, through the sky. Any bones or personal effects had long ago been carried away by searchers or wildlife. Just the plane's skeleton remained, the rusty green aluminum ripped and peeled like a beer can torn in half for an ashtray.

Finding the plane didn't bring him a sense of accomplishment. It wasn't even that much of a story, and now he had to hike back with wet feet and raw fingers.

Even in death, thought Todd, we're usually disappointing.

That night, he got drunk with the ursine man in the hot pool. His name was Bob Radtke and he spent so much time with his head under the spout that Todd suspected it was the cause of his baldness. Perhaps the impotable water was also a depilatory. Radtke was a high-school history teacher from Dillon, the nearest town of any size, and said he came to the resort—he used the word unironically—for one week every year.

"Got to get away from civilization, you know?" he said, taking it for granted that Todd would consider Dillon civilized. "Hike during the day, soak at night, look at the stars. Fucking *breathe*. What's your story?"

Todd considered telling Radtke the truth: that they were an average family from Greater Chicagoland who had arrived here only after a miscalculation that had more to do with the efficacy of an advertising campaign than any urge to visit Montana in particular. That he suspected his wife thought a week in the great outdoors would assuage the existential angst that had made him impossible to live with and would one day—most likely before the end of the world—ruin their marriage. That he was beginning to wonder whether she was right.

Instead he said, "I have two families, one in Chicago and one here in Montana. I spend all my time trying to keep them from learning about one another. It helps that I'm in sales. I know I should feel guilty about living a lie, but I just don't."

Radtke stared at Todd as if he were uncertain whether his leg was being pulled, then whistled low. "And that's your *Montana* wife I saw last night?"

Todd nodded.

"I can see why you wouldn't want to give that up," said Radtke. "Damn."

The way he said *Damn* made Todd feel so grateful he almost cried.

"Here, have a Cold Smoke, Chicago," said Radtke, handing him a lukewarm beer in a large maroon can. "Tell me about your family back home."

The next day, dehydrated from drinking five beers over two hours in a hundred-and-two-degree pool—and favoring the leg whose shin he'd barked on the steps climbing out—he followed Grace, Morgan, and Marissa up the trail to a ghost town called Coolidge.

Grace had promised them all the hike was only one mile each way. Just to be safe, this time they dressed for a proper hike, only to encounter locals wearing sandals as if it was nothing at all. In contrast to the previous day, the sun was shining and in the thin mountain air it was hot enough they all wished they'd worn short sleeves.

Coolidge was a relatively modern ghost town, having had its rise and fall during a silver boom in the 1920s. Unlike the squat, chinked log cabins Todd expected, instead they found gray frame houses flattened and splayed as though a catastrophic wind had blown them down from above.

The intense sun made it hard to believe they were even in the same state as the previous day's freezing hike. The better weather improved the girls' spirits and they shook off some of their sullenness, walking together with heads bowed to ensure their parents couldn't hear their conspiratorial chatter. This time they led the way, moving quickly as if determined to get the outing over with as soon as possible.

A trailside plaque identified key structures: the schoolhouse, the jail, the mill. As they moved slowly up the long, narrow site, Grace guessed animatedly about the functions of all the others, even though most were simple dwellings where cold and snow would have seeped through the cracks all winter long. One house, more intact than the rest as though it had been the last to become uninhabited, was covered in spray-paint graffiti proving intoxicated teenagers' deep knowledge of horror-movie conventions.

Markered onto one wall: *Always watches. No eyes.*

Across the stream, the sand-colored concrete foundations of the huge mill made Todd think of a lost civilization, something noble, Egyptian, and doomed. As they labored up the hill, faces and necks burning, Grace made it clear that the failure to put on sunscreen before leaving Bearpaw was a collective failure not to be borne by her alone.

Above the mill, technicolor water flowed out of the locked, grated entrance to the silver mine. There were no hand-scrawled admonitions not to drink it, but there was a sign advertising that the twenty-acre mining claim was for sale.

On the way back down they passed the peaked roof of a house, now situated in the middle of a stream; water raced through it, channeled by the sloping eaves. Todd climbed down and crouched on the bank, hypnotized. Had it slid downslope until it stopped in the streambed? Had the water changed course? Had some pioneer been driven mad by loneliness and sought kinship with the fish?

Sun glittered on the water as it foamed and splashed over rocks in the sun-dappled shade. The air smelled bracing and clean. Todd felt almost hypnotized as he took several photos with his phone and then a long video. The scene was eerie and mournful—How could you go home again if a stream flowed through it?—yet strangely peaceful at the same time.

Hearing his daughters giggling, he realized they'd been calling him and he hadn't even heard.

"Dad, it's just an old house," groaned Marissa.

Todd wiped the tears from his eyes before he turned around and climbed the bank. Pretending to laugh at himself along with them, he lagged behind as they hiked down to the car.

On the drive back to the resort, they stopped at a place called Crystal Park, where from her research in Chicago Grace had learned it was legal and permissible to dig for abundantly occurring quartz crystals. The parking lot was as crowded as any they had yet encountered in Montana, with families pouring out of cars with picks, shovels, rock hammers, rakes, and buckets. Unequipped to mount their own excavation, the Harrows walked a short distance to the digging area and regarded a pitted brown hillside that suggested a mudslide or a bombardment had taken place. Deep holes undercut tree roots, craters pocked the hill face, and sunburned children attacked the earth like diamond miners.

⟡

Todd and Grace were still outside the cabin when they heard shrieks from inside. Morgan and Marissa appeared in the doorway, wild-eyed and distraught.

"Our stuff is gone!" shouted Marissa.

"*All* of it," said Morgan.

"What do you mean, all of it?" asked Todd, alarmed.

"Well, everything that matters," clarified Marissa. "Everything with a power cord."

Grace pounded up the steps like a gymnast running toward a vault. She had confirmed the losses by the time Todd went through the door: everything with a plug, battery, or screen was gone while all their other belongings remained, seemingly untouched.

"You said there were good people here," Morgan accused Grace.

Grace shot a look at Todd. "I knew we shouldn't have trusted them."

Todd opened his palms to the sky. "They said they'd never had a problem with it before."

"My phone was here because I was charging it," said Marissa, beginning to weep. "I want to upgrade."

"This is your fault, Dad!" raged Morgan, and for a moment he thought she would beat her fists against his chest as she had when she was a toddler burning off anger over an upset already forgotten.

"I'm going to the office," declared Grace. "They're going to make this right!"

Todd pictured the muttonchopped paperback reader and wondered how long his country cool would stand up in the face of Full Metal Grace. Grace was used to dealing with people beholden to human-resource departments, conduct codes, and framed customer-service guarantees. He wondered how many minutes it would take before she threatened legal action.

"I'll go," he said quietly.

"That's not a good idea, Dad," said Morgan.

"You know Mom is better at this stuff," added Marissa.

"I'll handle it," he said, slipping out the back door, which was nearest, before any further protest could be mounted.

The main lodge was just around the flank of the hill, the pool and office beyond that. Instead he set a course upward, working his way past a derelict outhouse, planting his feet carefully on clumps of grass and navigating around fallen trees.

At the top of the hill was a meadow of startling beauty, where the setting sun glowed gold on a field of purple wildflowers he could not name but felt in some inchoate way he recognized. He saw a tree with four fully grown trunks rising from its root ball and thought, despite its deformity, it was possibly the most beautiful tree he had ever seen. Everything here had a name and yet he knew none of them. Was there still time to learn?

He walked until he found a depression whose steep sides and regular shape showed it to be man-made. Six feet deep, it was old, with grass growing up the sides. Todd imagined some long-ago prospector wandering these hills, digging exploratory holes, hoping to hit a motherlode each time and each time moving on.

He climbed down into the hole and, after sliding the sharper rocks to one side, lay down at the bottom. He closed his eyes and listened to the gentle sigh of wind in the tree branches, the pocking of a faraway woodpecker, the high whine of a mosquito. When he felt the tiny legs of a spider tickling the skin of his arm, he concentrated on the way his arm hairs transmitted the movement like a thousand tiny antennae.

Change wasn't as hard as he'd imagined. It was as simple as leaving baggage on the front porch with a sign that read *FREE STUFF.*

Back at his office in Chicago, while waiting for a software update to download and install so he can resume work on a task too boring for words, he thinks about the roof in the stream in Coolidge. He pictures the glassine water sheeting over a board and imagines the course of the streambed as it winds its way out of the high mountain valley and joins the Wise River, which empties into the Big Hole River, a tributary of the Jefferson River. Using Google Maps, he has followed the water's path all the way to the Missouri River and then into the Mississippi. Which passes just a few hours' drive from Chicago.

He thinks about glaciers melting, oceans rising. He imagines Chicago empty and the lobby of his building a foot deep in water with Asian carp finning past the security desk. As he watches the progress bar track the status of his download, he pictures the world without himself and feels, for the first time in his life, content.

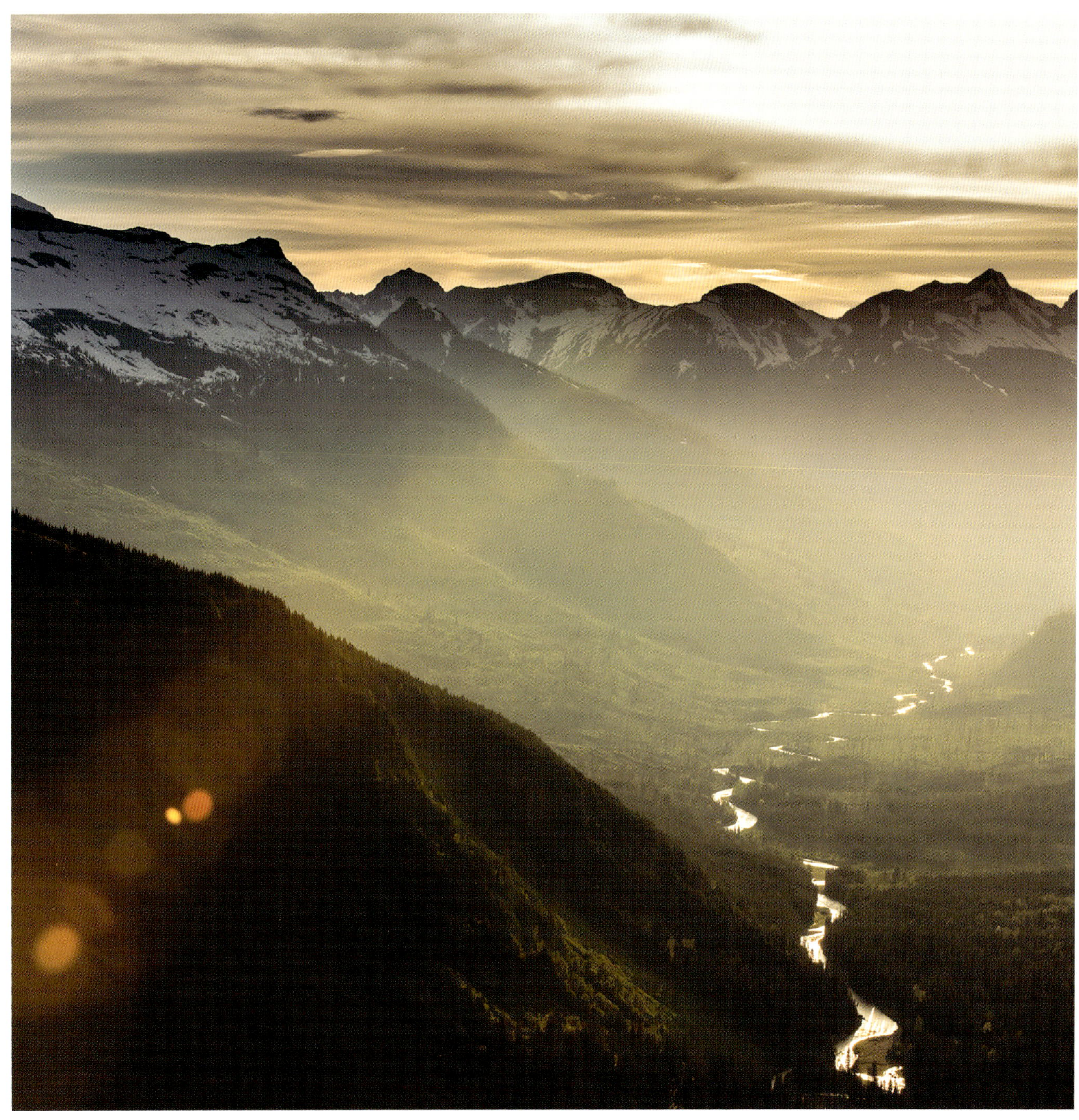

CONTRIBUTORS

Rick Bass is the author of more than thirty books of fiction and nonfiction, most recently *The Traveling Feast*. He has taught at the University of Montana and Montana State University, where he was the Western Writer-in-Residence, and in 2018 received the Montana Governor's Arts Award. He is a board member of the Yaak Valley Forest Council and Save the Yellowstone Grizzly.

Alexis Bonogofsky is a fourth-generation Montanan, goat and sheep rancher, and freelance writer and photographer who lives and works along the Yellowstone River in southeastern Montana where she grew up. Her writing and photography can be found on her website *East of Billings* and in various news outlets and magazines including *Mountain Journal*, *Montana Quarterly*, *Farm 406*, and *High Desert Journal*. For ten years she managed the Tribal Lands Partnership Program for the National Wildlife Federation. She received her BA in International Studies from Gonzaga University and her MA in International Development from University of Denver's Korbel School of International Studies. Her conservation work was featured in the book and movie, *This Changes Everything*, by Canadian journalist and author Naomi Klein and in the recent National Geographic coal documentary, *From the Ashes*. In 2014, Alexis was awarded the Cultural Freedom Fellowship from the Lannan Foundation in Santa Fe.

Christine Carbo is the author of the Glacier Mystery novels, an ensemble series set in and around Glacier National Park. Her books include *The Wild Inside*, *Mortal Fall*, *The Weight of Night*, and *A Sharp Solitude*. She is a recipient of the Women's National Book Association Pinckley Prize, the Silver Falchion Award, and the High Plains Book Award. After earning a pilot's license, pursuing various adventures in Norway, and working a brief stint as a flight attendant, she earned an MA in English and linguistics and taught college-level courses. She still teaches, in a vastly different realm, as the owner of a Pilates studio. She lives with her family in Whitefish. Find out more at ChristineCarbo.com.

Janet Skeslien Charles grew up in Shelby and attended the University of Montana. Her debut novel *Moonlight in Odessa*, which explores the booming business of e-mail-order brides, was translated into ten languages. Her second novel *The Paris Library* tells the true tale of the American librarian who defied the Nazi "Book Protector" in order to keep the American Library in Paris open during World War II. It will be translated into seventeen languages. Janet's shorter work has appeared in *Slice* and *Montana Noir*. She currently lives in Paris, France.

Longtime journalist and Delaware native **Gwen Florio** finally found her way to Montana in 2005. The first of her six novels was published in 2013. That book's title? *Montana*.

Born and raised in Shelby, **James Grady** graduated from the University of Montana, staffed the state's 1972 Constitutional Convention, and worked for Montana's US Senator Lee Metcalf in Washington, DC, where Grady now lives. His first novel, *Six Days of the Condor*, which was written in Montana, became a

Robert Redford movie and a Max Irons TV show. Grady's been a muckraking journalist, published more than a dozen other novels, three times that many short stories, and worked in movies and TV. He's received France's *Grand Prix du Roman Noir*, Italy's Raymond Chandler Award, and a Baku-Misu literary award from Japan. The *Washington Post* compared Grady's 2014 novel *Last Days of the Condor* to the works of George Orwell and Bob Dylan.

Keir Graff's grandfather was an itinerant preacher who fly-fished the rivers and streams of Montana. Born and raised in Missoula, Graff attended Hellgate High School and, briefly, the University of Montana. Under his own name and others, he is the author of six novels for adults, three novels for middle-graders, and short stories published in periodicals ranging from the *Missoula Independent* to the *Chicago Reader*. He is also the co-editor, with James Grady, of the anthology *Montana Noir*. Graff now lives in Chicago, where he has worked in publishing for two decades. He returns to Montana every chance he gets.

Laulette LeDoux Hansen was born in 1942 and raised on her grandparents' homestead near Montana's Big Sag. Her grandfather, a master carpenter who knew horses, taught his grandchildren to read the time and weather from the sky; her grandmother knew wildflowers, and played Schubert and Schumann on an 1898 Wing piano. Her father Ermal Hansen taught her to love music and flying. LeDoux taught Russian language and literature in Montana and elsewhere for twenty years while working as a consultant and interpreter in the USSR and US. She established a coffee business in Moscow, Russia, in 1991, and started writing songs at the age of 65. She lives in Missoula and Geraldine.

Jamie Harrison, who has lived in Montana with her family for more than thirty years, has worked as a caterer, a gardener, and an editor. She is the author of five previous novels—the Jules Clement series of mysteries (*The Edge of the Crazies*, *Going Local*, *An Unfortunate Prairie Occurrence*, and *Blue Deer Thaw*), which will be reprinted by Counterpoint Press beginning in 2020, and *The Widow Nash*, a finalist for the High Plains Book Award and the winner of the Mountains and Plains Independent Booksellers' Association's Reading the West Award. Her next novel, as yet untitled, will be released by Counterpoint in the spring of 2020.

Eric Heidle is a creative director, photographer, and writer with the rare good luck to be born in Montana and grow up riding in the passenger seats of pickup trucks. His family's long history in Montana is one of cutting hay, bending iron, chasing cattle, and digging for silver. Heidle's writing and photography has been published in *Backpacker* and *Montana Outdoors*, and his fiction has appeared on Montana Public Radio's "The Write Question" and in the anthology *Montana Noir*. His story from that collection, "Ace in the Hole," was nominated for a 2018 Edgar Award by the Mystery Writers of America. He lives in Great Falls with his love Dagni and a small horde of cats.

Sterling HolyWhiteMountain is a fiction writer and essayist who grew up on the Blackfeet Reservation. His work has appeared in volumes one and two of *Off the Path: An Anthology of 21st Century American Indian and Indigenous Writers*, *Montana Quarterly*, ESPN, and *The Atlantic*. He is currently a Stegner Fellow at Stanford University.

Allen Morris Jones is the author of the novels *Last Year's River*, *A Bloom of Bones*, and *Sweeney on the Rocks*, as well as a highly regarded treatise on the ethics of hunting, *A Quiet Place of Violence*. Co-editor of *The Best of Montana's Short Fiction*, he has also worked as a magazine editor, book editor, and publisher of his own small press, Bangtail Press. He lives in Bozeman, Montana, with his wife and young son.

Carrie La Seur's critically acclaimed debut novel *The Home Place*, an Indie Next pick, won a High Plains Book Award and was short-listed for the Strand Critics Award for Best First Novel. Her writing appears in such media as *Daily Beast*, *Grist*, the *Guardian*, *Harvard Law and Policy Review*,

High Country News, *Kenyon Review Online*, *Mother Jones*, *The Rumpus*, and *Salon*. She is a founder of the environmental nonprofit Plains Justice and the Billings Bookstore Cooperative. Her second novel, *The Weight of an Infinite Sky*, a rural Montana take on Hamlet, that was shortlisted for the Reading the West Award, is now available in paperback.

Maxim Loskutoff is the author of *Come West and See*. His stories and essays have appeared in numerous periodicals, including the *New York Times*, the *Chicago Tribune*, *Ploughshares*, and the *Southern Review*, as well as anthologies in the US and abroad. He lives in western Montana, where he was raised.

Antonia Malchik has written essays and articles for *Aeon*, *The Atlantic*, *Orion*, *High Country News*, and a variety of other publications. Her first book, *A Walking Life*, is about the past and future of walking's role in our shared humanity. A fifth-generation Montanan, she has lived and worked in several different countries but now lives in northwest Montana.

Maile Meloy was born and raised in Helena, Montana. She is the author of three novels, two short-story collections, and a middle-grade trilogy. Her fiction has appeared in the *New Yorker*, the *Paris Review*, and *Best American Short Stories*, and on *Selected Shorts* and *This American Life*. Her story collection *Both Ways Is the Only Way I Want It* was named one of the *New York Times*' "Ten Best Books of 2009." She has received the PEN/Malamud Award, the E. B. White Award, and a Guggenheim Fellowship.

Caroline Patterson is the executive director of the Missoula Writing Collaborative. She has published the short-story collection *Ballet at the Moose Lodge*, the anthology *Montana Women Writers: A Geography of the Heart*, and two children's books. Her work was included in the anthologies *Montana Noir* and *Bright Bones*. Her fellowships include the Wallace Stegner Fellowship in Fiction, the Joseph Henry Jackson Prize from the San Francisco Foundation, and a Montana Arts Council Fellowship. With her husband, the writer Fred Haefele, and her two college-aged children, she lives in the Missoula home her great-grandfather built in 1906, with the fireplace on the inside rather than the outside wall, because her great-grandmother said, "she could never spend a night in a house with a mortgage."

Jim Robbins has written about the West and western issues for the *New York Times* since 1980 from his home in Helena. He has also traveled around the globe writing for numerous magazines, covering the cloud forests of Peru for *Conde Nast Traveler*, the spicy peppers of the Yucatan in Mexico for *Smithsonian*, and the Yanomami Indigenous Territory of northern Brazil for *Vanity Fair*. He is the author of six books, three of them about nature and three about the human nervous system. His most recent are *The Wonder of Birds* and *The Man Who Planted Trees*, published by Random House, which are illuminating looks at the relationships between people and nature and investigations into how little we really know about our world.

Russell Rowland's fifth novel, *Cold Country*, will be published by Dzanc Books in the fall of 2019. Two of his previous novels have been finalists for the High Plains Book Award for Fiction. He has an MA in creative writing from Boston University and currently lives in Billings, where he is working on a memoir called *Be a Man* and consulting for other writers.

Joe Wilkins grew up in eastern Montana, where he spent most of his teenage summers working on a wheat and cattle ranch deep in the Bull Mountains. He is the author of a memoir, *The Mountain and the Father*, winner of a 2014 GLCA New Writers Award—an honor that has previously recognized early work by the likes of Richard Ford, Louise Erdrich, and Alice Munro—and three collections of poetry, including *When We Were Birds*, winner of the 2017 Oregon Book Award in Poetry. His debut novel, *Fall Back Down When I Die*, was published in 2019. He lives with his family in western Oregon, where he directs the creative writing program at Linfield College.

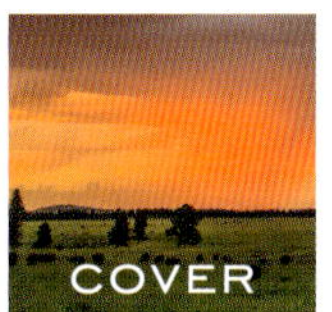

Little Snowy Mountains, Golden Valley County

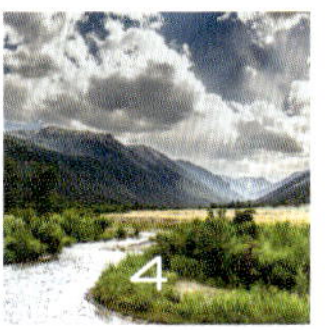

West Rosebud Creek, Stillwater County

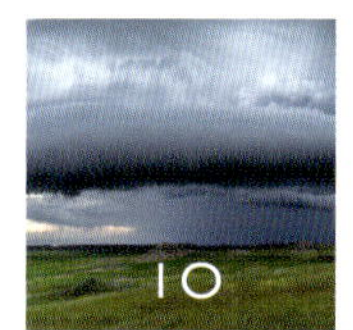

Charles M. Russell Wildlife Refuge, Garfield County

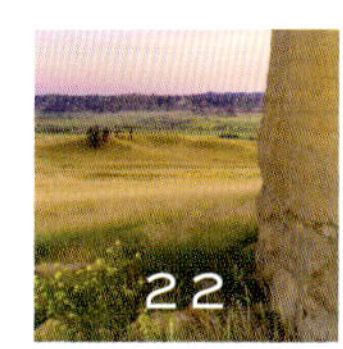

Off Highway 39, Rosebud County

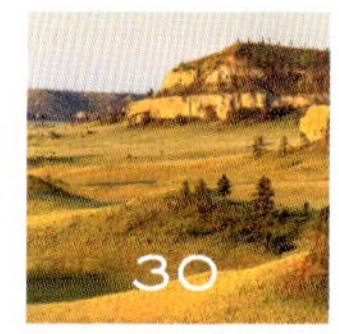

Off Highway 39, Rosebud County

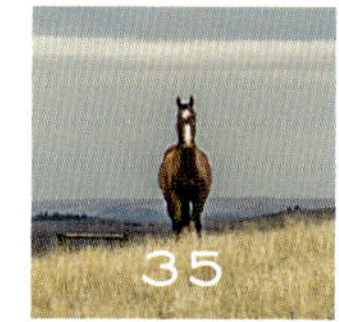

Pryor Mountain Foothills, Yellowstone County

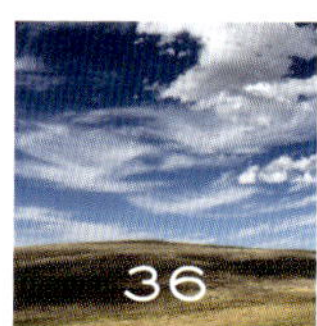

Eastern Montana prairie, Carter County

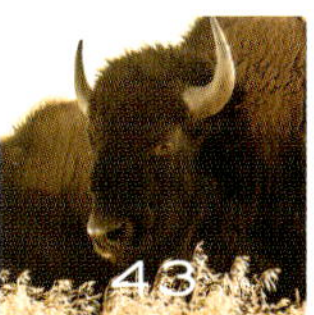

Fort Peck Yellowstone Bison

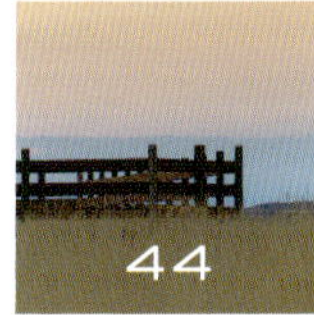

Fort Peck Reservation, Roosevelt County

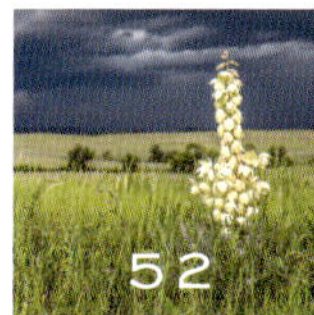

Yucca plant, Crow Reservation

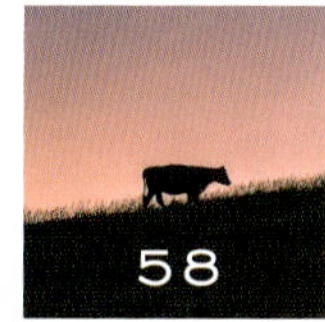

Near Gallatin River, Gallatin County

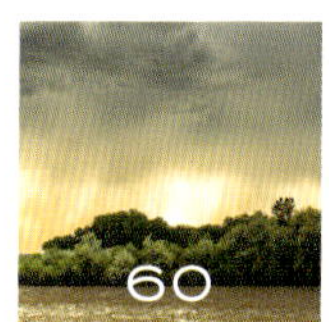

Yellowstone River near Forsyth, Rosebud County

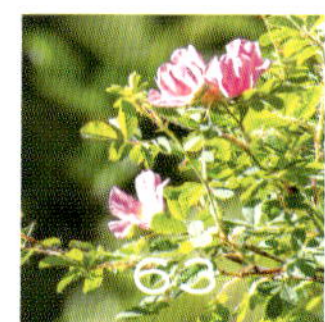

Wild rose near Gallatin River, Gallatin County

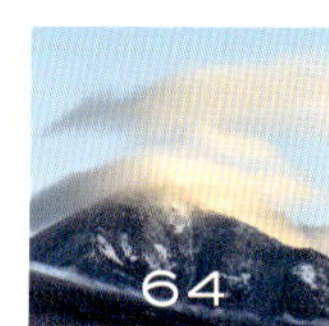

Near Livingston, Park County

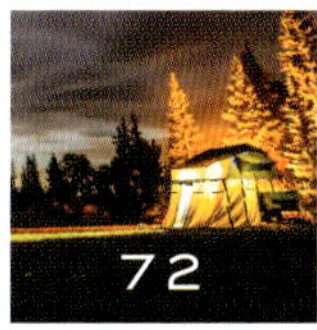

Custer Gallatin National Forest

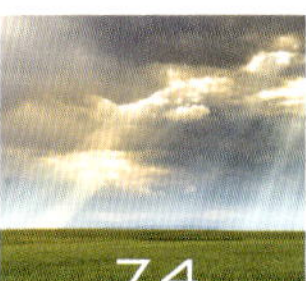

Near Billings, Yellowstone County

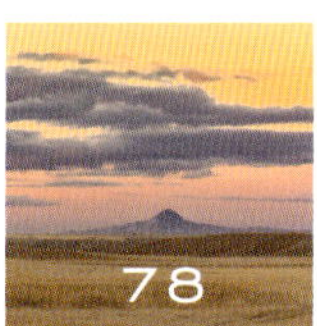

Sweet Grass Hills, viewed from Pondera County

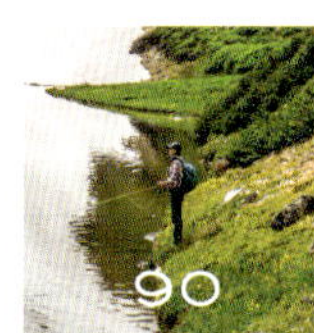

Beartooth Mountains, Custer Gallatin National Forest

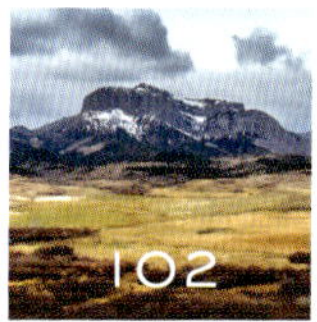

Rocky Mountain Front, Teton County

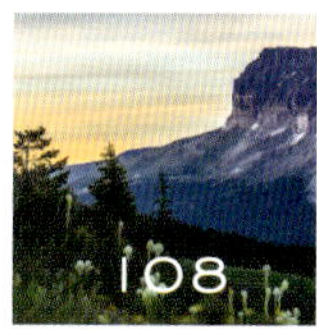

Glacier National Park

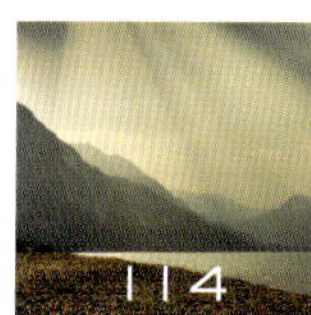

Mystic Lake, Stillwater County

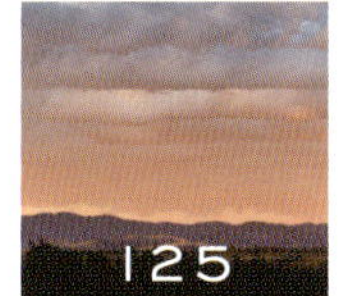

Bridger Mountains, Gallatin County

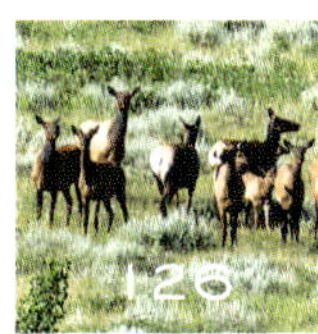

Elk near Luther, Carbon County

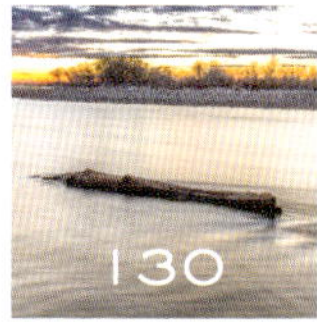

Yellowstone River near Billings, Yellowstone County

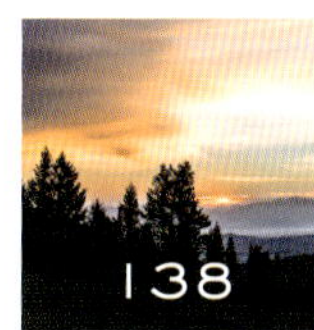

Looking east toward the Crazy Mountains, Sweet Grass County

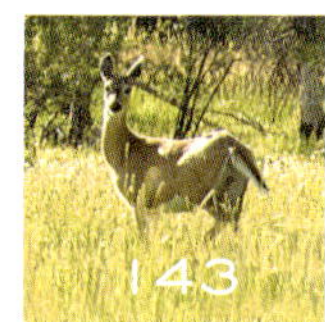

Whitetail deer, Swan Valley, Missoula County

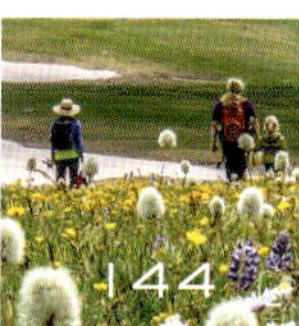

Near Glacier Lake, Carbon County

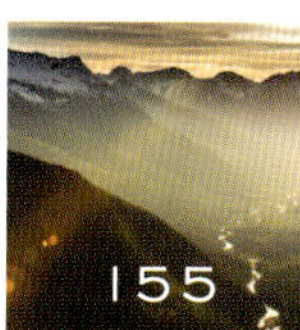

McDonald Creek, Glacier National Park

The editor would like to thank Tom McGuane for making the connection with MLR. Josh Getzler, Linda Joffe Hull, and Kirstin Scott also deserve recognition for their support and advice. And, as always: Marya, Felix, Cosmo.

The Montana Land Reliance would like to thank Tom McGuane for introducing Keir Graff to the organization, Alexis Bonogofsky for her photographic and literary contributions, Bruce Capdeville for his always prolific design, and Montana's landowners for helping protect the open spaces that shape us all.